Let's Do Theology

Let's Do Theology

A PASTORAL CYCLE RESOURCE BOOK

Laurie Green

MOWBRAY

Mowbray
A Cassell imprint
Wellington House, 125 Strand, London WC2R 0BB

First published 1990

Reprinted 1991, 1998

British Library Cataloguing in Publication Data
Green, Laurie, *1945–*
Let's do theology: a pastoral cycle resource book
1. Christian theology
I. Title
230

ISBN 0–264–67194–5

Typeset by Colset Private Limited, Singapore
Printed and bound in Great Britain by
Page Bros, Norwich

Contents

*This book is affectionately dedicated to
my mother and father*

Preface

It was out of my ten years' experience as vicar at Spaghetti Junction in Birmingham that I wrote *Power to the Powerless*, an account of how a group of working-class Christians came to make for themselves a theology that was vital and relevant to their urban experience. Their theology was reflective and yet active, committed and yet thoughtful, questioning and yet substantial. For the last seven years I have been working as principal of the Aston Training Scheme, a national ordination course. As I have travelled the country, I have been repeatedly asked by those who have read that first book, how they themselves might be able to go about 'doing theology' in their own parish, at home or in their workplace. I have also been asked to run courses and training days on such questions as 'What is the nature of theology?' and 'What goes on when we do theology?' This present book is an attempt to bring together some of my responses to these and similar questions, and I hope that it proves of service to those who want to try it for themselves. It is often a surprise to ordinary Christians to find out that they can be theologians, and if the reader does not warm to the word 'theology', I hope that by the time he or she reaches the end of this book they will after all have found something in it for them. A dear friend of mine who was in one of my earliest theology groups now refers to herself as a theologian, but she often remarks that until she got started in the group she still thought that incarnation was something that came out of a tin! I hope that others will be as delighted by what they discover as she was.

Countless people have helped me to write this book – some will never know how much help they have been. Many have been group participants; others have been the askers of awkward questions at conferences; some have been close associates and friends. Special thanks must go to the staff team of the Aston Training Scheme, Michael, Jeni, Bridget and Patricia, as well as the assistant staff and students who have put up with me for seven long years! Among others I am especially indebted to José Marins and Carolee Chanona in Latin America, to friends in the Urban Training field up and down the country, and to many educationalists who have helped me hammer my ideas into shape. That is not to say that I have finished learning about groups and theology, and I hope that the ideas in this book will be taken, developed and changed by others as their situations demand. I will always be pleased to hear how their group experiences have progressed and where improvements can be built into the ideas that I have developed here.

Especial thanks are due to Ruth McCurry at Mowbray for all the helpful advice and patience, and thanks to Jeni Parsons for reading many drafts. And finally, thanks to my family, Vicki, Rebecca and Hannah, who over the last few months have seen less of me than has the word-processor!

Laurie Green
Birmingham
October 1989

1

Transforming theology

Most people today seem to believe that the Church is out of touch. It does not touch their everyday lives, it does not touch their concerns, their routines, or their struggles. When asked whether or not they believe in God, however, many will say that they do, and many will go further and witness to an experience of the nearness of God in their own lives. Some feel that the Christian faith especially holds out a promise of meaning and value which they yearn for, and of which they have had some glimpse within their own experience. But ask them about the Church and it's a very different matter. I am often struck by the church notice board slogan which reads 'Christ is the answer'. I suspect that many would be prompted to respond 'Yes, but does the Church know what the question is?'

Christianity is a transforming and vibrant faith, which holds the key to the deepest concerns of our experience, and yet we are beset with a constant difficulty of trying to find a way of properly integrating our faith and our life; instead, we find ourselves smothering the faith with irrelevance, long theological words and complicated explanations. We have to admit that we, the Church, do not really do the Christian faith justice. At its best, of course, the Church does try to address the world, and faithful Christians up and down the country work away at the front line, binding up the wounds of those who suffer and engaging in the struggles of the day; and although much of that Christian faithfulness is hidden from the public gaze, it does, I am sure, bear witness to how faith and life are constantly being brought together in the lives of ordinary Christians. It seems to me, however, that this sort of Christian witness to the relevance and vitality of the Christian faith could be greatly assisted if Christians had better tools than at present for understanding the faith, and for seeing how very clearly it relates to their joys and their struggles. Then they would be able, even more vigorously and consciously, to bring together the deepest concerns of the world and the vibrant promise of their Christian faith. Those outside the Church would then be able to look at the lives and statements of Christians and feel that they were on their wavelength, and that Christians are witnessing to a faith that does indeed ring many bells consonant with an experience of God in their own lives.

I have a deep conviction that theology can be transformed in such a way that it can become a very productive tool in this endeavour. For theology can offer an exciting way of bringing together the crucial experiences of human living and the abiding truths of the Christian faith. This transformation of theology will of course be an ambitious enterprise because for many years theology itself has had a name for being one of the most irrelevant of all Christian practices; even church-goers are apt to think of theology as irrelevant. But I have seen theology revitalised in the hands of groups of ordinary Christians, and prove itself to have an amazing potential for the re-creation of integrated Christian living. It puts the faith back 'in touch' with life.

But 'theology' is a word that has got itself into a lot of trouble. Among politicians, at any rate, it now seems to have become a term of abuse to be hurled at anyone of a differing opinion – it has become the ultimate put-down! Recently, I heard Denis Healey slay his political debating partner in just this way: 'Well, you've now moved into the realms of fantasy', he remarked, 'this is just pure theology!' Theology is a matter near and dear to my heart, so it concerns me to hear the word used in this way – especially by those politicians I admire. But my problem is made all the more acute by the fact that there are also many Christians I admire who, likewise, would never dream of using the word 'theology', except in a derogatory sense. And who am I to blame them? What is it, after all, that most people think of if asked to imagine a theological debate? I suspect that some would picture a group of medieval scholars debating how many angels could take up residence on the head of a pin, while others would imagine a more up-to-date picture of a huddle of sceptical academics trying to dream up yet another awkward statement about the faith with which to hit the tabloid press. So where does that leave theology? It was a bishop of the Church of England who recently shared with me the concern he felt when his daughter told the family that she had decided that theology was the subject she would like to study at university. 'I have to admit it, my heart just sank', he confided. 'For my daughter to be alive to the faith of Jesus Christ thrills me, but to think of my poor child going through all that dim academic stuff really is a worry. Theology can be a very grey and heavy subject, can't it?' I had to agree with him that theology, the subject that used to be called the Queen of the Sciences, has had an extremely bad press of late; and is, in the minds of the majority, unfortunately, a 'grey and heavy' thing, hardly a subject to turn the world upside down. And yet it is also a fact that there are stirrings around the world that indicate that theology is capable of doing precisely that – turning the world upside down. In parts of Latin America, Africa and Asia a new interest in theology has blossomed, and has so empowered those Christians involved in it that their whole lives have been changed and they have felt liberated by their discovery of it. Even in the UK there are those who have found that theological study has thrust them forward into the political arena where they have been instrumental in important examples of social and political change. Now if theology is capable of all this, then surely our idea of it as a dull, heavy and fanciful subject cannot be altogether accurate. Perhaps we have the wrong idea about theology after all.

It was the same bishop who had shared with me his feelings about his daughter's university choice of theology who later that day shared the same concern among a large group of specialists in theological education and thus sparked off a storm of disagreement. There were those who felt that college and university theology was totally out of touch with today's concerns, while ranged against them were teachers from those very same colleges and universities who maintained that only their own academic style of study could claim to be theologically respectable. It is the aim of this book, however, to propose a far more ambitious way of being theologians, whereby the very best of what the traditions of theology have to teach us can be fully integrated into the issues that are hitting our society so hard today. I hope that in this way both camps of 'activist' and 'academic' theology can find a common mission, and serve one another in the quest to transform people and the society in which we live. This will of course call for a substantial reformulation of what we think theology to be, and will require that those who currently engage in academic theology, and those who reject that whole enterprise as unnecessary, may come to see theology as a far more wide-ranging activity than ever they might have expected – an activity in which all have their own indispensable part to play. But before we begin to formulate what this new approach to theology might be, let us consider the problem a little more carefully.

Book-bound theology

Recently, I had the fascinating experience of being asked by the Diocese of Bristol to give a series of talks on the challenging and intriguing theme 'Theology without Books'. I had to point out, of course, that on the face of it I did not appear to have a very good pedigree from which to address the subject, having already engaged in the writing of books myself. But the title 'Theology without Books' struck at the very heart of a matter that had long concerned me, because I have always felt that theology has suffered the fate of having been bound into the hard covers of a very academic approach to the world, and I have sought to understand why this might be and what, even now, could be done about it. When first I went to university as a young man to study theology, I discovered that I was expected to use college jargon and say that I had come not to 'do' but to 'read' theology, and one of the first duties that I was given by my tutor was to go out to the local bookshop and equip myself with what felt like a shopping-trolley full of great tomes. The clear message was that if I managed to read, mark, learn and inwardly digest all these volumes then I too would be able to sit in smoke-filled studies and debate the various theological arguments and points of view that were being propounded there. This, they told me, was what 'doing theology' really meant. But it seemed to me that they expected me to engage only in the study of other people's theology – to 'read' theology but not to 'do' it.

Well, that may all sound rather silly nowadays and I'm very glad to say that we have all come a long way since then, but there is no doubt that I still continue to receive very clear messages that there is no such thing as a theology without books! That is to say, in the minds of many, there is no way that theology can become an activity in which ordinary non-academic people can engage. It has been my experience, however, that it is precisely when theology is liberated from the confines of the library that it takes wing and becomes again what it has the potential to be. Exactly how this might be, and, even more important, how this might be facilitated, has become my abiding interest, and I hope to share some of my experiences in the pages that follow.

When I first began to think about the title of that Bristol conference, 'Theology without Books', I found myself looking at the possibility of a theology that is not limited to the academic, and this from two very different perspectives. First, there is that enormous proportion of the population who can read but, by and large, choose not to. Open any tabloid newspaper and you will see surprisingly little text. If you wander into W. H. Smith's or its equivalent, you may well be surprised to find that for such a reputable bookseller there are comparatively few books on the shelves. You will, however, find such stores fulfilling the growing demand for interest magazines on all sorts of subjects – ranging from motor-cycle maintenance to mothercare, from microwave cookery to military history. Everything under the sun finds a market when it is packaged in this easily manageable form, but the written style of the text in such magazines and tabloids will be chatty and descriptive – certainly not the sort of prose in which the average theological book will be produced.

But the problem about the printed page goes a lot deeper than its style of presentation, for there still appears to be a strange mystique in most minds about printed text in book form. It is expected that once printed text is bound into a book it then becomes irrevocably authoritative. Those who are deeply involved in the book world may have a blasé disregard for the printed word, but that is not how the vast majority of humanity views it. The printed text is still held in awe and people can easily feel put down by it. It has the capacity to disable people who in other ways seem to be wise and knowing, and they are even apt to mistrust their own experience if it is contradicted by the printed word. So when theology is so closely allied to the printed book, it too can take upon itself an awesome and debilitating aspect and frighten people off. With theology so bound up in books, it becomes difficult to recognise a truly theological statement when it is made by someone other than a scholar, and in terms that one would not expect to find on the printed page of a book. Their statement may sound too simple to be worthy of the name 'theology' because it is not wrapped up in theological language. Some graffiti that I spotted on a theological college wall sums it up quite well: 'Jesus said to them, ''Who do you say that I am?'' They replied, ''You are the eschatological manifestation of the ground of our being, in which kerygma we find the ultimate meaning in our interpersonal relationships.'' And Jesus replied, ''What?'''

Statistics indicate that many people harbour very real fears and anxieties about being asked to read or write in public because they have minimal skills in these areas, and these fears often go right back to early negative experiences at school. Such anxieties, fears and disabilities about books are manifest right across the country. But there is no doubt that there is a much higher incidence of those who either cannot read or 'those who can read but don't',[1] amassed in our inner cities, in outer run-down estates, in poor rural communities, and in other pockets of deprivation. A non-academic approach to theology is a serious and real need for people in these areas, and especially so when we remember that Jesus himself chose among his disciples (his learning fellowship) those who came not from the academic classes, but ordinary working folk who had practical experience and wisdom rather than academic skill. I feel sure that a fisherman like Simon would have been anything but a bookish theologian, and yet this man, whom Jesus called 'the Rock', led the Church into all manner of new theological discovery during the early years of its existence.[2]

But when I first began to think of that conference title, 'Theology without Books', I also began to ponder a second, and at first sight contradictory, issue about which so many of us are currently concerned. This is a problem that is more likely to beset those who have had a surfeit of academic education rather than those who don't read much at all. For many of the well-educated are finding that their academic books are actually beginning to close them off from some of the realities of the faith. I have a friend who lectures in theology at a large university and he recently shared with me his anxiety about this problem. He speaks of two related difficulties. First he tells of his own inability to find a way of relating the learned discourse of academic journals and the lecture hall to his own personal concerns, to the world at large, or to the local community in which he lives. And second, when he sets about teaching his third-year undergraduates, he is aware that they, like all the youthful generations that have gone before them, feel themselves to be on the threshold of venturing out into the world to commit themselves to some great task, and to this end they have opted to undertake a systematic study of theology. Their expectations of their tutor are that he should tell them where in all the great tomes on his shelves they will find *the answers* to facilitate their future life journey. They expect of him what has often been referred to as the 'banking theory of education',[3] where the student sets about learning the facts, knowing the texts, learning the systems of rational argument, in order that this theoretical theology may later be 'applied' in the world. This is an approach to theology that tries to differentiate between what we might call *pure* theology, which is ingested at university, and *applied* theology, which is what is later conveyed to those 'in the world'. The major difficulty with this differentiation is that it implies that there actually is a body of pure theological knowledge that can be learnt, and in this respect it treats the Christian faith in rather the same way as did the early heresies of Gnosticism.

In this connection, we must remember that the great 'classical' theologies that have been produced through the ages have grown out of their specific situations, and therefore have usually been the outcome of seeing theological questions through the eyes of a particular formal system of thought prevailing at the time – be it Platonism, Aristotelianism, Existentialism, Formalism, Structuralism or any of the other 'isms' that have from time to time become fashionable. As times change, however, so some of these prevailing systems lose their viability and authority for us, and when that happens we find ourselves left with a certain mistrust of the theology that seems to be wedded to that system of thought and values which we now find hard to swallow.[4] So, in many ways, what 'book theology' at universities seems to be lacking is any proper appreciation of the context in which it is being done, and the effect of this is that a theology dependent on one era or context is sometimes superimposed on another generation or situation without any consideration of the mistake being made.[5] Trying to 'apply' a theology thought to be in some sense 'pure' and not related to the situation out of which it grew can get us all into great difficulty, and result in the accusation that our theology is irrelevant.

The classroom, of course, can be a suitable place for disciplined reflection and some functional subjects can be learnt there; but the wisdom that is theology needs to be made in the very context of the issues of life. We therefore need to find a way of doing theology that brings the felt experience of life right into the heart of the enterprise, and yet at the same time is fully appreciative of the specificity of the context in which the resultant theology is formulated. We are looking for a theological method that does justice to experience and at the same time is fully informed by, but is certainly not subordinate to, scholarship and an understanding of the Christian traditions of faith.

So, for *all* our sakes, the attempt to find a new way of being theologians and of 'doing theology' seems to be a valid and worthwhile venture both for those who find books alien, and for those who have a realisation that all their books have actually kept them from valuing their life experiences as the raw material of theology. If theology can be liberated in this way from an exclusively academic approach, then ordinary Christians, together with the scholars, will be able play their part in, and take responsibility for, the exercise.

Participating in theology

By searching for a kind of theology that is inclusive of all types of people, we will enrich it tremendously. Not only will it be encouraged to address the questions with which ordinary folk have constantly to tussle, but it will also, and this is most important, allow for a whole new variety of religious and spiritual experience to be taken properly into consideration. And people who express themselves in very different styles from those who have handled theology in the past, will not only have different experiences to share but may want to share them in a variety of new ways. No longer will it be suggested that books are the only carriers of spiritual wisdom, but stories, proverbs, films, pop music, spirituals, poetry, handicrafts, dress, dance and so much more, may turn out to be carrying the people's expression of spiritual and profound experience, and may be doing so on behalf of that part of our culture that is not enamoured of the classroom or the chapel. If all this wealth of expression is brought to the theological task, then theology might begin to break out of its verbal captivity and use all the liberating avenues of body language to express the wisdom it seeks to focus. The Church has known for generations that the great truths of the faith will be confined and crippled if limited merely to erudite statements. This is why it has sacraments, art, music, service, care, fellowship and so on. St Francis put it succinctly when he advised his followers in the art of evangelism. He said 'Preach the gospel to all you meet. Use words only if necessary.'

A participative theology will not only allow for alternative styles of expression, but will also encourage the pressing issues of the day to be more adequately focused. For it seems that the Church is rather behind the times when its academic theologians continue to expend so much energy in that old debate as to whether or not theology is intellectually defensible in an age so wedded to the criteria of science. That may have been a pressing issue for many years, just as was the question of justification before it, but it certainly is not the key question for most people today. Today's questions are 'How can we Christians engage in a society which is so blatantly unjust and unchristian? What should be the nature of our relationship with this complex international society? How can we be Christians here in our daily lives, especially when the Church can often seem to be part of the problem of society rather than its salvation?' This challenge of how to be Christians in a difficult world is today's question, and additionally shares the virtue of being very similar indeed to the basic questions that are being focused and addressed in the New Testament itself. It is this type of question that can become the focus around which a new style of theological activity can begin to emerge, and it could unite the best of our academics and the best of those people who want us to concentrate solely on action; in this way, we might all begin to move together into an active theology that is based on questions of mission and society rather than questions that are no longer pressing for the vast majority of humanity.

So we will not be espousing a new way of doing theology just because it is educationally more sound (although it is), nor simply because it will help people to grow personally in the faith (although it will), but because it will address today's issues and allow the Kingdom of God vision to beckon us forward to participate in the transformation of society, so that all God's children may become the subjects of their own history, deciders of their own fate, rather than just pawns in the hands of ungodly forces. For Christianity should not be allowed to lull people into a false fatalism but, on the contrary, should be an agency for promoting active commitment for liberation, justice and peace on earth, just 'as it is in heaven'.

But to speak in these terms will of course lead us into all sorts of anxiety. To begin with, we may experience a fearful reluctance to engage in a form of theology that demands such risky action. This is very understandable, but to limit our understanding of the nature of theology so that it is in no way participative nor engaged, reduces it to impotence. As we shall see, one thing that will be required of us if we are to engage in a transformation of theology so that it might become a relevant and vibrant activity is that we will have to acknowledge that the Christian faith calls us to be open to God's transformation of ourselves in order that we may participate in God's transformation of the world. It will also require an openness to God's transformation of the world so that in turn we may be changed through it. Any of our faith endeavours, theology included, which hold back from engagement stand in the way of God's initiative in the quest for our salvation.

This transformed theology, being open to all, will demand that theologians engage in active involvement with the world in the quest for God's transformation of it. The word that has become a shorthand way of describing this sort of active theological work is 'praxis'. It stands for that reflection which of necessity involves action, and for the sort of action that demands reflection. Praxis is the intertwining of action and reflection, of commitment and spirituality, reminding us that any action without reflection may well be irresponsible, but reflection without action is sterile. As St James put it in his epistle, 'Faith without good deeds is useless . . . faith and deeds working together' (James 2.20, 22). Faith is the awareness of God's salvation, and it is that awareness which should both inspire our life's actions and reflect upon them. This is praxis, a constant marrying of action and reflection, and it is the key to 'doing theology'.

Let's do theology

So I want to say very firmly that all Christians worthy of the name should in fact already be theologians, although perhaps they would not use that title of themselves. Many Christians feel a bit frightened of making what sounds to be such a great claim. But human beings are gifted with a natural desire to try to make sense of things, and if theology is 'faith seeking understanding',[6] then many Christians will be prompted to try to make sense of the faith they have, and this activity makes them theologians. Very often, however, theology becomes an even more pressing necessity when a Christian is faced with an important decision to make, for when a Christian knows that action is required which should be well thought out in the light of the faith – action and reflection bound together in praxis – then it is out of such a life challenge that theology may best emerge. Let us look now at a simple illustration of this.

Freda is an ordinary Christian woman faced with a problem. She is sitting in the office at the back of a shop where she works. She has just learnt from the boss of the chain of stores that employs her that she must make one of her staff redundant if the shop is not to close. She has good relationships with her staff and knows their personal stories – but one of them has to go. First of all, she decides that the best thing to do is to read up on the law relating to employment, redundancy and so on, and then to check the facts of the case carefully with her boss and her colleagues. She might soon find herself praying about the situation of course, but this will not be the only thing that she, as a Christian, can call upon to help her in working out the answer to her problem. She may also find, for example, that she is helped by reflection with local Christians, perhaps at a Bible study group if there is one. Or maybe as she worships the next Sunday morning she finds herself singing a hymn or canticle that somehow or other puts her choices into better perspective. A talk with her vicar may prove helpful, or maybe she takes a Christian magazine and happens to read an article about the choices that Christians have to make in today's world. All this activity may help her in all sorts of ways to come to a decision about how she is going to cope with the situation that confronts her at work. She then talks with her colleagues at the store and they devise a strategy and implement it together.

The question now before us is 'Has Freda been doing theology during this process?' Much of what she has been doing – studying employment law, praying, worshipping and making decisions, for example – would not fit neatly into an old-fashioned definition of theology as 'reasoned discourse about God'; but my own inclination is to say that she has indeed been involved in the theological endeavour – perhaps unknowingly – because she has been reflecting in her mind and her heart upon the nature of God and upon what God would have her do in her situation, and then she has attempted to respond faithfully. She has not simply relied on the principle of pragmatism – practical effectiveness – but she has attempted to work carefully through the question of the nature of God's own operation and how God wants us to operate in the world. She has opened herself up to the prompting of God through worship and her relationships with the Christian community, and the outcome of all this has profound influence upon her behaviour at work. She has not been content only to be 'religious' about it, but she has taken the matter a little further in the direction of theology by being altogether more carefully questioning about things and she has critically judged the situation and God's nature in relation to it.[7] Let us take a moment to check and see what precisely she has been doing.

One of the things that Freda did was to *pray*. I suspect that it was that sort of prayer with which every human being is familiar – the prayer of anguish when we feel overtaken by experience and cry out 'Dear God, what on earth do I do?' It is an immediate attempt to put ourselves before God and have our minds and wills inspired by God's nature and presence. Sometimes prayer will turn more to the straight adoration of God, but I suspect that whenever I am overwhelmed by God's holiness and beauty, something is going on in my mind and heart which is fundamentally affecting what I know and feel about God and how I will think, act, feel and speak about God in future. I sometimes wonder if that means that even the adoration of God is in some sense a 'doing of theology'. The Eastern Church has always held that the theologian is 'one whose prayers are true', and I will certainly be maintaining in this study that a spirituality will lie at the very heart of all honest theology.

It is probably easier to work out whether or not Freda was doing theology at the *Bible study group*. Bible study certainly 'looks' more like theology than prayer does. It must be about God because it is God's word that is being studied, and usually it engages in careful thinking about that word; so, according to most definitions, it must surely be theology. But let us check that out. What if the discussion gets right away from the biblical passage and engages with a pressing matter of the day without direct relation to Scripture? And does the intellectual rigour of the participants have to be of a particular standard for it to be deemed theology? If it is necessary for the thinking to be concise and well focused, who draws the line to determine how 'clever' it has to be before it has enough academic integrity to merit the title 'theology'? After all, one person's 'clever' is another person's 'pedestrian'. To take things to an extreme we could very well ask, what if it's one of those meetings where the vicar goes on and on and the group falls asleep so that not much thoughtful engagement is evident? Do we need to have certain elements present – relevant text, clear thinking, full engagement – before we can truly call it theology?

Freda attended *worship* the next Sunday. Does this count as theology? Immersing ourselves in the experience of the worshipping community is to put ourselves in touch with the worship of God through the ages and to seek to be in communion with the Church on earth and in heaven. It is also to drink in the gracious Spirit of God and to offer our love with all our heart, soul, mind and strength. Is there any theology being done within that experience of worship? When an insight in a sermon stirs us and makes us rethink or carry our thoughts about God much deeper, then is that not a theological experience? When we find ourselves making connections between the Gospel stories and our own experience, is that not pushing at the very threshold of the theological endeavour? And what are we doing when we state the Creed together, if not giving assent to formulas about the faith that were worked out by theologians centuries ago as they tried to translate the Jewishness of the Christian faith into a predominantly Greek-minded world? Are we joining in their theological work as we stand and recite their formulas? And what is happening when we feel ourselves seized by the power of the sacraments? Their symbolism can be felt to be speaking to the very depths of our being, in potent dialogue with our souls. Can that be part of what it is to be a theologian? Allowing that dialogue to seize us and take us onto what sometimes seems to be another spiritual plane of awareness?

Freda then went to have *a word with the vicar*. What was happening in that conversation? Is not one of the vicar's tasks to help her to put her own experience and problem alongside the wisdom gained by the Church over many centuries? The priest or deacon should be a representative in some sense of that Christian experience which is much wider than just the local, but rather the accumulation of the experience of Christians through the ages as they have tried to work out answers to the thorny day-to-day issues of Christian living. She or he will have some appreciation of the gathered wisdom and experience of Christians who have gone before, as well as Christians of different cultures. Freda will thus be put in touch with something of the Christian story which may relate to her own part of the story, and she will be helped to check out where her experience resonates with the gathered Christian wisdom and experience. Reading a *Christian journal* is another means of entering into dialogue with the wider Church community, only this time at a distance through the written word rather than the spoken witness of her local minister.

Another thing that her vicar may offer her is the all-important critical edge or questioning quality which helps to translate her experiences of the faith into the hard stuff of theology. For it is true to say that much of our Christian religious expression in prayer, worship and so on, allows for wide and liberal use of symbolism, poetic language and licence; but she will now also be in need of some hard-headed precise critique if her decisions about work are to be made upon firmer ground than sentiment and fine emotions – as adequate and as proper as these may be in many areas of Christian faith, especially as an affective underpinning to our more rational and critical qualities of awareness.

Freda's theological activity did not end there, once she had done all her thinking at church. She then had to go and remind herself of the intricate details of the problem and, no doubt, as well as having read up on employment law, it was important to talk it through in concrete terms with her employees. *Checking the hard facts* of the case was part of her theological work, which did not finish when she stopped using the word 'God' or thinking only about 'religious' matters. We might even be inclined to suggest that she could still have been doing theology as she spoke with her workmates; for she was even then having to work things out in practical terms, making faithful Christian decisions and acting responsibly. It could have been that the decision at the store was that they would all band together and refuse to make a colleague redundant, but instead try to negotiate with the bosses for an alternative policy to be implemented. In that event she would have needed all her Christian wits about her, and that would have been facilitated by keeping in touch with Christian opinion and making sure that she did not become isolated from the Christian fold; in that way, she would have been more sure that her thinking and acting would remain in conformity with what was felt to be God's will. If she managed to accomplish this complex task of keeping her actions properly integrated with Christian understandings and the Christian community, we may well wish to say that even her *actions* themselves were in some sense theological.

So what is theology?

I suspect we could go on and on like this, continually expanding our notion of theology until we began to wonder whether we were ever going to find the limits of a definition of what 'theology' is. If we went on any further we might even end up saying that whenever a Christian is living, there is theology, but I doubt whether many would be happy with such a catch-all notion as that. I suspect that most of us would feel that we should keep our definition just a bit tighter.

One way to keep our definition more carefully focused is to consider what it may mean to call theology a 'discipline'. This word refers to the many different avenues of learning and study, ranging from the various physical sciences through to the human sciences like sociology and psychology, and on through all the arts and humanities, each avenue being referred to as a separate 'discipline'. Working alongside other disciplines, theologians will be trying to ask the questions that seem to be thrown up by God as we unearth more and more of the wonders of creation. A discipline is what a disciple, or 'learner', is engaged in, and Jesus asks us to follow him as his questing and questioning disciples in the Way, serving other disciplines by being with them in the risky adventure of learning and loving in the world. It will be theology's task, therefore, to wait observantly until the other scientific disciplines – especially the social sciences – have unearthed the raw material on which theological reflection must then do its work. Unlike these other disciplines, theological reflection itself does not have the tools to analyse the internal causal relationships to be found in the human and physical factors of God's world, and it should not boast that it does. But from its role as servant, it still has a distinctive function and cutting edge to bring to the raw material that other disciplines disclose. For theological reflection sets about asking how the transcendent God is being experienced within the raw material that other disciplines have analysed. To perform this function, the theological discipline will have to be intimately related to the other disciplines, not separated from them, and yet certainly dependent upon them. In order to picture the intimacy of this relationship I will be making a distinction in this book between 'theological reflection', which to my mind is this precise but limited and dependent discipline, and the broader concept, 'doing theology', to describe the overall enterprise which results when all the disciplines, including theological reflection, work together to create a faithful dynamic of action and reflection. But we will discuss this more fully as we proceed.

This understanding of theology's place in relation to the other 'secular' disciplines may be presumed to rely on an assumption that God and God's meaning is already present in the 'secular' world, waiting there to be discovered. This is a legitimate claim for a Christian to make in view of the intimate role we believe God to have chosen to play in relation to creation. The incarnation of Christ is just one example of this intimacy, and the very physical nature of the crucifixion is another. At every turn God seems to be heavily engaged even in the very physicality of the world – God's creation. The first act of God of which we are aware is the creation itself, and the whole biblical record points to the centrality of the world of human affairs as of prime importance to God – to the extent that God eventually goes so far as to die as the incarnated expression of love for the world. The realisation that God sustains the creation moment by moment is one of the legacies of the Jewish faith that Christians have inherited, but it is a specifically Christian insight to perceive that God is incarnated within it even yet in the lives, loves and concerns of his children. Theological reflection will therefore seek to understand and interpret the world through the eyes of its Christian faith using all the sacramental, credal and biblical insights that the Church has at its disposal –

but it will be God in our experience of the world which will be the focus of theology's attention.

But theology is not interested in knowledge about the world and about God merely for interest's sake – theology is not an end in itself. It is there to serve as a tool in the transformation and conversion of that creation – that people and society may conform through peace and justice to the Kingdom of God as inaugurated by Jesus Christ. Theologians are therefore those who engage with people in their situation in life in order to look at their shared experience and ask those questions about meaning that commitment to God requires. In order to do this adequately, Christian theologians will have to be in there slogging away at life issues and problems with everyone else, but bringing to bear upon the community's experience all that we can learn from our knowledge and love of Jesus and his ways with us. So an 'ostrich theology', which would prefer not to look the world in the face, is just not an acceptable option for us unless we are to deny our Christian incarnational responsibilities.

It may now be possible to draw together some of the threads of our thinking thus far, and hazard a preliminary definition of theology.

PRELIMINARY DEFINITION:
Theology is an active and critical ministry. It investigates and reflects upon God's presence and activity in our lives, and asks what that means for us.

But even this definition has its inadequacies, and each of us will have our own particular responses to it and see different ways in which it fails to do justice to what we feel theology to be.

First of all we may be concerned to notice that the definition as it stands does not include any mention of God in history. It seems to imply that theology is only something that can take place in the present. We might want to say that God has acted in the past and that we have a record of that in the Bible and other traditions of the Church. An appreciation of all the reflection of past ages upon God's activity must be part of our endeavour as theologians. We might want to reflect forward too, because part of our experience of God surely points us into the future.

Second, we may feel that the definition assumes that human beings are responsible for every initiative in the theological enterprise, whereas our experience of theology feels more like a *relationship* with God than just abstract talk about God. Some theologians have even said that human beings cannot make God the 'object' of any study, even theology, because it is always God, not human beings, who takes the initiative in the relationship. In other words, God is never object but always subject, and we have therefore to rely for any and every insight on being told it in the first place by God. On this reckoning, theology is to be defined as very much a receiving discipline. There seems, however, to be a critical flaw in this belief, for if God were directly responsible for 'telegraphing' truths to us in this fashion, then there should surely be much more agreement between Christians about the received truths of theology than there would appear to be, even given the differences we could attribute to the inadaquacy of our human 'receiving apparatus'. In fact, any cursory glance at all the conflicting notions in theology will prove that we are not simply repositories of received revelation. Theology should indeed be a relationship that we enter into with God and with one another but, as with any good relationship, it must be a two-way affair, and will demand that we be more than repositories of God's communications to us. But we can go even further than this, for an interrelationship with God is so crucial to the theological enterprise that it should even mirror its relational character by having a *collaborative* aspect at the heart of its methodology, and operate in such a way that it becomes the activity of the whole community working collaboratively together rather than remain the preserve of isolated individual theologians. It must be a thing that we do together.

Third, we have recognised in our preliminary definition that theology is active, but is it not also *transforming*? If theology only interprets and does not transform, then it is not an aspect of a living faith but of a dead one. The very aim of theology is to enable the transformation of Christians so that they become the conscious and active agents of the transformation of history at God's behest. In this way, Christian theological groups become the salt of the earth, the leaven in the lump (Matthew 5.13 and 13.33), so that the Church becomes more truly a sign of the Kingdom and so that peace and justice may become the hallmarks of our fellowship and our society. Our definition needs to stress, then, that Christian theology implies challenge, response and transformation. One cannot do theology without expecting change.

Fourth, we do not distinguish in our definition between Christian theology and any other sort of theology. Other faiths have great traditions of theology and philosophy that we ignore at our peril in this multi-faith society, but our committed belief in salvation through the action of the Trinity distinguishes our understandings of reality very sharply from theirs. Do we want to make this distinction clear in our definition, or do we prefer to remain very open to the insights that they bring to bear upon our work?

Fifth, our definition may sound as if we have always to start from scratch in our theological work. But do we not already have a treasure store of theologians to draw upon? Surely we already have some basic ideas and vocabulary that theologians throughout the years have created in order to help us in our theological endeavour. Incorporating this into our definition will surely encourage us to learn from their earlier successes and failures. It will also bring an historical perspective to the task and remind us that we are engaging in theology in company with those Christians who have gone before us and those who will come after.

In the light of all this, we might feel that our preliminary definition of theology has to be entirely redrawn, and the reader might even at this stage like to spend a little time reflecting upon the definition and redraft it accordingly. What I will now attempt to do, however, is to push ahead, hoping that even though a definition of theology may only now be emerging in embryo in these pages, it is nevertheless possible to discern some exciting new signposts on the theological horizon which will help build up a picture of a new way of being theologians together. Then, in the rest of the book, I will endeavour to spell out how that can be worked out both in theory and in practice and so arrive at a working definition of a theology that is ambitiously broad, and yet precise in its purpose and function. So first let us make sure that we have our ground rules more firmly established for that endeavour.

If you have ever tried to put up a tent in a howling gale you will know how important it is to get a few tent pegs firmly in place before trying to erect the tent itself. What I am about to do is somewhat similar, for already in our discussion there are emerging some strong outcrops that will serve as markers or 'tent pegs'; there are also other theological insights on the scene that we can now gather and place so that they will act as secure ground rules for the theological canopy that we can then begin to erect in the chapters that follow.

New theological horizons

As we survey the current theological landscape, there are many recent developments that may suggest elements and insights that will prove to be just the 'tent pegs' for which we are searching. For example, there have been new political theologies developing in Europe and liberation theologies sprouting up in the economically poorer countries of the world. A new surge of interest in charismatic faith is to be seen on both sides of the Atlantic and the Roman Catholic Church has been coming to terms with the second Vatican Council. Black Christians have been reintroducing the pentecostal tradition, and at the same time have been opening up their experience of being black to see how that helps our understanding of the gospel. Women too have been reconsidering their Christian identity as females and have suggested how this may foster a fresh appreciation of the very nature of God. The ecumenical journey now faces the additional challenge of multi-faith dialogue as an abundance of cultures meet on the streets of Britain. These are all relatively new features which have grown up on an already fascinating theological landscape. From this rich mix, there are six theological insights that I find so exciting and full of potential that I want to set them out now at the close of this chapter as my secure theological 'tent pegs'; we can then build upon them our new way of being theologians and of doing theology.

Each insight relates very firmly in my mind to a key element in the traditions of the faith, and so we may set them out diagrammatically before taking each in turn in more detail.

1 Full salvation must include liberation

The word 'liberation' has recently been emphasised in our theological vocabulary to focus upon two important and related Christian truths. The first is that God is interested in more than disembodied spirits. There has in the past been an emphasis in the Church upon the importance of the soul to the detriment of any concern at all about the well-being of the body, even though our Jewish forebears used the word 'soul' to refer to the whole of the created person. Later Greek influence led the Church into the mistake of concentrating so much upon the importance of the spirit that this entirely overshadowed any proper concern for the concrete historical realities which are also part of what it is to be human. The word 'liberation' reminds us forcefully that Christian salvation is not just for our spirit's sake. Salvation is for every aspect of what it is to be human – the historical, geographical and physical, just as much as the spiritual and intellectual elements. But the word 'liberation' goes on to enhance our understanding of salvation yet further.

With the privatisation of Christianity, which was begun at the Reformation and

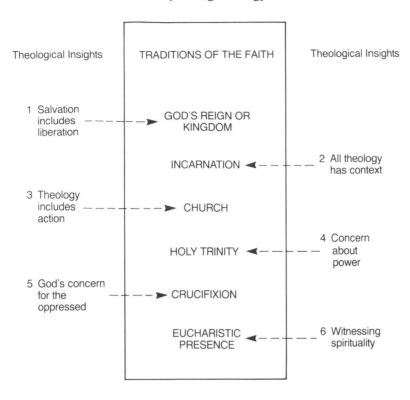

Theological Insights	TRADITIONS OF THE FAITH	Theological Insights
1 Salvation includes liberation	→ GOD'S REIGN OR KINGDOM	
	INCARNATION ←	2 All theology has context
3 Theology includes action	→ CHURCH	
	HOLY TRINITY ←	4 Concern about power
5 God's concern for the oppressed	→ CRUCIFIXION	
	EUCHARISTIC PRESENCE ←	6 Witnessing spirituality

which has been reinforced in our culture by the advent of psychology and the more recent re-emphasis upon the freedom of the market-place, there has also developed a helpful stress upon the importance of the individual before God, and the individual's choice in faithfully accepting God's freely given redemption. But as if to balance this emphasis, we must surely also remember that none of us is an island, separated from our fellow human beings. As the African proverb has it, 'a person is a person because of other persons'. There is no such thing as a fully human being who is not a human being in relationship to society. On the contrary, we are so much partakers one of another that my freedom cannot truly be complete unless the freedom of my brothers and sisters is also accomplished. If I should claim to be in some sense saved by Christ, then dare I rest until the whole earth is also free? But I can go even further than this, for when I look to the saving action of Christ I cannot but be aware of God's intention to save the whole world through Christ, not just a few individuals within it. So it is that when in St Matthew's account of the crucifixion we read that there was an earthquake at the very moment that Jesus died on the cross (Matthew 27.51), it is as if Matthew were graphically reminding us that Christ's death affected not only individual men and women but it brought about a fundamental change in the structures of creation – the earth itself was moved. At the crucifixion, then, God is concerned to save not only individual persons, but to put to right the very structures of creation, life and its relationships – and this must of course include the economic order and the political and cultural structures[8] of society too. To deny this would be to deny that God has a saving interest in the profound matters of our existence, the profound concerns of the children he has created. To embrace this fact is to affirm that true salvation works not only at the level of personal salvation, but also at the levels of community and social structure, thus allowing us to pray at the Eucharist that 'all Your children shall be free and the whole earth live to praise Your name'.[9]

Resonating with all this talk about bodily and structural salvation or liberation is that element in our commonly held tradition of faith which Jesus called the Kingdom or Reign of God. This is the structural manifestation of God's salvation for all humanity and all creation when the whole universe will behave in a way that conforms to God's holy and loving will. Within the Kingdom concerns will be numbered the structural questions of ecological stewardship, care for gender, class, ethnicity, politics – absolutely everything and everybody. It will be the arena where God's will is manifestly obeyed and cherished – the place of liberation.

The implication of all this, the 'tent peg' that we can drive home, is that in future our theological work must be concerned both for the structural aspects of salvation as well as for the transformation of individuals. Our theology must focus upon the issues of human freedom and fulfilment at the personal, communal and structural levels so that people can become the active subjects of their situations and not just pawns in the game of life; for while structures have the potential to liberate human beings and enable them to live in fellowship, body and soul, these same structures also have the capacity to hold whole groups captive. God's promise of this liberating freedom will also impart a strong joyous element into our theological adventure – we must know how to celebrate the Kingdom!

2 All theology has context

The second insight that should help as a secure 'tent peg' from which to develop a new way of doing theology has to do with context. This word 'context' – like 'praxis', which we met earlier – suffers a little from being very extensively used, but that is simply because it is a good word and does its work precisely. The point it makes here is that God does not reveal Godself in a vacuum, but always and inevitably by way of an experience. All revelation must be mediated through some experience or other and therefore it has a context, and a surrounding situation that itself becomes part of the revelation God presents. If we take an example it may become clearer. When Moses experienced God in the burning bush, he did not tell his friends of some disembodied abstract experience, but talked instead of a bush, a voice, a message and a command. The bush itself became for him at that moment a significant part of his experience of God. The historical surroundings, the place, the time, were all contributory factors to any understanding of the experience. Similarly, even if God is experienced in some 'out of the body' type of meditation, the meditator's state becomes a significant attribute of the revelation. This presents a problem for us, however, because we find that it is not legitimate to abstract a revelation from one context – to 'disembody' it – and to 'apply' it elsewhere without doing injustice to the specificity of the original experience. For example, the legal codes and expectations of the early Hebrews related to cooking, clothing, animal sacrifice and so on, and we find them expressed as if they were divine revelation in the Book of Leviticus and elsewhere. But such codes are very much limited by their historical and geographical context as a body of law seemingly appropriate to a very particular nomadic culture during the development of the Hebrew people and their cult. Few Christians today are mindful of religious circumcision or the wearing of mixed textiles, nor would they be prepared to take part in animal sacrifice or religious massacre of antagonistic tribes; yet such matters are all to be found in those biblical codes of law. The same discrimination would apply if I should take down a volume of theological sermons by Martin Luther from a library shelf. I should be startled at the contents, with all the swearing, cussing and foul language in so many of his sermons. I would have to remind myself that he was preaching not in twentieth-century Britain, but in the context of medieval Germany where he was leading the Protestant Reformation and where such expletives were commonplace among Christians. Or again, I will not understand very well the full implications of the theological writings of St Augustine until I realise that he was beset by the problems of trying to come to terms with the decline and demise of the Roman Empire which was coming adrift all around him. Now if the context is so important to our understanding of these biblical law codes and theologians of the past, then we must also remember that our creeds and all our other biblical material will have their original contexts too. God's revelation comes to particular people in particular places at particular times, and is never just shot into a vacuum. The surrounding culture, economic structure and political setting will all be important factors of context, and therefore significant factors for any understanding of the original intention of the revelation or the theology that was produced from it. It has always been this way; thus we should not be fearful if the theology we produce today seems to be related so intimately to the culture that surrounds us. To understand this is to appreciate that all theological statements are of necessity provisional and relative to their context, and there has never been and never will be a theology that is otherwise. Jesus made this clear again and again. He often spoke of the Mosaic Law of the Hebrew Scriptures as needing to be read against the background of its own earlier context, and he would then proceed to update it in the light of his own new context and its need.[10]

Experience in the mission field abroad has brought home to Christians today the importance of allowing each culture to make the Christian faith its own, for missionaries have realised what crass mistakes were made in the past by offering the Christian faith only in the terms of their own European-based contexts.[11] For example, was it ever really right to invite Africans to worship a Jesus with a white European face? But if we once agree that European expressions of faith should not be foisted upon African Christians in this way, then we must push that principle a little further and ask whether any culture should dictate to another what the truths of faith should be for that receiving culture. Can a middle-class Anglican culture, for example, ever tell a working-class or black British culture about Jesus without overlaying the gospel with all sorts of cultural prejudices of its own? But this realisation of the importance of context has not only raised problems, but has had very positive effects too for, as well as alerting us to the dangers of cultural imperialism, it has also liberated some Christians to begin to speak about God from within their own experience and context, and that freedom has spawned the exciting new developments of black theology, women's theology, and similar movements.

From this perspective of the importance of context we can now look again to our heritage of faith and find that our eyes are drawn to the fact of the incarnation of our Lord as a theological reference point. In Christ's incarnation, God chose to be revealed quite specifically within a particular context, culture and ethnic group-ing. One particular Jewish woman gave birth to him in a specific place at an observable time. Humanity's encounter with the Divine in Christ Jesus was com-pletely contextual. It was only after the resurrection that the faith was, in a sense, freed from the confines of its originating context, but that was only in order that it could find a home in other specific cultures. So it was at Pentecost that the message was heard by so very many people of differing cultures, but each in the context of their own mother tongue (Acts 2.8).

What this means for our development of a contemporary style of doing theology is that we must be sure that theology is allowed to develop from the people's own context and culture and is not bound up in an alien culture and thrust upon them from outside their context. Christ puts himself right inside the situation alongside the people's experience, and our theology should likewise be indigenous and contextual, originating from within the specific experience that people themselves have of God and God's world. We must also be sure to devise a theological method that allows for the careful critical reading of each context so that our theological work jumps to no abstract conclusions, but instead produces substantial, pertinent theology that is relevant to real people in their specific contexts.

3 Theology includes action

There is a growing appreciation of the fact that 'talk comes cheap', and it is not until we see someone in action that we can really judge their motives, their commitment or their competence. This goes for theologians too, and provides our third 'tent peg' for the development of a new way of doing theology. We emphasise the place of action in theology because it is only through doing that we really understand. By actually doing something rather than merely speaking about it, we begin to appreciate the thing spoken of in a totally new way and we begin to experience its fuller meaning from the perspective of participation. For example, it is one thing to read the script of a play, but it puts the play into an altogether different dimension of meaning if we ourselves act it out or are there at a performance. And so it is with theology. Academic theological discussion remains empty if it does not spring out of the experience of the Church's life. Perhaps this is why so much profound theology has been generated out of the experience of worship,[12] where the community meets intimately together to celebrate the great works of God. This is one reason why we can learn so much from the Church's sacraments – those acted signs of God's grace. All this means that we will not be content merely to 'read' theology but we will be wanting to 'do theology' by engaging in the dynamic interplay of action and reflection. This is not to say that doing is necessarily more important than thinking, but one without the other easily ends in muddle if not disaster. Jesus seems to have felt that both were important, but that in the end the quality of our actions would be our judge – 'By their fruits you shall know them' (Matthew 7.16 and 20). Although Jesus put much store by right teaching and reflection, at the end of the day the criterion of judgement for him was whether theological thought or action brought a remedy to human suffering.[13] If all that theology consists of is reflection upon reflections, then all that theology will be is a pale and distant image of the real thing. Theory is fascinating, but it tempts us to forget the real world from which it springs. Theory is useful when it stands back from a situation because it can thereby bring an important element of critique to bear upon it, but ideas that are worked out in theory may be altogether out of place in the world of things and human beings. But if our theology is integrated into the very heartbeat of Christian faithful action, then our theological reflection can become focused, relevant and attentive to the living God in each situation and can instruct our action so that it is informed and on target for Christian transformation. If action is part of theology, then we will be able to judge theology not only by its erudition, but also by the way in which it generates faithful lives.

As we look for a reference point from our heritage of faith which resonates with this question of active theology, we may be particularly drawn to the notion of the Church as the body of Christ, for here is presented to us a picture of the reflective, intentional community in action. A body not dreaming, not asleep, not merely reflecting, but expressive, pensive, prayerful and active – the body, an appropriate dynamic of reflection and action.

4 *The question of power*

The fourth element on the theological landscape that will help towards discovering a new way of being theologians, is the current concern about power, and I believe very strongly that to wrestle with the question of power is to wrestle with the character of the Divine.[14] First of all, it is not for nothing that we call God 'the Almighty', for Christianity shares with so many of the great faiths the conviction that all power comes ultimately from God – although how God chooses to use that power is one of the unfathomable mysteries. Christians maintain that part of that mystery is expressed in the statement that 'God is love' and this because God manifests power in love. When I truly love another human being I open myself to them in vulnerability and try to relinquish my power to control them. I also take joy in the fun of the interplay of our power, although I have to learn where the boundaries are to be drawn so that I do not hurt the other but respect the vulnerability which they are lovingly offering. I will show the depth of my love by my preparedness to risk my power, be that in showing courage to defend them or else in making the ultimate sacrifice of my power in suffering for them. It was this kind of powerful loving that was taken to its fullest divine extent in the passion of Jesus on the cross.

Power, then, is a spiritual question because it relates so intimately with the question of love. But often power is anything but loving, and is used to oppress and mar God's image in our fellows. Nor is it only a question of relationships at the level of individuals, but power operates at structural levels too: in international corporations, in economic and political forces and in institutional affairs. It involves questions of authority, wealth, control, status, class and much else. So these interrelated words, 'power' and 'love', thereby touch us at our most intimately caring moments and also when we are most detached and arrogant. They touch us in our personal lives and at every level where we are related structurally to others. When Jesus specifies in the Beatitudes (Matthew 5.3–12) that it is the powerless who are especially blessed of God, he confounds our prejudices about the nature of power. When he then promises even us a share in his power to heal, forgive and work wonders, he leaves us feeling overwhelmed by the abundant generosity of the Almighty.

It is the doctrine of the Holy Trinity that for me most resonates with this issue of loving power, for the trinitarian doctrine stresses that there is an intimate loving relationship of shared power and identity even within the dynamic of the Godhead itself. The Church may be split on the issue,[15] but within the Godhead there is no argument or disunity about who is the greatest or with whom the power should most naturally reside. Both within the Godhead itself and in God's way with creation, there is a preparedness to share power to become vulnerable. To this end God chooses to suffer with creation rather than to dominate it, choosing the way of the artist who deigns to work vulnerably within the limitations of the medium he or she has chosen as a means of self-expression in the world.

This question of power, then, is our fourth secure 'tent peg', and it has taken centre stage of late on the theological landscape just as it has in the realms of politics, economics and culture; and from this we can draw at least three lessons for our present purposes. First, our theology needs to be a shared community affair, open to all the pressures and risks that this may entail, but certainly no longer locked away safely in the confines of the classroom. It must become public domain material, and all the more vulnerable for that. And the relationships within the theological group must have no trace of domination about them either – the leadership and the expertise must be an open and shared responsibility. Second, within this open community there must be a 'speaking the truth in love' so that the critical honesty required of theological rigour may gently and firmly be supported within the fellowship. Third, the question of power, its nature and its exercise, must remain always of prime concern to our theology, since love is the power of the Divine.

5 God's special concern for the oppressed

We hear a great deal on the contemporary theological scene about God's 'bias to the poor',[16] and there is little doubt, to judge by the inequalities of opportunity even in current Western society, that the question of the poor must be of major concern to any Christian. We must be careful, however, to make it clear that God has a final concern for the well-being and salvation of all creation and that the oppressed have a special place in God's heart, not to the detriment of his love for all humanity but precisely because of it. But first, a word about the term 'the oppressed', which some people find a stumbling-block. In one sense the awkwardness and offensiveness of the word serves its purpose well, but others may find it helpful to think in terms of the older and more traditional phrase, 'those who are heavy laden'.[17] Such a phrase helps us to begin to feel the sense of burden experienced by those in our society who are bent under the strains of poverty, unemployment, ill-health and other oppressions which afflict so many at the bottom of the class structure. I would certainly not want to limit the use of the term 'oppression' only to the financially poor, for although it is at the economic base of society that the downtrodden feel that crushing weight of poverty, it is at the superstructural levels of our society[18] that we will also find those who are shackled and burdened by the oppressions of gender, minority culture, family pressure, housing, health, education and so on. It is often the case that these various pressures all build up together into a multiple deprivation of just one specific group, and this has led many scientific observers to utilise the word 'class' to distinguish those groups most or least at risk from these multiple burdens and pressures. Jesus chooses to ally himself with those who are most oppressed and who see society from the underside when in the parable of the sheep and the goats he speaks of himself being found in those who are hungry, thirsty, strangers, naked, sick and imprisoned (Matthew 25.35–46). It is only from the perspective of the least, the most downtrodden in any society, that a society may best be judged, and this because the poor are in the best place to see the realities of their society, because, unlike others, they are not protected from it in any way, but they are thrust up against it in a way that no other groups are. When we try to make judgements about our society it would be well to seek the vantage point of the oppressed, and to that end it serves us well in our theological work always to have before us the three pivotal issues of gender, ethnicity and class, for these and their attendant questions will most likely pinpoint for us those people who are being most hurt within any modern society. But as God's heart goes out especially to those who are least protected from the realities of a particular society's structures and agencies, so God seeks to save the oppressed and oppressor alike from the captivity in which they both are blinded and crippled. God's 'bias' to the poor is not to the detriment of his love for the rich, but is an expression of God's saving action at the heart of the whole dilemma. God's option for the poor is certainly not because the poor are good, but because God is good.

The theological reference point to which we may find ourselves being drawn when we think of God's great concern for the oppressed is the shocking historical fact of the crucifixion of Christ. Jesus shows his solidarity with the downtrodden from first to last, from his birth in a cattle shed to his painful execution as a political prisoner of conscience. But at the crucifixion, God holds Jesus up for all to see so that evil can be displayed back to itself.[19] In this way Jesus takes up the role of the suffering servant,[20] who brings the key to history in solidarity with the wretched of the earth and makes God's protest at innocent suffering. In such concern for the oppressed, God saves the whole human race.

Our best theological work will therefore stem from a prior commitment to the downtrodden. It will be through solidarity and constant sharing with those who are heavy laden that the issues of God's concern will undoubtedly surface, and it will be by being involved and committed that we will be given ears to hear and eyes to see.

6 Courageous spirituality for witness

It follows, then, that at the heart of any faithful theology there must be spiritual commitment. And given the tremendous forces that are today ranged against justice and peace, ours must be a courageous spirituality which is willing to live with all the risks of uncertainty and provisionality. Our theology must entail a spirituality that can stand the test of ill-treatment, ridicule and denial of status. We have unfortunately long been harbouring notions of spirituality and holiness as an otherworldly naïveté, but this sort of limp spirituality will not serve us in the harsh new cultural landscape of today where we will certainly need to be 'as harmless as doves but as wary as serpents' (Matthew 10.16). We will need an earthy and communal spirituality of obedience and celebration, which is so at home in its own milieu that it knows how to see God in the secular world around it, and drink up spiritual resources through the pavements of the city or the fields of the countryside. This sort of witnessing spirituality, about which I will have more to say later, will underpin so much of the community's theological endeavour.

An element from our Christian heritage that resonates so clearly with this notion of a courageous and witnessing spirituality is that of Eucharistic presence. Just as the body of Christ is somehow mystically present in the Eucharistic celebration, so also Christ is present in those who remain faithful. Their activity will not be frenzied and may only very rarely result in any momentous change, but they will remain at their posts in hopeful and active expectation. At the Eucharist the whole community should not merely be re-enacting a dead memory, but instead engaging in transforming action; and it is through that action that the community participates in the spiritual transformation of the world at large and looks for the coming of the Kingdom.[21]

The new theologians, then, must have these essential spiritual qualities so that together they may become so imbued with the mind of Christ[22] and his character that they find it natural, even amid the struggles of the downtrodden, to read the facts of the world through the perspective of Jesus.

In this chapter we have considered some of the difficulties that are forced upon us by a limited and conventional understanding of the nature of theology, and I hope we have prepared ourselves to engage in a broadening of its scope and meaning. We began with a critical consideration of a preliminary definition, and we have secured six markers or theological 'tent pegs' which should help us construct a new and more ambitious model for doing theology. These markers remind us that our new model must give special regard to issue of liberation, context, action, power, oppression and spirituality. We can now proceed in Chapter 2 to develop an alternative route into the doing of theology so that it may be both transforming and celebratory.

Notes

1 See the work of Jim Hart and Neville Black of the Evangelical Urban Training Project, for example, *Learning Without Books* (EUTP, PO Box 83, Liverpool L69 8AN).
2 See, for example, the Acts of the Apostles, chapter 10.
3 The 'banking theory of education' is a term used by Paulo Freire and others to describe an understanding of education as the imparting of factual content by the teacher which is filed and stored by the students, whose task is to live off that capital and to draw interest from it by reproducing that content on demand. See, for example, Freire's *Pedagogy of the Oppressed* (Penguin, 1972), chapter 2.
4 cf. unpublished paper by T. Richard Snyder, 'Some Thoughts on Contextual Education', New York Theological Seminary, USA, January 1973.
5 See R. Schreiter, *Constructing Local Theologies* (SCM, 1985), chapter 1 on Translation and Adaptation Models of theology, and later sections on how to use the observation tools of semiotics to understand cultures. See further, Aylward Shorter, *Toward a Theology of Inculturation* (Geoffrey Chapman, 1988).
6 'Faith seeking understanding' translates the Latin definition of theology, *fides quaerens intellectum*.

7 A clear distinction is made by some liberation theologians between 'religion', which is the uncritical indulgence in symbolism in order to express faith, faith being understood to be a human awareness of God's freely given grace, and 'theology', which is taken to be a much more rational and critical mode which comes after religion. See, for example, Clodovis Boff, *Theology and Praxis: Epistemological Foundations* (Orbis, 1987), pp. 110f.

8 'The concept "structure" functions to point to the patterns or regularities that transcend or precede or condition the individual phenomena we can immediately perceive. The bridge is more than the cables and girders that compose it; the psychic "complex" or "syndrome" is much more than the thoughts and reflexes it organises; the "class" is much more than the individual persons who make it up; a "religion" is much more than a bagful of assorted practices. It is this patternedness that the word "structure" tries to enable us to perceive within all the varieties of its appearance' (John Howard Yoder, *The Politics of Jesus* (W. B. Eerdmans, 1972), p. 190).

9 Eucharistic Rite A, paragraph 52, *Alternative Service Book* (CBF, Church of England, 1980), p. 144.

10 For example, Matthew 19.7-9, On the matter of all theologies being contextual, see Schreiter, *Constructing Local Theologies*, pp. 93ff.

11 cf. Vincent J. Donovan, *Christianity Rediscovered: An Epistle from the Masai* (Indiana, 1978/SCM, 1982). See also Roland Allen, *Missionary Methods* (1912).

12 We find many examples in the Bible of theology being generated from liturgy; cf. the letter to the Hebrews and the Book of Revelation. In the Hebrew Scriptures the great festivals likewise gave rise to theologies of Passover, Exodus, and so on.

13 cf. Mark 2.9-12, 'Which of these is easier . . .?'

14 cf. Genesis 32.23-32. When Jacob wrestles with God at Jabbok he is wrestling with questions of power, authority and blessing.

15 The Roman Catholic and Orthodox Churches have long been divided concerning the *Filioque* clause in the Creed, translated 'and the Son' when included in the Nicene Creed, which some believe puts the Holy Spirit into a hierarchical subservience to the other two persons of the Trinity.

16 Bishop David Sheppard, *Bias to the Poor* (Hodder & Stoughton, 1983). A more recent and systematic survey of reasons for taking this stance is to be found in Leonardo and Clodovis Boff, *Introducing Liberation Theology* (Burns & Oates, 1987), pp. 44-6.

17 Words taken from Matthew 11.28, 'Come unto me all that travail and are heavy laden, and I will refresh you', which are used in relation to the prayers of confession and absolution in the Anglican rite for Holy Communion.

18 Some see society as ultimately based upon the infrastructure of its productive, technological economy. Constructed upon this infrastructure is the superstructural culture of society, which will include factors of education, housing, health, ethnicity and so on. Oppression can be found in each area, poverty being within the infrastructure for example, and racism within the superstructure.

19 See, for example, John 12.32, and compare the lifting of the fiery serpent by Moses (Numbers 21.4-9), where those who had been bitten could see it and be healed.

20 cf. Isaiah 50.4-11.

21 cf. Tissa Balasuriya, *The Eucharist and Human Liberation* (SCM, 1979).

22 cf. Philippians 2.5 and 1 Corinthians 2.16.

2

A new way of being theologians

During my predominantly urban ministry, I have developed a style and method of doing theology which has quite naturally emerged from the needs of the people and situations with which I have been engaged. It has proved to be creative and productive for those with whom I have lived and worked, and it has grown from the theological insights just described – the 'tent pegs' which hold it firm even when under the strains of the issues generated by our new economic and political situation.[1] All this has inevitably prompted me to try to clarify what the nature of the method is, and, slowly but surely, a picture has come into focus. I want to offer that now, but on the strict understanding that theological groups do well to develop and redesign the model as their own predicament determines. On that basis, many have found the model that follows quite helpful.

It was some years ago when I came across a diagram in a book on industrial and educational psychology[2] that was intended to describe a method of learning which paid due attention to the experiences that adult students brought to the classroom. The diagram attempted to display how elements from experience could be brought together with elements of theory. I remember how I began to play with the idea of substituting into that diagram new words and phrases which could convert it from a conservative learning model into a pattern for personal and social trans- formation, and thus produce a picture of what I meant by the phrase 'doing theology'. After much trial and error with the small group of urban Christians with whom I was then working, I ended up with a spiral diagram that owed much to my reading of Paulo Freire and Juan Luis Segundo, two fascinating thinkers from South America.[3] Most of the descriptions of theology that I had met before had made the whole theological process sound more like a method of control and conditioning than an open system of discovery and transformation; however, the more I developed my spiral diagram, the greater my conviction grew that here was a style and approach that would serve people who were more concerned to be open to the Spirit's operation in the world rather than merely learning theological constructs of past eras. All that was some years ago and it was not until much later that I realised that what I had been doing then was trying to reinvent the wheel! For it was on meeting a number of Roman Catholic friends who had recently returned from Latin America that I learnt that there already existed a spiral model of doing theology which they referred to as the Pastoral Circle or Cycle – the similarities between that and my home-grown spiral were remarkable. The Pastoral Cycle had been developed by liberation theologians working from a model originally created by Father Joseph Cardijn, a Belgian priest who had been the inspiration to many Catholic workers and students between the wars. He had attempted to find ways of moving Christians to a more careful analysis of their situation by asking them to 'see, judge and act' upon their experiences. The Catholic justice and peace movement had taken that framework and developed it significantly, and, more recently, Joe Holland and Peter Henriot in North America have inspired a movement there towards what they call 'Social Analysis'. In Europe, such organisations as INODEP have been sponsoring similar routes into theology.[4] I found so many parallels between all this work and what we had spontaneously been developing here that I was even more convinced that we were mutually on the right track.

Although my spiral diagram conforms largely to the Latin American Pastoral Cycle, the way of working it which will be described in this book is very much home-grown, and has been developed from many hours' experience of using the model with a variety of different Christian groups in Britain.

Let me then present, in diagrammatic form, how I think we should go about the business of doing theology in the complex society in which we live. As I have suggested, I have found it most helpful to think of the process as a circle, cycle or, even better, a spiral, which moves around continually from action to reflection and from reflection to action; it is this constant interplay between the two that we have earlier called 'praxis'. To earth my description it may be useful to make reference to an example so that we can see how the spiral works in practice, although I will of course be going into more practical detail in subsequent chapters. Freda, whom we mentioned in Chapter 1, presents an ideal example, because her situation of having to make a decision at work about a staff redundancy is a typical starting point for doing theology. Thus the spiral starts with *experience*.

As was constantly stressed in Chapter 1, our theological work must always remain conscious of the encounter with experience. This is fundamental to any earthed theology, and so this is where we must start. We begin, when doing theology, by trying to become as conscious of the real situation that surrounds us as we possibly can. We will not be wanting at this stage to engage in a thorough analysis, but instead to make sure that we really are aware and conscious of the feelings, emotions and impressions that the experience engenders. No Christians can engage dispassionately about God, and thus it will be much better for us to take as our starting point for theology an involved encounter of participation in something that touches us deeply as human beings. The experience we choose to consider may be a very active one, like running a rowdy youth club evening, or it might be passive – more of a predicament than an activity. Or it may be a situation demanding a response, like that of Freda hearing that an employee had to go. In any event, there is a situation that confronts us or an activity to cope with. And it is interesting to note how often the situation which grabs us to do theology will have this common element of worry or anguish about it. 'How are we going to cope with this?' or 'what on earth can we do about that?' is so often the starting point for

a relevant and exciting piece of theological work, even though it begins on a
negative and worrying note. This may have something to do with God's special
concern for those who are heavy laden; but, in any case, it is a fact that good
theology is more likely to derive from a problem than a statement, more likely to
arise in a prison than a palace.

It is this felt experience that can be our starting point, with all its implicit
assumptions and emotional sub-strata. As we engage this aspect of the Doing
Theology Spiral, we will tell stories about how the experience feels and hear from
others in the theological group how they are feeling, and what sort of experience it
is for them. Of course, no one comes to the experience from a vacuum, and so, at
this early stage, opportunity is made to explore some of our prior feelings and
prejudices, for good or ill, about the experience or issue. As Christians, we will
also want to express something of our inner understandings of what meanings and
values lie behind our immediate perceptions of the situation and share some of
those feelings together. Often this can be done through prayer and worship, as well
as by the utilisation of either discussion or non-verbal exercises in the group. In
any event, the group will try at this stage to make sure that they have properly
identified just what the experience is and that they have a feel for something of the
significance of the experience; to discern what their investment is in the situation
and finally to become more aware of the issues that are at stake and the questions
that are begged by the experience. When they have made this preliminary engagement with the issue and experience, it becomes possible to move on to more
concerted analysis of what is happening in the situation. This is done by moving
around the spiral into the *exploration* phase.

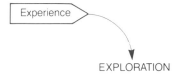

Exploration is key, and yet it is a stage often skipped by hasty would-be
theologians. Having told stories of how they feel about the experience or situation
in which they are participating, it is no good the group assuming that first impressions have in fact presented a precise and accurate picture of what is happening.
The only way that a theological group can come anywhere near knowing what is
really going on is to immerse themselves in a thorough analysis of the situation in
which it is set and really make sure they know their stuff. If Freda had heard only
the first word or two that her boss had spoken to her, and then switched off from
listening to him in order to go straight down to her Bible study group, she might
well have missed some vital information that would have made an enormous
difference to the whole situation. Likewise, if she had not taken time to read up on
employment law, she would never have known of the wider implications of her
predicament.

We too have to use all the disciplines at our disposal to get right under the skin of
the situation about which we are endeavouring to do theology. We need to use our
critical imagination in order to ask perceptive questions thrown up by our initial

appreciation of the situation, and then set about gaining as much information and insight into the experience as we can using whatever disciplines of enquiry are necessary. It makes very good sense to use experts in the fields of sociology, psychology and the humanities, as long as they are invited in just for this part of the exercise and not allowed to let their own agendas dominate the group's life. But the group's own ability to 'read the signs of the times' and a large helping of street wisdom will often be just as important in this analysis as academic knowledge. The group will need a listening sensitivity to the situation and the people within it. They will want to itemise, analyse, search back through the history, and gain perspectives from other sources. They will need to ask questions about individual agents around the scene, look at the structures that are operating and ask questions about their power. It may even be possible, and perhaps important, to put the experience into a national or even international perspective – especially in these days of the EEC and transnational companies. It will be important to see who is benefiting and who is losing out in the situation, what values are or are not operating, and in what direction the whole issue seems to be heading. The group will need to know the situation inside out, for the clearer it can be at this exploration stage, then the more their later theological reflection and activity will go to the jugular of the experience.

Having explored our experience, the next stage is that we think and *reflect* about it all.

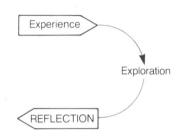

From the first moment of engagement in this exercise, the participants may already have been aware of all sorts of Christian assumptions that lay behind their initial impressions of the situation, and it was important to think and pray about those assumptions even at the outset. But in this reflection phase it will be necessary to make a concerted and conscious effort to see how the Christian faith relates to the experience, now that time has been taken to analyse and explore its implications more carefully. The situation being experienced must be brought into direct intimate contact with the Christian faith and all that the Christian community means for them. In this way, the group will be able to check the situation against that Christian heritage, and check the heritage against the situation. Bible study, prayer, worship, hymns and songs, the creeds and councils of the Church, the theologies of times past, the present social teaching of the Church,[5] the great themes of the faith like salvation, creation, sin, thanksgiving, and so on: all these and much more will be at the group's disposal as it engages in theological reflection upon the experience. Just as Freda went to her church to worship and to her Christian house group meeting, and talked it through with the vicar and read some literature about the subject, so the group will need to reflect carefully upon its experience in all sorts of ways. Freda may well have considered some of the Old Testament prophets' injunctions about the nature of justice in society, or been helped by hearing a collect about human responsibility and God's grace. The stories of creation and the Garden of Eden in the Book of Genesis may have thrown light on the difficult balance that must be struck between being productive and being responsible stewards of God's creation. Jesus' discipleship group may well have modelled to her something of the sort of solidarity that she and her colleagues were striving to emulate, and so on. As did Freda, each theological group will try to bring forward those treasures from the Christian heritage which seem to resonate with the experience that they are currently encountering. And this activity will help them to discern whether the story they are telling in their lives might truly be considered as part and parcel of the Jesus story, or whether their words and actions are just the telling of their own separate story – an altogether different story.

We can also learn from Freda that this whole reflective exercise is best not done in isolation. She needed others around her for her to do her theology and the same will be true for us. The group helps in a whole variety of ways and not least because – although at first sight it may not appear to be the case – the theological depth of most Christians is quite astounding once they find their voice, and we would not want to ignore that great resource. But this potential can only be tapped if all Christians are encouraged to participate in theology – even at this reflective stage. To begin with, they may need a lot of support and encouragement, and this the group can give, but we must never forget that theology is the activity of the whole body of Christ, and we waste that wide resource if we try to individualise it and separate it from the community.

In Chapter 5 I will say a lot more about this reflective element in the theological cycle, and those later detailed comments will require a slight modification of this part of our spiral diagram, but at this stage it is more helpful to keep the picture as simple as possible and see how the next stage in the process of doing theology develops out of reflection. For next in the cycle comes that element we might wish to call *response*.

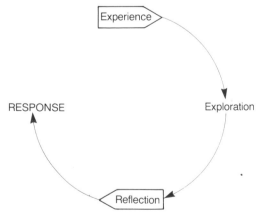

We can sit and reflect till the cows come home. If that's all theology is ever going to do for us, then we would be right to ignore it. But the essential style of the sort of Christian theology being described here is that it gets back into the action at this point with new insight and drive. To this end the group asks itself, 'In the light of all the experience, exploration and reflection, what does God now require of us?' This is where faith and action go hand in hand once again. This is where theology becomes concrete again, and cashes out in experience, for the group sets about experimenting with a range of different responses to see which one works best in practice given the new insights derived from the theological reflection phase. Freda, you will remember, had many options. She could choose to sack one of her staff, or reflection might have prompted her to try to engage in new negotiations with her employer. Such negotiations would have been just one of a number of possible theological responses she could make. Of course, responses can take a whole variety of forms, from tough action to silent presence, or indeed it may even be that a group's response is to continue doing what was being done in the first place, but this time with much more insight and understanding. Action without reflection can be irresponsible, and so the theological spiral allows us to survey many different responses based upon a fuller appreciation of the analysed situation. The task then is to judge which response is best in the light of Christian reflection upon the whole experience. Such a considered response, based in the faith, will be a 'spiritual' activity even if it is very practical and down to earth, because it will derive from a hunger to see God's will done. It will probably need the resources of what I have termed a 'courageous spirituality' to accomplish it.

Having discerned the response God seems to demand, be it of an active or passive nature, the participants then go ahead and do their best to implement it. But this is only to find that this responsive action puts the group into a brand-new predicament, for they have come full circle into experience again; but this time it is a different experience, the experience of a *new situation*.

Things are not guaranteed to work as well as this every time, of course, and inevitably we sometimes fail to risk the consequences of our new discoveries and refuse to move on to the new situation or experience; we prefer the safety of the old, even when our hearts know better. In the diagram I have tried to indicate this possibility by drawing in a dotted line from 'Response' back to where we started from; but even so, I doubt whether it is possible to find ourselves back in exactly the same place, for so much will have been experienced on the way.

But if the group chooses to respond more creatively, then they will move into a new situation which is in fact a new starting point, an experience that will require a new exploration, a new set of reflections and new responses. Following the cycle round like this will not just be going round and round in unproductive circles, because each time the group moves into active response it will find itself in a new place; not just moving over old ground, but a moving spiral taking us forward all the time. What we have then is a spiral of action and reflection, of experience and contemplation, of praxis. The diagram will now look like this.

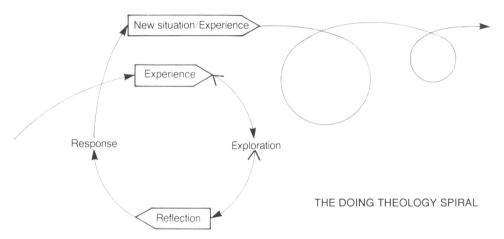

THE DOING THEOLOGY SPIRAL

Once having engaged with the situation at the different stages around the cycle, the group finds itself in a good place from which to look back over the various phases and check whether the outcome of their endeavours has been constructive and faithful. Moving into a second cycle of exploration, reflection and so on allows the group to evaluate the whole theological process from the perspective of their new situation. This evaluation is an important part of the whole process, as is the continuous opportunity for celebration – celebration of all that has worked out well and celebration of the opportunity to be part of the discovery and comradeship that this style of doing theology always offers the group.

However, any diagram will have its limitations, and there are some glaring simplifications in this diagram which will require further clarification. It may be of course that the group that seeks to do theology will prefer to redraft this diagram or produce a different model altogether. Nevertheless, I hope that the general impression of the model I am proposing is now clear, and during the course of the chapters that follow I will seek to explain in more detail each phase of the Doing Theology Spiral that I have presented. Suffice it here, however, just to add a few points for the sake of clarification.

First, the distinctions between each phase of the cycle are certainly not always as clear in practice as the diagram might imply. For example, the diagram makes the distinction between exploration and reflection much sharper than it is in reality, but this is done because it is a constant fault of theologians that we do not *look*. We jump to conclusions, leapfrogging the exploration phase, much preferring to work only with preconceptions and ideologies rather than with observable and awkward phenomena. Having stressed this need to look and explore as logically prior to reflection, I nevertheless find it helpful sometimes to draw the arrow between exploration and reflection as a two-way link to remind us that in reality we cannot have one without the other.

In precisely the same way, it is impossible for a human being to have an experience without some prior reflection playing its part in that experiencing – this is simply the way we subjective creatures are made. We are predisposed to interpret our world by virtue of our very looking, our very experiencing.[6] But again I find the distinction made in the diagram between experience and reflection serves as a helpful reminder lest we forget the importance both of experience and interpretation. As it is, the diagram stresses the importance of involved encounter (experience) as well as the value of that detachment which is necessary to some extent both in analysis (exploration) and in interpretation (reflection). Having done justice to the distinctions, we are then in a better position to see how, taken together, they combine as praxis, thus emphasising the physical and incarnational base-line of our Christian faith.

This brings us to another factor that cannot adequately be represented in the diagram, but which will certainly become apparent in the subsequent chapters. It is simply that experience can play a very significant role in all the phases of the cycle and not only in the first phase. This is because with the use of the right group methodology, even reflection can be 'experiential' when that is appropriate. By using the insights of adult education and learning theory, there is no need to limit ourselves to a distanced, boring or theoretical style of operation in any part of the diagram, and I hope to make that much clearer as the book proceeds.

It is important here to clarify further my use of the terms 'doing theology' and 'theological reflection' as I have used them in the spiral diagram. In the chapters that follow I will reserve the term 'theological reflection' for that aspect of theological activity which is centred upon the reflection phase of the cycle, where the explored experiences are brought into engagement with the great traditions of the faith and questions are asked about where the transcendent God is active within creation and our experience of it. That particular reflective activity is, in my terminology, just one aspect of a much larger process of discovery and response, the whole cycle, and to describe this I use the term 'doing theology'. Theological reflection alone, although understood by some to be all that theology consists of, is, I believe, dependent upon and responsible to the other aspects of the Doing Theology Spiral and is therefore only one particular element within the total endeavour that is theology. The tight definition of theology as one particular scientific discipline among others is what I specify as 'theological reflection', whereas I reserve the term 'doing theology' to refer to a much wider and more ambitious process of reflective action which incorporates many disciplines and phases. The importance of this distinction cannot be overemphasised, because it allows us to see more readily how the argument between activists and academic theologians may in fact have been worsened by a confusion of terms and definition.

But there is one more important issue raised by the diagram and it is indicated by the boxes that appear around the words reflection, experience and new situation. These signify that, since the whole process is essentially cyclic, it is perfectly possible to move around the diagram having started from a variety of points, and not only from experience. For example, we may have started into the spiral process from an inner realisation that something is seriously wrong with our reflection and our thinking. For example, we may always have assumed our own denomination to be the only true one, and other so-called Churches to be neither Christian nor authentic. If we then read an account of the beliefs and practices of another denomination that contradicts all that we had assumed and we now become convinced that its adherents are Christian after all, and that the denomination has authenticity, then we are confronted by a problem. This is because the intervention of these new thoughts has brought dissonance to the harmony of our previous system or construct of thought. This tripping up of the mind by a new realisation is what learning theorists call 'cognitive dissonance'.[7] The dissonance presses us with a need to do some fresh sorting out in our minds and lives. We are therefore prompted to move from this reflection into some new response that will enable a fresh analysis of the situation to be made. This means that we can find ourselves starting into the cycle of doing theology from a point different from that initially expected; not from experience but from cognitive dissonance within our reflection. The important thing is that although for most people the point of entry into doing theology will be in some committed experience, there is nothing wrong with starting from wherever it feels natural for the individual or the group and to get moving around the Doing Theology Spiral in whatever way turns out to be possible and most productive. The boxes in our diagram serve to remind us that we should start from wherever is most natural and effective.

The important thing is to keep moving on from one phase to the next so that the whole cycle of the Doing Theology Spiral is rehearsed again and again. The diagram is a simplification of a quite complex process, but I think it is the more helpful because of its simplicity. For the aim is that, with practice, the whole process may become second nature to any theological group so that they find themselves following the cycle quite intuitively, without having to make constant reference to a complicated blueprint. The cycle moves along into new discoveries and new places at each turn of the theological spiral, and in this way it reminds us that theology is just one vehicle on a Christian journey, which never allows us to remain for long in one secure place. The Doing Theology Spiral is just one supportive tool for following Jesus in the Way.

A South African example

It will be helpful now to look at some examples of the Doing Theology Spiral in action so that we can keep our thinking earthed. Since southern Africa can never be far from our minds, I want first to relate a story which comes from the South African Institute for Contextual Theology.[8] A small group of young South Africans, black and white, decided to do some theological work together, and took the Church as the focus of their interest. They had no formal theological education, so where were they to start? We could imagine them starting from the models of the Church to be found in the writings of St Paul or the early fathers.

They could have heard expert expositions of scholarly books on the subject. But instead they chose simply to describe to one another their own concrete *experiences* of the Church. They described the Sunday services that they had attended, sermons they had heard, doctrines they had been taught, Christians they had met, the church buildings, and different denominations they had come across. Everyone of course had plenty of raw material to offer because it was concrete, here and now experience, and far from abstract. It soon became clear that their feelings about the Church were full of ambiguity, and in their group they expressed those feelings of anger and frustration forthrightly. They were very critical, and yet they also felt that the Church was of very great value and significance to them. From this experience they realised just how full of contradictions their Church was. So much for the experience phase of the spiral.

Next, they moved into exploration and set about enumerating, listing and analysing the grounds for the contradictions of which they had become aware. They explored a whole range of contradictions: the Church's disunity despite its aspirations to be one and catholic; its fine words about apartheid and yet its lack of action in the matter; divisions within it between its professionals and its uneducated members; they lamented the fact that there were certain people of status who held power in the Church, yet they had all heard Jesus' words of admonishment: 'It shall not be so amongst you' (Mark 10.43). Even the grand church buildings came in for criticism when compared with the tiny shacks in which the people themselves had to live. So it was that in the Church and in the preaching of the clergy the whole group recognised momentous contradictions. From this exploration they then moved on to the reflection stage.

Some of the group wanted to rush headlong into a response by setting up their own 'pure' Church which would have none of these contradictions, but other group members suggested that before they did that it would be well to sort out what their picture of an ideal Church might in fact be. To do this the group began to look to the Scriptures. They looked in the Hebrew Scriptures at the idea of the nation of Israel as the People of God, but as the biblical history unfolded before them they did not feel that the nation had lived up to that ideal at all. So they moved on to the New Testament, and they looked instead at the picture of Jesus and his group of disciples, who were in some sense the first Church. But even there they could see the same contradictions and betrayals emerging. And so it began to dawn upon them that they had perhaps been looking in altogether the wrong place for a picture of the perfect society. They should not have been looking at the Church for perfection after all, but rather at the idea of the Kingdom of God which figures so centrally in Jesus' teaching. From their reflection upon the New Testament they could see that while the Kingdom was perfect and always in some senses ahead of human experience, the Church was always with us in the here and now, as part of our struggling, failing, hoping history. It was this realisation that sobered the group and made them more self-critical, and more aware of their own imperfections as they compared their meagre responses with the vision of the perfection of the Kingdom of God. They too were involved to some extent in the same contradictions that they had noticed so glaringly in others.

But the group's theological reflection did not confine itself to the Bible. The group decided that they would need to get to the root causes of the Church's problems if ever they were going to play their part in overcoming its contradictions. They therefore tried looking in church history books in order to discover the historical causes and processes which they sensed undergirded the contradictions. However, they got nowhere. They found themselves struggling with the history books; they realised that there was something worth absorbing there, but they themselves could not fathom it. So they opted to invite along a person who was a specialist in church history, not to lecture, but to answer a set of very specific questions that they had crystallised and had worked out for themselves. 'When is the first time in history when there was a contradiction in the Church?' 'How did they handle money when they set up the South African churches?' and so on – questions about ideologies, economic systems and vested interests. And they heard answers about influences in the Church from the time of the Roman emperors through to the establishment and maintenance of the South African Church. They were particularly interested in the relationship they could now see between the missionaries and the colonialists. And they interpreted the facts they gained from the specialists in a way that made sense for them. They felt that their Church had been caught up not only with the ideology of apartheid, but also with the ideology of *laissez-faire* capitalism and its division of people into 'workers' and 'employers', 'us' and 'them'.

The outcome of this process of reflection was a new appreciation in the group that the contradictions within the Church were extremely dangerous and destructive of persons when ignored and hidden from view. These same contradictions could, however, become creative and productive of change if brought into the open and realistically faced up to by Christians. The historical facts about the Church were real in themselves, but they were also symbolic of the wider community, and they could therefore be used to help explain why the problems exist today in the wider South Africa society. What was needed were people who would speak out plainly about the contradictions so that the Church could become realistic about itself and emerge as a visible sign of hope and honesty, a community of people on their way to God's promised Kingdom. This they decided was to be the thrust of their response.

They set about explaining all that they had discovered about the Church whenever and wherever they were given opportunity. They invited the clergy in and asked them to preach about their findings in their own churches. They asked the clergy to work with them in their consciousness-raising activities. Many searched the Gospels to see how Jesus had chosen to proclaim his message, and this helped them find ways of sharing what they had discovered about the Kingdom and the Church's struggles to achieve it. Some of the group's teaching made the poor whom they visited feel more confident and hopeful, and this was reminiscent of the New Testament accounts of how some of Jesus' evangelism was received by those in need. At other times, the group's actions and teachings were less successful, but this failure resonated with many passages in the Gospels too. They had started from their own felt experiences of Church, and now they had worked their way once around the theological spiral only to find that they were back with a fresh experience and with new things to discover. They had been prompted into responsive action by the cycle, and this with new resolution and fresh understanding about their task and identity.

This example highlights a number of points about how the cyclical method of doing theology may be facilitated.

First, as I have already stressed, the group had a clear preference for *starting from their own experience* – their actual, concrete experience of the Church – and not from some abstracted concepts about what the Church might have been. Within that experience there was, as we have predicted, a whole range of preconceptions, emotions and a Christian faith already interpreting to some extent what was experienced; but starting from everybody's experience was the key.

Second, we notice that it was obviously a *community effort*. A people's theology is not the result of an individual working alone at his or her books. Obviously, there is more chance of a group being creative than an individual, given the old adage that two heads are better than one, but additionally, and perhaps more importantly, if risky responsive action is expected of group members then two things are essential. First, they must have the support that comes from group solidarity, and second, they must themselves have had a hand in the reflection that has led to the responsive action – or else they might not be convinced enough to see the action through. Thus it was essential to work as a group.

Another aspect of how this action–reflection theology looks in practice is to be seen in the South African group's preparedness *to ask questions* honestly and fearlessly. It may not have been polite at the time to ask the Church institution about its financial relationship to slavers and merchants of the past, but in the end it was certainly more productive and theologically creative to ask straight questions. This questioning had to be thoroughly self-critical too, and it was good to see how they eventually came to the realisation that they were themselves responsible members of the Church they were criticising. In addition, their critical questioning approach also made sure that any prepackaged answers and authoritarian posturing by teachers or leaders would soon be cut down to size. It is instructive to notice too how this South African group seems to have gone instinctively to the question of power in their discussion with the church historian, for they sensed the importance of the answers he would give. When I was studying political theology in New York some years ago, my professor had the irritating habit of thumping his fist on the table and demanding 'Power! Who's got the power? If you don't know that, you'll never make theologians!' I have since come to see just how right he was to push the point home.

That leads to the fourth major lesson to be learnt about theological method from our South African example, namely *how knowledge should be used* by the group. Wherever the process of doing theology makes it necessary to find out more about history, sociology, economics, biblical interpretation, or whatever else, the experts in one form or another may well need to be consulted and the information they may be able to provide has to be drawn out of them. But the overall power must at all times remain within the theological group itself. Any amount of information can be drawn out from people, from books or other resources, as long as that information truly throws some light on the questions that arise out of the experience of the group itself and its life. The use of information for any other purpose – to prove a point, to defend a stance, to maintain the status quo or to avoid the real issue – would be an abuse of the power of information and would detract from the integrity of the enterprise. We must be careful, then, how information is shared in the group, for it can be a powerful put-down or control.

The fifth and final point to draw from this South African example is that it puts great *stress upon the practical*. It begins and ends with the practice of Christianity. It begins by looking at what church members do in practice and it works its way towards love in practice. Some Christians seem more intent on making sure that people should think correctly about their faith than that they should live out their faith in practice, but the South African group seemed to me to get the balance about right.

A British urban example

So much for our South African example. But lest it be implied that this cyclic style of doing theology is only possible in the Third World, let me also share an example of its use in Britain among a small group of elderly women who had been meeting together for some years to knit for the Leprosy Mission. Over the course of time their numbers had dwindled, but faithful members still met once a week to share a cup of tea, to knit and raise money for the charity. As years went by, enthusiasm had waned but the knitting was still being done. I therefore suggested that they might like to engage in some thinking about their knitting and I described the theology spiral diagram to them. We were to begin, as usual, with the experience. The women spoke together first of the sheer enjoyment of producing a knitted garment, second of the companionship engendered by their meetings, and third, of their sense of concern for lepers. Then, after sharing these feelings, we moved on to more detailed exploration. We looked more analytically at the mechanism of knitting, in which a long woollen thread is manipulated by means of needles into complex patterns and garments, which offer durability, warmth and beauty. Then, after exploring this process of creativity, we moved on to consider the composition of the group itself and began to appreciate the variety that was represented there. Thirdly, we explored the issue of leprosy, and shared a slide presentation all about the subject.

Having thus explored, we moved round the cycle to reflection. The first of our reflections was related to the process of creation in which the knitters had been involved. The women were aware that in the Book of Genesis, God is pictured as the Almighty Creator. As they read the stories of creation they felt more appreciative of the joy that God must have felt during the creation, for they themselves had had a little glimpse of that joy even in their own small attempts at creativity. The difficulty and methodical complexity of some of their knitting patterns mirrored the measured and disciplined forms of the first Genesis creation account, where God is pictured as taking a steady and stately six days of creativity to bring order out of chaos. The second creation account recorded in Genesis, chapter 2, mirrored for the women the other aspect of creativity that they had experienced – the spontaneous and effervescent bubbling over of the creative act. Now they could appreciate just how much God had enjoyed the process of creation. From there, they moved on to concern themselves with the make-up of their group and reflected on the diversity within it. This diversity, they felt, had produced a much more interesting and buoyant group and they recognised the extent to which they relied on the variety of gifts that such diversity offered. They felt that this mutual reliance upon the creative gifts of others in the group was mirrored in what St Paul had written about the Church. Each spiritual gift was important, he said, for each was the distinctive offering that a member makes to the whole body (1 Corinthians 12). This interrelatedness of each member and each gift with the next became a central feature of the group's thinking. If just one stitch in the knitted garment should be dropped, then the whole garment would be at risk of becoming undone. Likewise, the significance of each individual, however lowly in the world's eyes, was considered by Jesus to be of infinite significance in God's eyes.

When they finally turned their attention to those who suffer leprosy, they were soon able to make the connection between what they had so far learnt and the fact that Jesus had taken especial trouble to reach out to those whose bodies had been spoilt and marred by disease – where the creation had come to grief – and he had bound those lepers back into the body of human society; no longer outcast, but precious, and once again integrated into human society. The dropped stitch had been reworked into the garment. How pertinent the connection was between the group's creative knitting of single stitches into whole, complete garments and the healing and inclusion into society of those who had experienced the separation and disintegration that leprosy wrought. It was this reflection that prompted the little group to move on to response, to further committed action. They decided that they would try to enlarge their knitting circle and offer membership to those who, like the lepers, were usually barred from society. They sought out the housebound and frail and visited them regularly in order to sit and knit with them where that was possible. They also brought their learning to the attention of other Christians by setting up a display stall in the church entrance hall. They took responsibility for a service of worship where hymns and readings told stories of creation, of lepers being healed and society finding new wholeness and completeness. And, finally, they found their group growing, not only numerically, but, from having been a rather lack-lustre gathering, they were now a vibrant and inspired group determined to continue the search and make their contribution towards a better society.

This example of the little knitting group illustrates how exciting even the most minimal theological activity can become for those involved in it. The group had no formal theological training and knew themselves to be well past the age where great projects were any longer manageable. And yet they accomplished great things!

Getting stuck

One final example may help to illustrate another facet of the Doing Theology Spiral. This example is once again a British one, the full story being already told in my book, *Power to the Powerless*.[9] There I tell of a group of working-class Christians in Birmingham who set about the study of the parables of Jesus only to find themselves propelled by those stories, and by their exploration of the needs of the neighbourhood, into the establishment of a Community Advice Centre at their church. But having once got the whole project up and running, and after years of preparation, they found to their horror that nobody came to their centre for information or advice. Had they only been a church action group, the whole project might well have faltered and collapsed at that point, but instead of this they dutifully continued round the Doing Theology Spiral into a fascinating exploration and reflection upon their new situation. It looked and felt for all the world as if they had failed and had been left on the shelf, but rather than close the project there, they reflected on how it felt to be underused, and from that basis they came up with an amazing 'spare-part-on-the-shelf' theology – a theology of unemployment, old age, disability and marginalisation. In addition to this, they found that the Bible could point them to more positive ways of understanding their waiting and 'stuckness', for when they remembered that Jesus too had been led out into the wilderness prior to being allowed to begin his ministry, so they realised that they too should use their waiting time constructively in preparing them-selves more profoundly for the ministry that lay ahead. This time of reflection led the group into new responses so that eventually visitors came flooding to their Advice Centre project. Thus, both they and the wider community found empowerment.

But even when the Advice Centre project seemed to be so successful, the group's theological reflection did not end there but moved on to consider new things. They journeyed round the spiral once again and found themselves moving into a fresh exploration of the experience they were now having in the Advice Centre. As they did so, they began to perceive that their new-found 'success' was only superficial. Their information service was easing *symptoms*, but it was not touching the under-lying *causes* of the issues that were evident in their community. On one occasion they might find themselves rejoicing that they had helped an elderly person gain the health care they had so eagerly awaited; but at the next moment they would realise that thousands of others were still waiting in the health queue, and while they had helped one it was only at the expense of those who would still have to wait at overcrowded hospitals. Through this constant reflection on their action, they came to realise that they were in reality still quite powerless in the face of such issues. But to this realisation they again brought insights from the Bible and from other sources. They had recourse to look carefully at the trial scenes of Jesus and his crucifixion. They read magazines and newspapers about power, saw films, heard what the theologians of old had said about evil and powerlessness, and from all this reflection they were led again into new commitments to their community and to God.

What this Advice Centre project particularly illustrates for us at this juncture is the crucial importance of seeing the process of doing theology not merely as a closed circle which, after one circuit, is completed, but as a spiral which is open-ended and is in some sense never-ending. After their first circumnavigation of the cycle, the group's response appeared to have ended in failure; for when they evaluated the Advice Centre project they observed little success. But they moved on from there to a continuation of the process, taking this 'failure' as the new situation from which to explore and reflect. On the other hand, when the project appeared on the surface to have succeeded, they spiralled around the process once again and explored the true nature of that so-called success. Only in this way did they keep the project itself flexible and on target, and at the same time its parabolic and theological nature always remained obvious.

Action and reflection

In each of the examples that we have considered it is quite evident how doing theology moves us from experience into reflection and then from reflection back into experience once again – a dynamic process that we earlier referred to as praxis. The diagram represents this continual interweaving of action and reflection. But its unity could be unnaturally divided so that in one section, to the bottom and to the right, we would have exploration and reflection, those elements that are predominantly reflective, and to the top and to the left (experience and response) we would have those two elements that are predominantly the active elements of theological work. Our diagram would then be split in two like this:

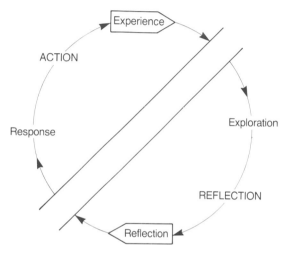

This dividing of the cycle into two is a constant and real danger, for many theologians have started out with every intention of completing the whole cycle, but have then become so immersed in reflection that they have forgotten to return to the action half of the diagram and they finish their theology with just reflection and fine words. Come to that, many parish churches fall for exactly this tempta-tion, and separate out their action from their theological reflection. Throughout the week their church and church hall may be full to the gunnels with active groups, everything from day centres and toddlers' clubs to unemployment drop-in centres. But all that activity may be completely separated off from the worshipping community. The latter do their theological reflection on Sunday mornings, but maybe do not even know the people who are involved with all the action that goes on during the rest of the week. This is anything but a united cycle of action and reflection. The worshippers may be lulled into thinking they are part of an active and integrated church, but in fact they are just one half of a fractured cycle. If those who were active would only engage in theological reflection about their acti-vity, and if those who were worshipping would take the risk of also venturing into responsive action together, then the whole parish enterprise would have more faithful theological integrity. The cycle would be made whole again.

From our examples we can appreciate that the spiral model of doing theology can operate at almost any level. It is appropriate to be used at a Church Council meeting, when an important decision has to be made. It has proved a helpful tool in enabling local churches to work out their strategies for future mission. It can encourage little groups into finding their feet and their purpose again. It can help those who are suffering to make a little more sense of their plight and restore courage. It can help the already stretched small congregation to set its priorities. It can be used by the highly articulate or by those who are yet to find their voice. It can be used quietly on retreat, it can be energetic in the cut and thrust of the work-place. But the Doing Theology Spiral really comes into its own when it is used by groups who have a deep commitment to transformation. Then it becomes more than just an educational method, but an instrument of the Kingdom. I have known it used by people who have had no such prior commitment, but the exploration and reflection phases of the process have so opened their eyes that they have found themselves becoming more committed to transformation as the process has gone on. This was certainly the case with the women who had been knitting together for Leprosy Mission; they ended up with an altogether new perspective and an urgent commitment to the establishment of an accepting and 'whole' society. Their particular response may not have been earth-shattering in the world's terms, but they did make every effort to work with God in the community, to break down the sinful barriers of isolation, and that was very significant.

The doing theology diagram does not pretend to be some infallible blueprint; on the contrary, it is merely a straightforward and commonsense way of letting God's word speak to our experience and of letting our experience speak to God and to one another. The method certainly raises some very important issues and poses challenges, but at this stage I would like to save those questions till a later chapter. Instead, I shall look in more detail at each of the four phases of the Doing Theology Spiral and ask how we might actually go about all this in practice. In the course of the next four chapters I will therefore concentrate on each phase of the cycle in turn. While this approach might run the risk of separating each phase off from the next rather too emphatically, it will nevertheless have the advantage of clarifying just what is happening at each phase of the Doing Theology Spiral. Let us then consider in Chapter 3 the first phase, the phase of experience, and see what that looks like close up.

Notes

1 A fine description of the current state of Britain, both economic and social, is given in John Atherton's *Faith in the Nation* (SPCK, 1988).
2 D. A. Kolb (ed.), *Organizational Psychology* (Prentice-Hall, 4th edn, 1984).
3 See, for example, Juan Luis Segundo, *The Liberation of Theology* (Gill & Macmillan, 1977) and Paulo Freire, *Pedagogy of the Oppressed* (Penguin, 1972).
4 See, for example, Joe Holland and Peter Henriot SJ, *Social Analysis: Linking Faith and Justice* (Orbis, 1983) and the work of the Center of Concern, Washington, DC 20017. The Paris-based Ecumenical Institute for the Development of Peoples (INODEP) facilitates programmes of training in the techniques of education developed by Paulo Freire.
5 See, for example, Bishop R. L. Guilly SJ, *In Pursuit of Human Progress: An Outline of Catholic Social Teaching* (CAFOD, 1988). Christian denominations will have produced their own synodical papers and special published reports. Such teaching will be

particularly interesting for groups wishing to find out what various denominational authorities are saying about the theme they have chosen to study.

6 Our prejudgements distort our perceptions so that we 'see and do not see, hear and do not hear' (Matthew 13.13).

7 For a concise survey of the implications of cognitive dissonance, see John Hull, *What Prevents Christian Adults from Learning?* (SCM, 1985), pp. 36–102 and 123–43.

8 The Institute for Contextual Theology is at PO Box 32047, Braamfontein 2017, South Africa, and publishes a whole range of material drawn from their own experience.

9 Laurie Green, *Power to the Powerless* (Marshall Pickering, 1987). Available from Poplar Rectory, London E14 0EY.

3

Getting started

Making the experience come alive

Many churches are fearful of doing theology because they feel that they already
have so many drains on their time and energies that the thought of setting up yet
another group fills them with dread. Usually the group will be a new one, coming
together specifically in order to begin to do theology, but the method does not
necessarily require brand-new groups to be set up. It does however demand that
we take more time in planning the deliberations and actions in the groups we
already have. Once the method is fully implemented, however, group participants
often find themselves empowered to do things of which they would never before
have felt themselves capable, and so in the long term the load on any one person or
group eases considerably. In the short term, however, it is an extra commitment.
Other people may be fearful of utilising the method because they sense that it may
lead them into areas where answers are difficult to find and where they feel out of
their depth. As a poor swimmer, I have to confess to knowing how that feels, but I
would never have learnt to swim at all had I allowed myself to be disabled by my
fears. And in any case, Jesus tells us that we will only gain our life if we risk the
possibility of losing it (Matthew 10.39).

Let us look more specifically now at how the first phase of the Doing Theology
Spiral can be approached. This is the part of the cycle where we own the
experience and try to get inside it as much as possible in preparation for a later and
even more thorough analysis at the exploration stage. Let us recall first how the
experience phase stands in relation to the whole exercise, by reference to the cyclic
diagram.

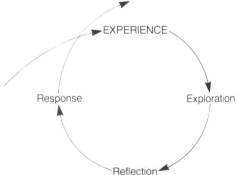

There are three elements or tasks to accomplish within the experience phase.
First, it will be necessary for group members to get to know one another quite well
and begin to share something of themselves in the group. Obviously, as time goes
on the group members will become close associates, but right from the beginning it

will be important for them to get used to the group and to begin to feel that they can trust it and open themselves up within its circle. Next, it will be necessary to focus upon an issue or theme around which the theological work will be done. This focus may relate directly to the locality in which the group live, or it may have to do with a common piece of work in which all the members are engaged. It could, on the other hand, be a fresh theme that the group has never thought to focus upon before but that clearly fascinates the group enough to devote time and attention to it over a period. When the group is clear about its focus, the members will then need to share their first impressions of the issue or theme that they have chosen. They will not at this stage need to be scientifically precise about the theme, but the intention rather is that they should share their feelings, inclinations and preliminary thoughts together so that they have the theme sufficiently identified between them. Let us take each of these elements in turn and describe in more detail how we might go about achieving each one.

Getting to know the group

Our spiral diagram tries to indicate that we never come to an experience as if from nowhere, but we bring with us a whole range of prior experiences, reflection and beliefs, and all these will affect how we respond to our present situations. By sharing of ourselves at this early stage, the group is better prepared to appreciate that each participant will be coming at things from a different perspective and will have different things to offer during the development of their theology together. It will also be important to build up a team spirit in the group so that all the members know they have something worthwhile to share and that the team values all their gifts. A pleasant room to meet in, a warm welcome and a friendly atmosphere will be essential to the success of the group, and time should always be taken for plenty of 'getting to know you' opportunities. There is no need to rush this important element of the group life, for time taken now will pay great dividends when it comes to being able to share deeply together and to work together well during the later stages of the theological enterprise.

It might be helpful to describe one such sharing exercise in order to see how the more informal 'hellos' can be supplemented by opportunities to go much deeper. The exercise I will describe is best done once the group has been drawn together and participants are beginning to get to know one another at least a little. It gives opportunity for the members to share one with another something of their own faith and values. I have described this exercise in detail in a published worksheet entitled *My Faith, My Story*.[1] Each participant has a piece of paper on which to make some personal jottings or drawings which, it is explained, will remain confidential to them. Then in a meditative way they are asked to think slowly back to some early memories and take time to recall where they grew up, the first school friends they remember, what it was like to leave school, their first job, their early loved ones, their first encounter with the faith, and so on, right up to the present. They are then asked, while still in this meditative mood, to decide on two or three major turning points or factors in their life story and to consider whether they feel God was present in those moments or not. By this time in the process there is usually quite a lot of quiet reflection in the group. We can either end the exercise there and have everyone share how it went, or we can take things further by remaining in a meditative mood and asking the members to select in their minds a couple of stories or people in the Bible that mean something to them – Bible stories they warm to in some way. They are then asked to reflect on what it might be in their own life's experience that has led them to select these particular stories or passages. All sorts of groups find this exercise quite liberating, especially if everyone gets a chance afterwards to chat about how the experience felt for them.

There are many variations on this theme. One is to ask people to draw a line which represents their life journey, and to place upon it simple drawings or words that remind them of events, special people or places in their life story. Sometimes music can be played so that participants relax enough not to have to keep interrupting other members while they are still completing their pictures. Then everyone gets a chance to introduce their picture to other members of the group and, after this, members are asked to think together what place each feels God may have had in their life picture. It is a simple method but very effective. After such a faith-sharing exercise it is helpful to have a short time of quiet meditation in the group so that each life experience can be treasured and valued before God.

Some groups may find it more helpful to have the picture of a tree with roots, trunk and branches introduced to them. The roots represent each individual's past and background, the trunk represents their present and the branches represent their vision of how the future should be. When each participant has had a few minutes to draw their own tree, they spend time drawing or writing on to it the appropriate things about themselves at each level. The group can then share that and chat it through together. It is always a joy if similarities can be found in the various stories, and the group may wish to draw a combined tree symbol for the whole group if they feel that they already share enough common experiences or hopes. All such exercises, and there are many variants upon these themes,[2] help to weld the group together, introduce members one to another and also get them into the habit of valuing their own experience and making connections between that and God's activity in their lives. All these things will be very important in these early stages of the theological endeavour.

During the course of these preliminary exercises it is to be hoped that the group members will be trying to express the values that they hold dear and this will all help to uncover something of the theology with which they come to the group. For although few if any will call themselves 'theologians' as yet, they will all be carriers of an implicit theology by which they already operate their faith in the daily routines of life. Even members who would not normally call themselves Christians may find that they are imbued with some sort of 'popular faith' or 'folk religion', which is their attempt to express something about God which they feel but perhaps have great difficulty in defining. They might therefore use superstition, community wisdom, corporate activity and the vestiges of Christian stories and symbols, all wrapped up together, to try to express something of the flavour of their experience of the Divine, and it will be good if the group can help its members express something of all this at an early stage. Many regular church-goers will be more reliant on this 'folk religion' than we might expect, but all this has a chance to come to the fore at this early stage so that it can be utilised and properly transformed as we progress through the various stages of the theology cycle.

When the group feels it is beginning to create its own identity by means of these 'getting to know you' exercises, then it is always helpful for members to give their group a name. If the group members know already what the direction and focus of their concern is going to be, then they may build that into their name, but often a group name will originate from the feelings the members have about the group itself. I have known groups call themselves the Mustard Seed, the Seekers, the Salt and Pepper group (when there were an equal number of black and white members), and so on. Having the team name their group helps members feel they belong – that they own the group and its process and that they have some responsibility to it.

This whole process of getting to know ourselves as a group may only take a couple of meetings if members know one another well already – but there is no substitute for an outing or a common activity to really weld the group together in these early stages.

Discerning of focus

The next task for the group to accomplish in these early stages will be to choose a specific focus around which the theological work will be done. Now that they are getting to know one another well, it will be easier to be sure that whatever focus is chosen really does carry all the members of the group and is not just the personal interest of one or two of the team. It must be a shared choice if the enthusiasms of the whole group are to carry them through to the accomplishment of the whole process. So it helps if the chosen theme can be something that really is of signi-ficance and concern to the whole group and that touches all participants at a reasonably deep level. The more commitment the group can have to the chosen theme, the more vital will be the theology that flows from it.

It may be a very church-centred concern that strikes them as important, such as the experience of sitting in church Sunday after Sunday and becoming increas-ingly bored by the worship. Members may decide that they all share an interest in trying to find out just why they are so bored and feel sufficiently committed to do something about it. It might, on the other hand, be a very positive experience about prayer that they choose as their focus. Some members may be very gifted in prayer and so the theme interests them, while others may be committed to the theme for the very opposite reason and want to find a way to pray which can get them started. On the other hand, perhaps there has been a lot of illness and death in the community lately, and the group feels that it is time that they really got to grips with the difficult question of why God allows suffering to happen. However, it may be that the group has come together around any already agreed focus because it is not a new group at all but a group that meets regularly for a particular purpose. It may be a Leprosy Mission knitting group, as in my earlier example, or a youth group that has to look at a recent drug craze that is hitting their town. Or maybe they are the Parochial Church Council which has some decisions to make about the parish.

Whether the group has chosen the theme or whether it has already been decided, if the group can have an enthusiastic commitment to the theme, then that is likely to be productive of theology. If they are not all that interested, then it would be as well to look for a focus that really concerns them. But if that enthusiastic commitment relates in some way to the concerns, struggles and

predicament of the oppressed, then my experience is that the theology is even
more likely to issue in a transformative and exciting group life.

We may in the end be spared the trouble of having to make a decision about
what theme the theological group should focus upon, because it comes to us of its
own accord. I remember being involved with a Mother and Toddler club where a
number of the mums began to talk about their fear of becoming boring and
nervous people. They felt that the outgoing energies that they used to have when
younger had somehow atrophied now that they were tied to the home. They even
said that they could understand parents who ended up beating their children,
because they themselves had sometimes felt those uncontrollable emotions of
frustration and panic at being totally at the beck and call of their toddlers. We
decided to meet again the next week with this very issue in mind, and to do some
serious Christian thinking about the problem. Even though these mums were not
regular church-goers, they were very pleased to do some experience-based
theology for a few weeks around this difficult issue because it was one that was of
great importance to them. Very often indeed, issues will come to the group from
the community in which it is set, and one only needs to be on the local grapevine
for a short time before the issues and concerns are being very loudly articulated.
Lots of parishes have been prompted by the *Faith in the City* report[3] or the Hereford
Report on Rural Mission[4] to undertake a parish audit of their community and will
find that just such a focus can be a very productive theme, while others will find the
same sort of generative commitment in a similar exercise in relation to their
stewardship or evangelism planning. From such exercises it can very often follow
that a community issue or need is very sharply focused, and so evolves a new
theme around which the theological work must obviously be done.

Given the various theme options that may have come to light in the group, it is
very important that the participants themselves decide which one they would like
to take as their major focus. To do this, it is as well to subject all the possible
themes to a number of criteria. Clearly, the most important rule is to choose the
theme or issue that the group members feel most committed to, and feel most
strongly about. It is also worth considering which feels to be the biggest and most
pressing problem, as well as which theme the group feels is manageable for them,
given their resources. Through this process of elimination, one issue or theme is
discerned as a front runner. If that theme can be reasonably well and simply
expressed, and if it can be fleshed out by the group with stories from real
experience, then the decision has been arrived at.

There is no reason, however, why a theme should not be changed and
redeveloped if in retrospect the team begin to lose interest or commitment in the
original focus. More often, however, a group will develop or refocus the theme in a
slightly different way from how it was originally envisioned, and this happens as
the group gathers more information and experience in the early stages of the
theological spiral. Even in the process of taking this one theme round the spiral
once or twice, all sorts of implications and depths will be unearthed of which they
were not at first aware, so that the original theme focus may change and reform as
the process unfolds. In general terms, then, the rule seems to be, start where the
group feels it is possible to start and let things develop naturally. Let down our
bucket where we are and we will surely find water.

Sharing first impressions

Having begun the process of getting to know one another and feeling some sense of group belonging, the team then moved on to discern a focus for its theological work together. The third element of this experience phase of the cycle that they must now undertake is the sharing of participants' first impressions of the subject that they have chosen to study. They may have taken as their focus an individual's experience which is valued by the whole group, an issue that they all find important, an institution and its needs, or a locality in which they all live, but whatever the focus the task will now be to identify that theme in an impressionistic way by producing some preliminary descriptions of it and as far as possible by sharing experiences and initial feelings about it together.

First then, the group should try to describe in broad outline what it is that they have chosen to look at. If the members are asked to gather up pictures, newspaper cuttings, photographs, magazine articles, videos, songs and so on which they feel relate to the theme in some way, then a very interesting session can be spent sharing these preliminary findings. Outings to plays, films or places that have something to do with the theme are ideal experiences for opening the group up to further awareness of the feelings related to the issue. If it is a church-related issue, then there may be another church that has itself looked at the material and an exploratory visit may make our own group members aware of how similar or different their own feelings are about the issue compared with those whom they visit. As the group gets into its subject so there will probably be a lot of stories told that relate to the theme, stories from their own experience and stories from friends or relatives. As the stories are shared, time can be taken to check out how people feel about the stories, and the story-teller should be helped by the group to be aware of how the story makes them feel as they tell it. All this activity will help the team build up a general picture of their experience of the theme or issue.

If the group now takes different aspects of the theme and writes or draws them up on separate big sheets of paper, they may then be able to brainstorm a whole range of words which come to mind as each aspect of the theme is considered. These suggestions will act as a helpful opening up of some of the wider implications of the theme, but will also help the group discover their preliminary feelings about the subject. If the chosen theme is race, for example, brainstorming may suddenly make participants aware of the associations they make in their own mind when such words as black, white, soul, sari, Pakistan, Wales, England and so on are focused on in the exercise. The brainstorming exercise helps the group to share something of their preliminary feelings about the theme in general and about the various separate aspects of it. If possible, these early feelings need to be brought into the open, because group members will probably be coming to the theme with all sorts of prior ideas, emotions and prejudgements. Such feelings are not always easy to specify, and so it is often helpful to have groups draw in chalks or paint what they think of when the subject is raised. They can then have plenty of time together to share their pictures and discuss them together. Photographs, stories, role-plays and so on may also help to trigger the feelings that group members already have about the issue. They may wish to share what they feel are the high points and the low points, their sorrows and joys, their ignorance and frustrations about the subject, and it is helpful if they can tell one another whether they presently feel things relating to the theme are fine as they are or whether they feel they want things changed.

All this activity should help the group to move to the point where they can express in some way or other just why it is that they feel a commitment to the theme – why it grabs them. They may even find that they can begin to express where their hearts tell them God is involved in it all. Just to sit quietly and meditate on the issue for a moment can often help at this point, for in this way the group has an opportunity to fix upon the sacredness of what may appear on the surface to be a very secular concern. To place a candle before a picture that represents the issue for them can be a great aid to meditation of this sort.

By the time the group has finished this phase of the work, they should to some extent have begun to discern who is involved in the issue and who is being affected by the situation they are studying. They should be able to say how they feel about it and how it affects them, and why it is that they feel gripped by the subject. They should be much clearer about the issue and know what are the basic questions and problems that it produces. They should also have a notion of what thoughts, feelings and experiences they have had about it all in the past and, more significantly, intuitively they may already be sensing something of where God is present in it all. If this is the case, the group may wish to celebrate that in worship and song together.

Checking the method

If all this has been accomplished, it will be time to move on from the experience phase to the phase of the cycle that we call exploration. But before going too far round the process of the spiral it is important that the group has some notion of what the aim of the whole exercise is, and some agreement about how they are going to set about this endeavour of 'doing theology'. It can be very disconcerting to be a member of a group and to be asked to engage in various activities without having any notion of why you are being asked to do them. Someone therefore should have the responsibility of explaining the Doing Theology Spiral at this early stage, so that all the participants can decide whether this is the approach they want to take. The power must be left with the group to determine their own agenda and they may decide to vary the spiral in some way to suit themselves. It is to be hoped that the transforming and active style always remains, but the spiral diagram must be open to the group to modify as they will. It's their group and their theology!

Working in the group

Now that we have a clearer notion of what is involved in this first phase of the Doing Theology Spiral, it should have become apparent that certain group styles will be more appropriate to this sort of theological work than will others. I have indeed known a group where the exercises so far described have not worked well owing to the fact that the ethos of that group was all at odds with the aim of the particular exercises. For although the cycle does not rely upon sticking rigidly to any one system of orthodox doctrine, it is wonderfully enhanced if fostered by the right group ethos. It will be as well therefore to take time aside for a moment to describe in more detail the style and ethos to be found in those groups that have worked most successfully around the spiral. The rest of this chapter will therefore be devoted to an examination of how an appropriate group style may be engendered and to a description of some of the most helpful tools that can be used to assist the theological group process. For those who have experience of working in theological groups of this type, or are acquainted with group process and adult education methods, then much of what I have to say here will be second nature, but it is important to record some basic points nevertheless – and especially for those who are engaging with this sort of process for the first time. I have, in addition, included what I hope will prove to be a list of helpful books and resources in the Bibliography.

The group

It will be evident already that I make the assumption that this sort of theology is essentially a group exercise rather than the pursuit of private individuals. Fundamental to the theological cycle is its affirmation of the mutual sharing of experience and reflection and the honouring of the experience of others. There is also implicit within it an acceptance of the fact that theology belongs to the whole body of Christ and that a collaborative and co-operative style will therefore serve it best. We have our best example of that in the way Jesus called together an intimate fellowship to be his first discipleship group.

The use of groups will be found to be especially appropriate to working-class cultures where the informal small group is at the heart of everyday life. However, it is helpful in other cultures too, for the small group provides the relaxed and intimate atmosphere that is so conducive to deep sharing. As fellowship and mutual understanding emerge in the group so the quality of the sharing and the preparedness of its members to be vulnerable to one another will also develop. The pooling of experience and spiritual insight which is then possible in this sort of sharing atmosphere far outweighs any advantages that an individual theologian working alone may have.

It has been proved that human beings learn best by being actively engaged in the learning experience and so educationalists have made it their business in groups to provide experiences specially designed to this end – sometimes referred to as 'experiential education'. We will be detailing many such 'learning by experience' events in the following chapters, and they will nearly all require a group setting if they are to succeed. As our description of the cycle proceeds so the element of action implicit in the later phases of the cycle will become more evident; here too the group emphasis will be important, for this sort of action-orientated theology may eventually prompt the group to venture into projects that no individual would ever be able to organise alone. If the action decided upon should turn out to be somewhat risky, then it is of utmost importance that the members have one another's support and solidarity to rely upon. So, for these and other reasons our theology will best be done in groups. But what sort of groups should they be and where might they meet?

The people

Groups may be of varying size – anything from three or four to about twenty or thirty. But such large groups may be split into smaller groupings for much of the work, coming back together as a large group as and when desired. I would hope that our groups can always include, if not dominant elements of the poor, then at least a significant presence of those who are not in positions of power or advantage in our society – those whom I have earlier called 'the heavy laden'. This will encourage a more down-to-earth and experientially centred theological style in the group, and will also help us to focus our picture of society more sharply. Often in the Gospels we find Jesus teaching that it is the outsider or the socially marginalised, like the Samaritan, the leper or the poor widow, who becomes the sign to the insiders, so we need to attract into our groups those who feel at the margins of society. But if such folk are going to feel ready and able to articulate their experiences and feelings in the group, then it will be even more important that a great deal of trust and honesty be engendered within it. Unfortunately, theological courses that the Church usually makes available, unintentionally exclude almost all blacks and working-class people by making them feel on alien territory, rather than at home among friends. However, some Christians quite clearly have a gift for hospitality and really help a group to be warm and welcoming, but groups will have to be aware of many cultural factors if they are not to be unwittingly exclusive.

In the New Testament, Jesus certainly seems to have offered us in his discipleship group a helpful model of the sort of group that is best able to do theology. Many of his disciples would have been from poor or marginalised groups, but others he had invited to make an option for the poor (cf. Mark 10.28 etc.) so that they deliberately left the security of what they had and followed him in the Way. Our own groups today may not include those living in poverty, but it is to be hoped that at least an intentional commitment will be made by its members to get alongside and share the experience and the cause of 'those who are heavy laden'. Each and every group member will have particular gifts to bring to the theological task, and so if our group represents a breadth of experience then so will the theology that is produced from within it; and it will be all the better for that, just as long as no minority voice is obliterated because of any feeling of alienation from the group.

Most groups will of course have some mixture of classes and sub-cultures within them and so the enabling task will be to keep an eye on where the power lies in the group. The group itself will need to be very aware of the balance of black to white, male to female, Methodist to Anglican and so on, that it has within it. And when newcomers or non-church people arrive, again care has to be taken that they are truly included by the group and not overwhelmed by any exclusive Christian jargon or excessive 'fellowship'.

The place

The group usually finds it helpful to have a home base to call its own, somewhere it can feel secure. This all helps to build the self-confidence of the group, and the right kind of confidence is a key to success in doing theology. I would suggest that the meetings of the group should never be known as 'classes', which may be reminiscent of painful school experiences, but rather be described as groups, teams, meetings or workshops. The home base needs if possible to be within walking distance of people's homes and safety precautions have to be taken nowadays if the meetings are to be held in the evenings. These points may seem insignificant but are essential if people are not to be excluded from the meetings. Successful black-led churches therefore usually provide door-to-door transport for their members in the inner city. 'Step-by-Step', a training project set up by the Bishop of Stepney in East London, makes the helpful point that many people, especially those from the working class, are very dependent upon their friendship- or family-networks, and thus meetings should not risk disrupting those culturally important contacts.[5] They therefore hold their sessions in series of threes – three Wednesdays running and then a break for a couple of weeks. There is no substitute for personal invitation and coming along with a friend, especially if participants are wary of churchy things, and the most successful groups may be those that work on the principle of personal invitation. A room at the local club or pub, the back room at the Mothers and Toddlers Club, the unemployment centre, the church, or the front room at a neighbour's house – there is a whole range of venues that may be appropriate. But groups should not confine their activities to classroom-type venues. There must be times too for outings and visits to places that are of special concern to the theme that is under discussion. Visits to other groups, project work, worship celebrations and so on may happen in many different places and will not be confined to the group base.

The leadership

Most church groups will find it fairly easy and even comfortable to be told answers, and it is often so much easier for the 'leader' to conspire with that wish. It saves the group having to do any tough theological work for itself and it feeds the leader's ego wonderfully well! It is a very real temptation. But if the group is to work, the leader will need to guard against this temptation, and instead become a vulnerable learner among fellow learners in the group. This will allow us to talk not so much of 'the leader' as of a 'shared leadership'. It used to be that a Bible study would consist of the group sitting round listening to the vicar speaking eruditely about each verse from the notes he had copied out of his commentary the night before. That may have made everyone think that the theology they were imbibing was strong and secure, but it was something of an illusion and the group learnt little. One way to get away from this style is to rotate the hosting and the leadership for each session, or ask different members of the group to be responsible for different aspects of the group's life. One can be the timekeeper, another the host, another the 'memory' who takes a note of events or decisions and recaps for the group if it feels itself getting lost. Worship will constitute part of the life of the group, but a style of worship must be found with which members feel comfortable and which is appropriate to the focus of their theological investigations. Very often it is here that certain members of the group, if given the opportunity, will prove to have liturgical gifts, and may lead prayer, hymns or worship presentations with great flair.[6] It it always desirable to have some brief moments of prayer during each session, and it has been my experience that the sharing of the Eucharist has been a very important occurrence too. But all this will depend upon the wishes and style of the group itself.

Another way to take the emphasis away from one leader is to have no agenda or papers around that the rest of the group cannot easily see. Instead, large pieces of paper are pinned on the wall or put on the floor with felt nibbed pens provided for all to add their comments. In this way all agendas, information notes and ideas can be owned by all members of the group and the power of information is thus shared by all participants. This approach also gives another member of the group a leadership responsibility – being in charge of the paper and pens. And if someone else is a fund of songs and choruses then they can take their turn to lead the celebrations of the group. However it is organised, it is always possible to take the spotlight away from one leader and share the leadership around.

Confidence building

Some of the basic rules for establishing groups must always be adhered to. First, having once brought it together, plenty of time must be taken to build up the group, remembering that different group members will need to be enabled in different ways. Some will need to be encouraged to speak up, while others will need to stop hogging the limelight. Most individuals will need encouragement, and to assist in this the group itself must be helped to gel and have trust in itself and in its own membership. It is important to cultivate a group awareness of the resources that are within it, so that participants do not look constantly outside themselves or to the clergy for some safe authority from which to secure ready-made answers. Those who are responsible for hosting or being group leaders must know and use the names of all members and use some simple exercises to encourage people to trust one another in the group. Asking people to share about very safe subjects is a simple way to engender trust. To have a number of pictures or articles around at the start of the session that relate to the theme of the meeting can prove to be a helpful starter, and if people are asked which they prefer of the objects or pictures then the conversation will not be difficult to get into and it will lead helpfully into the subject in hand. Most leaders will remember to do some such thing to help the group at its very first meeting, but we are inclined to forget that each and every time we meet, we need a 'starter' exercise of some sort to help the group re-form. If we forget this, we may realise only halfway through a meeting that some more nervous member has not really got themselves started in this particular session, but by then their nervousness has escalated and it has become doubly difficult for them to begin to play their full part in the group. So we help everyone to 'break their duck' and say something at an early stage of every meeting, not just at the first session. Simply asking everyone to share briefly what has happened to them since the last meeting will suffice. Time spent in this way always helps the group to share more intimately later, for it can feel very intimidating to be asked to share an important thought or feeling with someone you've never heard speak.

Above all, we need to make sure from the outset that everyone knows that their contribution is valued, and we must therefore offer a great variety of styles of operating in the group so that everyone has a chance of expressing themselves in a way with which they are happy. Some people will be helped to express themselves by having the group draw or act, others by chatting in twos or threes. Others respond well to pictures, others like lists on a flip chart or to draw diagrams, while others will prefer straight discussion. We must try very hard not to have our groups based all the time on the style of operation that the leader prefers. This is another reason why it can be very helpful indeed if the leadership rotates around the group. There is an amazing wealth of material now available which offers helpful advice and ideas for getting started and making sure that the group style remains open, interesting, inclusive and to the point. Again, the Bibliography at the back of this book should prove helpful.

It is absolutely crucial to be aware of the degree of literacy in the group or else we can frighten people off straight away if we expect them to read. My rule is never to pounce on anybody expecting them to read a large chunk of text, however erudite and confident they may appear on the surface. If we want to ask for volunteer readers, as for example when we want to mime a Bible passage as it's read out to us, then I think it is best to photocopy the text and divide it up into very manageable short sections so that the task can be easily shared round the group – and then only among those who readily volunteer. Bibles can always be made available as well for those who want to see the whole passage later on.

Despite all our emphasis on groups, there are some who find groups a frightening and intimidating prospect. Such folk need very gentle encouragement and the security of knowing that there will be no pressure on them to do things or say things that they do not want to do or say. Many people express concern about groups but, once they have experienced them, find membership a delight and a liberation. Clearly, though, patience and sensitivity must be exercised if groups are to be experienced by all their participants as facilitating and not intimidating experiences.[7]

Those of us who live and work in the so-called urban priority areas know that group attendance will fluctuate, and this is often because people who are living on the margins of society will constantly have crises to deal with. One evening Mrs White couldn't make it to the meeting because her daughter was having difficulties with her husband; the next meeting she was absent because some lads were making trouble in the street and she could not come out. The next week she got a little evening job, and so it went on. But Mrs White was still a member of the group and the group knew it. They told her about the meetings each week and she sent messages about her points of view. Commitment is not always expressed in the way we might expect, but my experience is that when a group is working on the Doing Theology Spiral then there is a remarkable degree of commitment to it on the part of its members, however that may be expressed.

Tools to encourage the theological process

As the group begins its life together, it tries to be as open and warm as it can be. However, while having a joy and celebration about it, it must retain that vital cutting edge which will make it productive and more than just another pleasant gathering. As the group journeys through each phase of the cycle in turn – experience, exploration, reflection, and response – there will be certain common tools that can be used to enhance the process of theological discussion, analysis and group life. Let me now briefly describe some of them so that we can make reference to them in future chapters.

The first tool may be referred to as *problem posing*. Raising creative tension through critical questioning is known by adult educators and group theologians as 'problematisation',[8] and it is an essential ingredient if the group is to move forward with its theme and at the same time save itself from becoming too self-regarding. Put simply, problem posing is the process by which we take any common statement and turn the form of the sentence around so that it takes on the form of a question. This allows us to see what the problem is that has been hidden by the statement. The South African group that was the subject of our earlier example, instead of constraining their work with the statement 'the Church has contradictions', turned that statement around and asked instead 'Why are there contradictions in the Church?' 'What are these contradictions and where did they come from?' The little group that met to knit for Leprosy Mission were not content simply to state that lepers were outcasts. Instead, they turned that statement into a problem and asked, 'Why are lepers outcast? Why should anybody be set aside by society?' Quite often in our doing of theology we will get stuck and not know which way to go. One straightforward way out of the impasse is to 'pose the problem' and ask 'What is the problem that lies behind the statement?' In this way critical questioning will carry us forward to the next step. Dom Helder Câmara offered a wonderful example of this process when he said, 'When I give food to the poor, they call me a saint. When I ask why the poor have no food, they call me a communist.'

Another very helpful tool that facilitates the group's theological process is the *brainstorming session*. This is an appropriate phrase to describe a process where the group agrees for a short period of time not to block any notion that may come to mind. The group settles on the word that most describes what they want to think about together, and then one of their number draws or writes that word in the middle of a sheet of paper for all to see. The members of the group then call out – just like in a word-association game – any words that come into their minds when they think of that keyword, and one member writes those words on the sheet of paper. It is very free association that is called for, and the rule is that no one questions a contribution, even if it seems unrelated or even bizarre. It is a chance for the group imagination to run wild and come up with all sorts of leads, some of which, it is true, may on later reflection turn out to be dead-ends. But to question a contribution stops the imaginative flow and, what is more important, makes that member feel their contribution is not worthy of inclusion in the group's life, and that is a cardinal group sin. Once the paper has enough contributions written or drawn on it then the group can look at each suggestion in turn to see what it makes of them. When the group has an idea of what each contribution means, then a coloured ring can be drawn round just a couple of the very best suggestions which the group feels it wants to follow up. Brainstorming is one of the easiest of group exercises and yet is so useful when the group is not sure quite what to do next, for it really does free the imagination in a most refreshing way.

I have already mentioned another helpful group tool when we were considering group leadership. This is *the memory*. It sometimes happens that a group may function really well for one of its sessions only to find later that no one really remembers what was said or done there. My experience is that the keeping of a confidential group record of events can prove very beneficial. A simple cassette recorder can be used to this end with great success. A group member is responsible for keeping the tape running during the session and then listens to it once again just prior to the next meeting so that they can remind the group of some of the important phrases, statements or happenings that struck them as significant as they listened. The group may want to write some of those points up at the beginning of their next session so that they can be owned and developed, but in any case the same tape cassette is used once again and the current session is recorded over the last one so that the confidentiality is obvious to all. Photographs and pictures of previous sessions and events can also act as a fine 'memory' for the group. This can help to keep things moving forward in each session and it ensures that one meeting builds upon the last without boring the group members with the reading of minutes of the previous meeting.

Throughout our description of the phases of the theological cycle we will also be referring repeatedly to the use of the *expressive arts* as another way to enliven and open up the group's theological work. Using a multiplicity of media gives opportunity for all types of people to express themselves at levels that they may not have explored before, and in addition it limits the degree to which those who are verbally articulate can dominate the group. Painting or chalking pictures, working from TV and videos, slideshows, photographs, dance, cartoons, tapestries, banners, clay modelling, murals, and so on, may all have their part to play. I was once in a group which included Julie Harper, an accomplished artist. She helped us first to get the feel of expressing ourselves by drawing shapes but then let us loose with paper and poster paints. We had had a number of discussion sessions on the theme of 'suffering' but it was not until we were given the paints that our deeper unexpressed feelings began to see the light of day. We may be really surprised at the depth of expression and discovery which the use of these media engenders.

In the latter part of this chapter we have taken time to consider what style of group life is most conducive to the doing of theology; the Bibliography that I have included at the back of this book will direct the reader's attention to more detailed and technical material on this question. Our brief sketch should however have given a sufficient flavour of this participative group style, and we can therefore turn our attention now to the next phase of the theological cycle, where the broad observations which were our focus in the experience phase can be scrutinized more precisely in the exploration phase. Those earlier impressionistic sketches of the issue the group had chosen to consider can now be turned to more detailed description and the group's anecdotes can be turned into finer analyses.

Notes

1   This process is written up in full in Laurie Green, *My Faith, My Story* (UTU Worksheet no. 4). Available from Urban Theology Unit, 210 Abbeyfield Road, Sheffield S4 7AZ.
2   See Bibliography for resource books.
3   *Faith in the City*, the Report of the Archbishop of Canterbury's Commission on Urban Priority Areas (CBF, Church of England, 1985).

4 *The People, the Land and the Church*, the Second Hereford Rural Consultation 1986 (Hereford Diocese, Board of Finance).
5 The Step-by-Step programme has recently been reviewed and revised. More information can be obtained from Step-by-Step, Stepney Area Office, 7 St Andrew Street, London EC4A 3AB.
6 See Bibliography for resource book suggestions.
7 On adult resistance to learning groups, see David Goodburn, 'Needs', *British Journal of Theological Education*, volume 2, number 1, summer 1988.
8 On the 'problem-posing concept of education' or 'problematisation', see Paulo Freire, *Pedagogy of the Oppressed* (Penguin, 1972), chapter 2.

4

Exploration

In moving on from experience to exploration, we will first need to consider the nature of the exploration we are seeking to make. Next we will go on to describe the many avenues open to us to gather information about the theme. Finally, we will give attention to how to make sense of the information that we gather. But before looking in detail at each of these elements of the exploration phase, let us refer yet again to our diagram to remind ourselves where this phase fits into the overall spiral of doing theology.

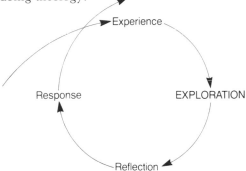

From anecdote to analysis

During the experience phase of the theological cycle, the group got to know one another, they decided upon a theme that was to be the focus of their theological work together, and after owning up to their prejudices and their hopes and fears, they then considered the theological or faith commitments with which they came to the theme of their study. To help them do this they shared stories and anecdotes, drew pictures, gathered magazine and newspaper clippings, and so on until they felt that they had a generalised impression of the subject that they had chosen as their focus. But at this exploration stage of the spiral, the group must now move from those impressionistic anecdotes into factual analysis, from generalised sketches to specific description. But even as they do this they must guard against becoming too clinical about the experience that they now seek to explore. Maintaining this balance between experience and analysis may not necessarily be easy, but in any action–reflection praxis there will be a need to stand back a little from the situation in order carefully to analyse the hard facts of the issue, while at the same time it will be important to keep well rooted in the experience of it, for in this way it will be easier to judge both its critical and its felt nature. To this end we will need to move constantly back and forth between the feelings raised by participation in the issue, and the more clinical and systematic investigation of it.

The importance of moving from experience into analytical exploration is illustrated by thinking for a moment of the typical television documentary. Very often such a documentary will leave viewers *feeling* that they now have experience of the issue that the documentary has covered, but the learning may often have been only at an emotional level, without necessarily giving viewers very much *information* to go on. The programme will have included many emotive pictures and suggestive camera shots designed to give expression to the feelings the issue evokes, but the programme may not necessarily have offered much hard factual information to the viewer. I often come away from a television documentary feeling that I need some way of checking that my emotions about the issue have not been manipulated. This is indeed the danger of story. Story is very emotive, but it does not of itself give very much opportunity for a more objective verification. Some feel that one story can be judged by another if it is placed over against it, but it remains difficult to know on what basis one judges one story as valid and another as false if there is no factual information to go by. The opposing myths and stories of Northern Ireland are sometimes of this emotive nature, but they are rarely to be taken as the basis from which to determine the rights and wrongs of the situation in that grief-stricken land. To do that we need hard facts, statistics and the sort of evidence that stories are not intended to provide. And yet without the stories to back up the facts, the statistical information remains cold and clinical and gives no impression of the importance of the emotions that lie behind the facts and figures. We need to gather facts, but we also need to listen to the stories in order to keep our balance during this exploration phase of the cycle. If, for example, the group should be considering the issue of freedom, then as well as collecting data about slavery and captivity it would be well for the group to visit one of the old slaving ports such as Liverpool or Bristol. There have recently been some very fine booklets published that will guide the group round the old slave buildings and enable them to visit the pertinent sites. Similarly, a visit to a theatre or a film that relates to the question of slavery or freedom would help to round out the picture derived from the group's gathered statistical and historical information. If a visit is out of the question, then the same purpose might be served by having one or two members experience for themselves what it is like to be tied up and captive for a brief period during one of the meetings.

A group visit to the planning department of the city or town can prove to be a more interesting way of gathering community statistics than hours spent reading through masses of statistical data, or if the group is studying homelessness and destitution, it might be helpful to engage in an exercise known as 'the plunge'. This method invites group participants to volunteer to sleep rough themselves in the city for a night with just a few pence in their pocket and find out at first hand something of the reality of destitution. These sorts of exercises and visits can easily be developed around the chosen theme so that the exploration phase of the cycle can be interspersed with fresh experience of the questions at issue. Not only does this help to make the detailed exploration more exciting for the group, but it also liberates them from too clinical an analysis and helps to broaden the base upon which the analysis is founded. In this way we do not suffer what Martin Luther King called 'the paralysis of analysis', by which he warned of the dangers attached to getting so stuck into analysis that we forget action, become divorced from the felt realities of the experience, and become scared by the vastness of the subject at issue. The very best way to manage this balance of analysis and experience, of reflection and action, is for the group themselves to remain engaged throughout with the realities of the issue so that even if one evening a week is spent in analysis of the statistics about the situation, the felt realities of the problem are never far from their consciousness. For example, if the group is studying the issue of homelessness but during the week they are also offering their spare rooms to homeless people, then they stand a good chance of engaging in a well-balanced piece of participative work and study.

Using the analytical tools

When a theological group engages in exploration, they will be gathering as much precise information about the issue or situation as possible, and to this end there will be a wide range of tools at their disposal. First of all, the members of the group will themselves have various *observation skills* which can be used to check out some of their earlier assumptions. They will look, listen and use all the natural inquisitive interest of their senses. But they will also need to utilise checklists, data research, and other analytical and observation tools that derive from the social sciences and the arts.

The *social sciences* include such subjects as sociology, psychology, economics and politics, and many of these disciplines are ideally suited to the exploration of localities, groups or issues. But when these disciplines are used in our exploration, some may become anxious lest, when accepting a particular scientific approach to the analysis, there is the attendant necessity of accepting the philosophy behind each particular approach. Since sociology has been so heavily influenced by Marx, and psychology by Freud, participants may fear for example that in utilising techniques from these disciplines they may find themselves buying into Marxist or Freudian philosophical assumptions as a consequence. But we need have no great fear, for it is possible for us to utilise many of the tools of these disciplines without arriving at Marxist or Freudian interpretations. As we move round the Doing Theology Spiral we will be given ample opportunity for questioning and criticising any findings in the light of the insights that come to us from our theological investigations, just as we will be checking our theological explorations by means of our discoveries from other disciplines of study. This will enable us to utilise other disciplines without being subservient to their ideological assumptions.

The *arts* will likewise present us with a whole range of material which seeks to focus, clarify and interpret the issue we are studying – material in the shape of novels, works of art, videos, cultural events and so on. But as soon as we encounter this sort of artistic material, we inherit problems relating to the cultural and class derivation of the material itself. Great care has therefore to be taken to use insights that come to us from popular culture, television, pop music, trade unions and rap poetry, as well as from the Tate Gallery, Covent Garden and the classical poets. If a good spread is available, then the group will be able more accurately to compare and discern the nature of this analytical and interpretive material.

Whenever we begin to use the disciplines of the social sciences or the arts, we encounter the problem of *professional advantage*, for those who are well acquainted with these disciplines will have an obvious advantage over those who have never before looked at sociology, history or classical literature. It takes confidence and an attentive ear on the part of those who know their subject if they are to enable the group rather than disable it by their knowledge. We all know about the type of vicar who will not keep quiet at a Bible study meeting. The South African group that we referred to in our second chapter got around this problem by inviting the experts in to answer only such questions as they themselves had prepared from their preliminary investigations of the subject. The expert was allowed to answer these questions and do nothing more, and in this way the group were not overwhelmed by too much weighted information.[1]

Gathering analytical information

Sometimes masses of data about the issue will emerge from within the group itself but, more often than not, the group members will have to go out to meet the issue and unearth information 'out in the field'. To help them do this systematically, groups often find it helpful to have a framework to work from that lists a number of areas of investigation so that the group can take time to explore how each area relates to the issue under consideration.[2] So that the whole group understands the plan being followed, the framework is written up for all to see, as follows:

> *Areas of Analysis*
>
> 1 Historical
> 2 Geographical
> 3 Social
> 4 Economic
> 5 Cultural
> 6 Religious

Let us take each area in turn, to see how this analysis is done; as always, though, it must be up to the group itself to determine which areas it selects as appropriate to its particular setting. In the description that follows, I will outline how each area may be investigated and give an indication of just how detailed the analysis can become when at its best. Most groups will, however, be working to certain time constraints, and thus have to select those areas where they can most usefully concentrate their energies. For the sake of breadth, though, I will indicate a whole range of factors under all of the headings. First, let us consider how the historical analysis may be approached.

1 Gathering historical information

If we ignore the history of an area or issue then we will be treating it as if it had no context in time, as if it came from nowhere and, by implication, is going nowhere. It is only when we appreciate the history, or the story so far, and understand the social trends, the myths and expectations about the issue, that we can set about the question of how we might participate more fully in writing the next page of the history.

If the chosen issue is rooted in the locality, then we will probably be helped by the use of maps. The local library is usually full of old maps and it is possible to have them photocopied. By buying sheets of transparent acetate and the right marker pens, it is quite easy to draw from later maps on to the acetate sheets and then overlay them on to the oldest map that the group can find. If this is done in colour, then a clear visual picture begins to emerge of how the neighbourhood grew up and how the issues have developed. Local people very often show great interest if they hear that the group is to mount a mini exhibition of old local photographs and the meetings of the group begin to bubble once a sense of local identity and pride develops. And it is not only among the older folk that enthusiasm is evident. Younger people can also become excited by this historical analysis, as if thirsting for a sense of their own historical identity and for their roots. Visits come into their own once again at this point, because many of us have an extraordinary ability to live in an area for years without getting out and discovering all its nooks and crannies. Even in the cities, many citizens have never walked along some of the old industrial canal footpaths for example, even though some of our cities are riddled with them. Some groups enjoy inviting in outside speakers to give talks or slide-shows about the history of their community, while others love to draw charts and diagrams and make taped interviews of elderly residents, or make photographic, tapestry or video presentations of their history – their story.

Other groups will not be starting from a consideration of their locality, but rather from some issue or other that concerns them – perhaps racism, schooling, running a youth club, or a concern to make the Church Council more relevant and decisive. Thinking up new ways into exploring these areas can be quite an exciting challenge, but again it will be important to take account of the history. How long has the issue been around? What did people first think about it? Collecting cuttings from old newpapers and magazines sometimes helps to fill out the background. Very often, specialists need to be brought in who have read the books on the subject and they can be quizzed to see what the history has to tell us. Again, even with an issue-based group, a pictorial and sometimes mapped history can be drawn and displayed on the wall of the meeting room so that it is more comprehensible to all. It is also helpful to plot on our maps and in an accompanying loose-leaf scrapbook the major stages through which the issue has passed.

The group should by this stage be in a position to highlight the major turning points in the historical survey, and from this they should begin to perceive certain patterns of change emerging. There have probably been major external events that have played their part in the story, like war, major building initiatives, national policy decisions in the Church, and so on. And as the history emerges so it will be necessary to look at the past not only from the perspective of those who gained from it, but also from the point of view of those who suffered as a consequence. The group will need to work out who and what the major agents of change were, and where their power in the situation came from. All this will help us appreciate and understand the trends and patterns that carry through into the present.

2 *Gathering geographical information*

Our checklist directs us next to the gathering of geographical information. If our concern is with the locality, we can once again start with maps. This time it is worth obtaining a reasonably large-scale Ordnance Survey map and marking on to it all sorts of social features. If the group cannot obtain a map of its own, one can be borrowed from the library and a copy drawn that is adequate for the purpose. The group can go into as much or as little detail as they have time for, but it will be helpful to draw on to the map at least something of the following. As well as indicating important geographical features, road systems, public transport facilities and so on, it will be significant to take note of the incidence of such things as car ownership in the locality. The group should pay attention to the fabric of the area and mark on to the map the locality and types of structure that have been built. The approximate age and type of housing can usually be simply colour-coded, as can different types of industrial or farm distribution. Buildings of special religious interest can be labelled, such as the churches, chapels, mosques, temples, and so on. Public amenities, shops, pubs, clinics, parks, schools, telephone boxes etc. can helpfully be located, but it is important to keep the map clear, for too much detail can muddle the picture it seeks to clarify. Again, if there is a lot of complexity in the area, the detail can be drawn on to acetate sheet overlays so that by laying them on to the main map, significant trends or coincidences can be discerned and noted. The dates of the development or rehabilitation of the different areas can all be plotted in this way, as can those areas that show a dominant ethnic group in residence or ownership. The age of the population in various locations very often relates to the historical development of urban regions, so it is helpful to plot age trends in various streets and districts if they can be determined easily. All these statistics should be readily available from local government offices, the planning department or the city engineer,[3] but, for more specific information, the group should get into the habit of following leads and ferreting away until it has the information it requires.

This sort of exercise helps to build group confidence and solidarity, and this may become quite significant when more formidable obstacles are met later. Sometimes, opposition will be encountered even at an early stage, as was the case when I wanted information about the degree of lead in the atmosphere in the area of the city in which I was then living. There was extreme unwillingness to let me have the figures, in case I published them and caused a scare. The key is to keep on digging, for if there is unwillingness to give information, that often gives an indication that the information really is worth having! Each and every area will have its own peculiarities, and only the group itself will know best how to do the mapping exercise for its locality; but one thing will always be important to find out – who, in the last analysis, has control of the area? Who owns it and who can make decisions about the future of the community?

We may have chosen to look at an issue that is not easily mapped, such as the health service or the quality of local education, but a little imagination on the part of the group will pay ample dividends. Mapping local health authority areas, local surgeries and ambulance distribution may help to pin down the more abstract issue of public health, while mapping of Third World trade networks may help broaden our perspectives on issues that have to do with economics or industry.

Geographical analysis of this sort should help the group to see the spread and implications of the issue – even to the national and international level. Rarely is a local issue as confined to one community as may appear on the surface, for a local issue often turns out to be just the local symptom of a much larger and broader-based reality.

3 Gathering social information

The group will also need to discern more carefully the nature of the social relationships within the community or issue being studied. What types of family and group structures emerge from the study and how do the people concerned pass on their informal learning? The latest census figures will help the group find out quite a lot about the population of an area, and the ready assistance of a planning department statistician can be a great asset. It should be possible to find out in broad terms where people are employed, who are unemployed, what sorts of skill are registered, whether people are married, single, bringing up children alone, and so on. It will often be important to know how mobile local people are, and whether the youngsters leave the district as soon as they have the chance. Informal 'front doorstep' conversation will give an insight into what the local people do for their recreation and leisure, if they have any, and how they relate together in clubs and in families. There may be informal gangs, interest groups or even another study group looking at the community, who should be met. The local doctor, social worker and police officer may have altogether different perspectives to share, but the group will also try to find out who in the locality is considered by the community itself to be important. Street networks and communities are crucial factors in any locality and can lead the group into a much better understanding of how a community lives, plays and works.

If the theological group is focusing upon an issue rather than a community, it will still be very important to find out who the people are that are involved in the issue. Where are decisions made and who takes them? Where is the power in the situation? These will be key factors to discern and gauge. The group might ask itself 'Who wants to see change and of what sort?' 'Who is against change and why?' 'Who can change things and who can not?' Analysis of the interests of the forces of law and order, communications media, education, and so on, will all help to chart the social forces and powers that are at work regarding the issue. Descriptive diagrams of political structures and photographs of important political figures should not be too difficult to come by, and such charts will help the group discern who exactly has power in any situation, whether that power be at local, national or international level. Only when it is known where the power is, will it later be worth lobbying and seeking the support of councillors, MPs, courts, parties, interest groups and so forth.

4 Gathering economic information

Next we must turn to the economic structures. The group will need to gather as much information as it can about how money relates to the issue or locality it is exploring. It will be necessary to present as clearly as possible how wealth is produced and distributed in the community or in relation to the issue being studied. Where people work, whether local or at a distance, what they do and how much they earn, may best be displayed by means of maps and charts. The group must find out if the industries related to the area or issue are labour- or capital-intensive, what technologies are used, and who controls the production and the employment patterns. If there are attendant service industries, information about this needs to be clearly presented too. The group should try to describe how the wealth thus produced is distributed, what people do who are not in paid employment, and what taxes operate in the community. Money is always a factor in any situation and it will be necessary to know as much as possible about its power and influence over the issue or community being studied. It may be important to know if there are investments involved, and under what conditions those investments are made and what returns investors are expecting. What local people do with their money is also a key feature for a community study, and this must be described if at all possible.

5 Discerning the culture

There are certain key indicators that we can look to for pointers into the culture of a community.[4] For example, the group may begin by looking to see where and between which groups conflict exists, and how that conflict is dealt with. It should not be too difficult either to find out how a community is seen by its residents or those who work in the area, and here again there will be indications of the system of meanings and values that is operating within the community. For example, some residents might say that although the area has its problems, they would not want to leave because their family is there and because it affords easy access to their local place of work. From that sort of response we can learn that family ties and employment are considered of importance to those residents. Very often there will be all sorts of myths about the community, together with prejudices about residents in various streets. Inter-cultural rivalry may be rife, especially when there is 'race' involved. There will be a variety of lifestyles apparent in most communities today and friendship groups usually tend to focus around such similarities. It is always interesting to see to what extent income and wealth play their part in distinguishing such sub-groupings.

The local culture will also carry symbolic stories about the community. When vicars past and present are the focus of these stories, then they may very well colour how the local residents view the Church. Symbols within the community may be understood in different ways by different groups, and if an issue is the focus of the group's theological work, that issue itself may turn out to be symbolic of something greater than itself. The church building, for example, may stand in the community consciousness as a symbol of continuity, or as sacred place, or perhaps community care, or even as a symbol of privileged status. The discernment of symbols and their meanings will be a key indicator of the culture that surrounds the focus of the group's concern.

Another helpful and informal way of getting to the system of meaning and values carried in the community culture is through the use of *pictures*. A photographer or an artist may produce pictures that are typical of the locality or central to the issue being studied, and then interested groups are asked to talk about what they see going on in the pictures. Do they interpret a photograph of the boy running down the street as a picture of a vandal, a child having a game, or as a young man hailing a taxi? Is the policeman in the picture interpreted as a 'bobby', a friend, or an enemy? Some social and Christian organisations produce pictures and posters that beg social questions, and they can be used in a very similar way.

The stories and anecdotes that derive from the community or that surround the issue can also be explored a little further by asking the story tellers where they first heard the story, why they tell it in the way they do, whether other stories that they know are very similar and so on. In this way a profile of the stories can be drawn up so that a better appreciation can be gained of what the stories are seeking to highlight in the life and culture that carry them.

There are some cultural issues that are best dealt with by a very direct approach. Racism, for example, is often not very obvious to the onlooker until some basic questions are asked, such as 'Exactly how many black people are employed in your college and in what capacity?' Audits and questionnaires of this type can sometimes be obtained off the peg from agencies specialising in these issues,[5] but often it will be necessary for the group to create the questions themselves. Questionnaires are extremely difficult tools to operate scientifically, but it is nevertheless well worth while for the group to put together a series of questions to ask the public, even if only as a simple check on the statistics that come to them from other sources.

In gathering cultural information, photographs and interviews with local leaders will come into their own. Local murals, folklore, local stories, traditions and questions of lifestyle can be drawn, sketched, photographed, or even presented in collages made up from newspaper or magazine cuttings – school-children are usually quite skilled in this art and can play a big part in the group at this point. All the information that is thus gathered about lifestyle, class, self-consciousness and cultural identity will help to make clear the meanings with which the local culture has invested its experience.

6 *Religious factors*

Religion, the sixth element on our list, will be another important cultural factor to consider, and different religions will foster different family and employment structures as well as a variety of attitudes and responses to issues. The place of children, money, women and men, food and drink, music and leisure, will all be greatly influenced by religion and its attendant culture. To have a notion of these basic differences within a community will be of great value to a group studying its locality, but religious factors may also be fundamental to a group that has chosen to address an issue rather than a locality. For example, one group who were wanting to consider the question of evangelism discovered that a local Christian youth club had decided to give free copies of a paperback Bible to all its members, not realising that the Muslims among the youth interpreted this act as symbolising a renunciation of the Christian faith on the part of the youth club leaders, because in their Muslim culture a Holy Book would not have been so cavalierly distributed. We will need to build up understandings of various religious cultures if we are to appreciate how issues are perceived and interpreted by differing groupings.

Even within the culture of non-church white communities we may be surprised to find religious images and theological concepts forming one of the major threads of the system of meanings and values of that culture. This sort of religion we have already referred to as implicit or folk religion. Quite clearly, most people already have some feelings and thoughts about religion and this reservoir of faith is extremely important to address, for even though it may be very far from anything that may be called Christian, it may well contain all sorts of vestiges and images of the Christian faith. It is important that we take this popular religion very seriously in the course of our theological work, for it can be where the majority of folk have to begin and within it we may be surprised to find a great deal of theology going on already!

There will be many other powerful images all around in our local cultures, in our newspapers, in local folk memories, in children's stories, in jokes, films or popular novels, which relate in one way or another to the theme or locality that the group is considering and all these will prove informative factors in the analysis. Modern advertisements too are full of the most revealing images of the myths of society and its theologies, and the television offers an abundance of sources for reflection. Taking just a little time to try to discern how each of these structures play their part in building up society's understandings of the issues will pay dividends as the group does its theology together.

So it is that our theological groups amass a wealth of data and information about the situation, locality or issue that they have chosen as their focus. They may follow my suggested framework of analysis and look at historical, geographical, social, economic, cultural and religious factors in turn. They may have time to be as thorough as I have suggested in this description, although most groups will of necessity have to be a little less ambitious, choosing to look at those sections of the analysis that seem to them to be of most importance. But whichever approach they use, it is to be hoped that they will by this stage have a sound grasp of how the situation feels and looks.

The group is likely to become much more confident during this phase of the work, for it begins to take all sorts of initiatives in seeking out data, interviewing local councillors, Members of Parliament and other responsible authorities. This process of information gathering requires determination and discipline and cannot be rushed, but careful preparation will pay dividends later. The problem, issue or whatever it is that has been chosen as the theological theme, can be broken down by the group into a range of sub-issues by brainstorming and investigation. Constant questioning of What? Why? Who? Where? When? and How? teases out the issue and the group uses every method to hand to describe it, write it, picture it, role-play it, photograph it, make banners about it, and celebrate it, until they really do feel they know their subject.

The exploration of ourselves

Before the group members begin to try to make sense of all the data that have been amassed, it is important to check out what part the group participants themselves play in the issue or locality they have chosen to study. It may be, for example, that they themselves are part of the problem and never knew it! I therefore suggest that at the exploration stage groups take a little time to explore themselves more thoroughly.

By sharing with one another how they are feeling at each point in the whole exercise, the group members will begin to know where statements, angers, fears and biases are coming from. If a couple of members are having terrible fears about their own employment security, for example, then that is bound to colour their feelings, for good or ill, when employment issues are discussed in the group, and it is important for the participants to know this. But just as significant as knowing about the feelings of individuals within the group will be self-knowledge for the group as a whole. Now that the exploration is well underway, do they still, for example, see themselves as an evangelistic group, a Christian action group, a simple friendship group, or what? Their class relationship to the locality or to the issues being discussed will be an important factor too, for no doubt their situation in life will give them a particular group perspective on each problem raised and they will need to be aware of that.

Many groups meet under the auspices of a larger group or institution, such as the Church, and such groups will need to analyse that parent body to see how it relates to the theme in order that they may better perceive how that may influence their own perspective. If, for example, the group we are working with is a church group, then it might be helpful to make a careful analysis of the congregation, along with an appraisal of how the congregation itself views the group. It would be helpful to log the size of the congregation and its membership and consider what ecclesiastical boundaries the church might expect the group to confine itself to. A profile of the leadership, lay and ordained, of the membership, their homes, employment, if any, status, wealth, interests and so on, will all fill out the picture. A list of the formal activities of the church in its worship and its attached societies and clubs, together with a notion of its financial base and the availability of the buildings, will be of great importance if church resources are to be called upon in any way by the group at a later stage.

The historical perspective will be just as important here as it was during the exploration of the community, for the group will want to be sure whether the church has a history of action or passivity, how it has been involved in the past, on whose side it was perceived to be, and on whose side it actually was. If it is possible to describe it, then the style of faith of the overall congregation is well worth consideration because it may be, for example, that they are actually operating at a folk religion level when the minister or vicar is assuming otherwise. If the group decides to do its theology without analysing such features, it may well have some surprises ahead when asking the congregation to support its endeavours. And this brings us to the all-important issue of the relationship between the group and the larger congregation. It is as well that this be analysed with as much clarity as possible at each stage of the enterprise so that appropriate strategies can be determined during the whole process. If, for example, the group has taken the sensitive issue of the baptism policy of the church as its prime focus and intends to explain its findings to the wider congregation, the group needs to have some idea of where the congregation has stood and now stands on the issue if it is to present its findings in an understandable and acceptable fashion. There will probably be other church groups in the locality too, and the degree of ecumenical activity and potential should be gauged, for it can be very significant during later phases of theological activity.

For those groups that feel themselves to belong to institutions other than the Church, it will be just as important for them to analyse how their parent bodies tick and the relationship they themselves have with them. It will also be helpful to know how other similar organisations in the community view the parent body and how well they get on.

During this process of gathering of data and information about the group's concern I have known participants become expert analysts. They have worked with statistics and lists and have used surveys and questionnaires. They have conducted interviews and made investigative visits. They have written plays and stories, constructed dialogues and skits, used that 'brainstorming' method I spoke of earlier, repeated chants or made up choruses. They have made banners, painted murals, produced slide-shows, videos and tapestries, all as aids to describe and analyse the focus of their concern. But having done all this, the next step is to try to begin to make some sense of all the information being amassed and to see if there is meaning within it.

Making sense of the information

As long as the issue originally chosen by the group is one that interests them and in which they have some personal investment, then it is extraordinary how exciting this whole business of exploration can be for the group. I have known groups to be sitting up into the night, not wanting to disperse, as they find out more and more together about the nature and shape of whatever they have chosen to explore. Group members will also begin to discover and disclose their own various gifts, be it the use of the telephone, drawing posters and charts, reading magazines or books, gathering music, making photographic studies, interviewing and so on. All this time the group will be attempting to bring together what at first sight is a mass of unconnected information and stories, and to present it all in some manageable form. But as they do, they will begin to discern certain patterns and trends emerging, and they will inevitably try to make some sense of all the data and to interpret them in some way. In order to do this in a disciplined manner it will be necessary to be aware that there are at least three major ways of interpreting society.

The three dominant understandings of societal relationships are the traditional, the liberal and the radical. The *traditional* understanding sees society as a natural, almost biological, phenomenon which gently renews itself like the seasons, in a cyclic fashion. According to this understanding of society, power relationships will be based on the acceptance of authoritarian benign control and, on this basis, change will be viewed as deviant, since the system itself is understood to be natural and right. According to this view, anyone who is in difficulty in society is deemed either to be in need of punishment since it is they that are at fault, or in need of a 'hand-out'; but there can be nothing wrong with society itself to have caused their difficulty. This has been termed the 'empirical' explanation of pheno-mena – almost a 'what you see is what you get' explanation and no more.

The *liberal* model of how societies function asks us to view things rather differently. Here, change is thought of as necessary, but only on an evolutionary and gradualist basis. Power in society will this time be viewed in managerial terms and there will be a seeking after what is felt to be a proper balance in all things. 'Progress' and 'success' are the two key words, and 'reform' is considered to be the way to achieve both. People's difficulties are, according to this way of thinking, real and collective, but can be put right by allowing the social system to grow and develop naturally for the better. This understanding of society has been called the 'functionalist' explanation,[6] and it is generally wedded to a *laissez-faire* economics and management style.

The third option available to us in the interpretation of all our data is the *radical* model. The radical interpretation does not expect slow evolutionary development, but looks for rapid transformation of society, engendered by creative conflicts within it. Power will this time be perceived as something that should be shared and aspirations will be towards the benefit of the whole community by means of participation. Change will be expected to occur on this model more as a result of imaginative leaps rather than the gentle copying of 'natural' patterns from the past. People's difficulties will be thought of as symptoms of the constant struggle that goes on between conflicting groups; progress will result not from reform this time, but from a restructuring of society and the replacement of the way things are with a new system of relationships. This radical understanding is sometimes called the 'dialectical' model of social relationships, and indicates that society is seen here as a whole complex range of factors and groups constantly pushing and pulling at one another.

Within the Church at large, there is likely to be resistance to change; therefore, the traditionalist view tends to be the dominant interpretation of the data that are collected. In the group, however, the unearthing of so much information may prompt its members to see change slightly differently, so there may be tensions. Generally speaking, most of us probably utilise a mixture of all three models when we make our interpretations of society, but it is as well to be aware of the various options, just in case we are tempted to overlay the facts too heavily with certain interpretations in order to make them fit neatly into our own preferred models of change.

So the group's responsibility now is to make some interpretation of the data that have been amassed, but how should they go about such a daunting task? This will require a certain amount of self-confidence in the group, for there is no doubt that this aspect of exploration – or social analysis as it is sometimes called – can be a rather difficult process. The essence of the exercise is at heart a very simple one, however, and the key is to ask as many probing questions of the information as possible; in this, the 'problem posing' technique of making statements into questions will help us immensely. To assist us in the formulation of these probing questions, I have found that many groups are helped by a simple threefold checklist. Again, I like to write this out for the group so that they can see what the agenda is. This allows them to change it or develop it if they feel they would prefer to follow a different approach. My threefold checklist is as follows:

Making Sense of the Data

1 LOOK FOR CONNECTIONS
2 LOOK FOR VALUES
3 LOOK FOR CAUSES

Let us consider each element in turn.

1 *Looking for connections*

This is an attempt to see how one piece of the jigsaw fits with all the other pieces so that a picture can begin to emerge. When I was working with a theological group at Spaghetti Junction in Birmingham,[7] our historical analysis had revealed that even in the time of the Roman legions the locality in which we lived had been an important intersection of roads and bridges. This not only resonated with the recent building of the Spaghetti Junction motorway interchange itself, but offered us an interpretation of many of the factors of deprivation that we had discovered in the community. We felt that it was because our locality had always been seen as a traffic routeway rather than a community in its own right, that it had never been taken care of by the powerful forces that had driven their canals, railways and motorways through the heart of our area. This was an example of how one piece of historical information became an important interpretative piece of the jigsaw, allowing us to see the whole social picture more clearly.

Another way to look for connections is to remember that most issues have repercussions at various levels – the personal level where I feel the situation myself, the local level where the community together experiences the problem, the district level where the wider community is involved and, beyond that, the national level and the level of international affairs. So, for example, unemployment may hit me personally, but it will also be possible to consider the issue at all the other levels I have mentioned. And when these different levels are appreciated, we begin to notice more sharply the structural nature of many of the issues we face. So, for example, if we are concerned about the local doctor's surgery always being crowded, by asking questions about health at the different levels indicated, we become aware that all the information that we have collected about economics, geography, culture and so on, will relate in some way or another to what at first sight appeared to be only a local issue about the nearby doctor's waiting room. Sometimes our maps show up common or linking features too. If, for example, an older area of housing is also the area of immigrant population, this may help us interpret those factors in some way. And so the pieces of the jigsaw begin to fit together and connections are discerned. When the broader picture comes a little more into focus in this way, then we are able to move to the next point on the checklist.

2 *Looking for the values*

Hopefully, our investigations of the issue or community will have unearthed something of what motivates the people involved, and their hopes, concerns and ideologies will have come to light together with an understanding of what systems of moral value they work with and what they want from the situation. Different concerned groupings will probably have different ideas about the issues and will be working from different values and ideologies. But despite these differences it is usual that there will be one set of values which, by and large, are controlling the situation, and it will be these 'dominant' values that we will be keen to locate. What these values are will have been hidden deep within some of the answers that were given in questionnaires, interviews and conversations. However, if these dominant values have not been clearly stated, it may sometimes be easier to see what the intrinsic values are by looking honestly at the situation for ourselves and asking ourselves the awkward questions about the power and powerlessness that we see there.

An exercise that can help us discern the dominant values may be described as follows. Having drawn a number of lines to represent scales of value, we then mark on to those lines where we would place the people and agencies that we have investigated during our process of exploration. For example, we might write up at each end of a large piece of paper two opposing value words such as 'competition' and 'co-operation'. The group can then discuss where along the line between these two opposites they would place the various groups, characters and situations that they have met during their exploration. Having done this a few times for different groups, the words 'competition' and 'co-operation' can be exchanged for any other value words that the group would like to try. Such value words might be 'unity and diversity', 'material and spiritual', 'peace and violence', 'freedom and control', 'equality and hierarchy', 'money and people', 'giving and taking', and so on, just as the group thinks best. After some practice, the group may begin to discern which are the overriding or 'dominant values' that are at work in the situation, and those words can then be written up in big letters and some drawings or photographs attached for emphasis.

3 Looking for causes

Once we have some of the basic value systems named, it may then prove possible to pinpoint the institutions and the main persons who seem to us to be the holders and carriers of these traditions and values in the situation, together with those who have power to sustain them. Our investigations may even help us to see where it is that the people derive these sets of 'values', and our historical analyses may help us to discern where they may have originated in the first place.

Once we have moved to asking these important questions about where the power is in the whole process, then we may be able to determine amidst all that we have observed, what we believe to be merely the symptoms of the problem and which factors or persons are the underlying causes of those symptoms. There will be a whole series of questions that will help us to determine what these causes are. We can ask ourselves, for example, in whose interests the present situation is structured, and who stands to benefit from changes that have occurred within it. From this we might be able to tell whose interests are the most powerful in the situation, and whose interests and welfare are more likely to be overlooked. We will be helped by asking where we see the three crucial elements of gender, class and ethnicity at work in those basic causes that we have discerned. It will be productive too to ask what part the deeper structures of technology and capital are playing at each level as we have described them. If we constantly ask the question 'Why?' of all the factors that are emerging in our analysis, then eventually we will pinpoint those factors that we believe to be not merely surface symptoms, but the underlying causes that have actually shaped or are still shaping the nature of the issue or locality being considered. It is here that our 'problem posing' technique can be very helpful in checking each factual statement that we make about the issue or locality, by turning each statement into question form. As we go through each element of our analysis, the historical, the social, the economic, cultural and religious, so we can ask the question 'Why?' and then try to rank in order of priority what, in our estimation, the two most important causal factors are in each area and what values underlie them. We will only be in a position to make provisional judgements at this stage, but later, when we have looked much closer at our Christian values and traditions, we will be in a better position still to judge the evidence according to gospel criteria. At this stage, however, we can at least make some useful provisional judgements about what the underlying causes are of the situation that we have been investigating.

But as we focus these basic causes ever more sharply, so we also have to remember to ask where we see ourselves in the whole situation, and to what extent we ourselves may be a contributory factor in the issue being studied. I remember seeing a group quite recently that had decided to look at the question of racial discrimination in its local community, and it was studying a picture which one of its members had found in a magazine. The picture portrayed a group of young angry white fascists eyeball to eyeball with a gang of black Rastafarians. The startling discovery for the group occurred when they were asked simply to decide which group in the picture they felt most akin to and which group seemed to be most alien. While they had been dispassionately and clinically unearthing facts, they had been able to distance themselves from the situation, but now they were shocked into realising that they themselves were part of the equation that they had been exploring. They saw themselves in the picture. This is one of the reasons why it is so important for the group never to hide from acknowledging their own part in the situation, but instead to remain engaged as committed and self-aware participants.

Moving forward

I have taken time to spell out in some detail the various avenues that may be explored during this whole process of exploration, but many groups will be aware that they will simply not have the time to work through this extensive agenda. I have belonged to groups that have spent as long as a year on this exploration phase alone; they have done things very thoroughly – and it has paid off in the end. But other groups only have three or four meetings to devote to this exploration phase, so they must choose what methods and approaches seem most manageable. Each group must go about their theological work in the way they feel is most appropriate for them; however, the more precision they can muster, the better will be their theology in the long run.

But before moving on to the next phase of the theological cycle, the group would do well to begin to look a little more to the future and to the possibilities that they sense even now within the situation. It is well worth the group sketching out for itself what it believes to be a number of likely scenarios, based upon what they have so far observed. Given all the facts that are now spread all over the walls of their meeting room, what do they believe may happen in the future? Have they discerned any clear trends in the situation and, if these continue, where will it end? Have they any great hopes for the situation and what are they? Are there any great dangers observable which need to be named? Who will be hurt most and who will gain? What would need to happen to stem the tide of any bad dynamics discerned by the group, and what would need to be fostered to help the good to prevail? What is the group's likely prognosis?

And second, before we move on, it may be useful for the group to make another preliminary check on what resources it now feels that it has amassed. These may well have changed even during the process of the exploration, for by now it will be obvious that all sorts of personal strengths and gifts have come to light in the group. It may also have occurred to them that they are in touch with new external resources too. Maybe they have made all sorts of useful contacts during this exploration phase, and these may help them in future when they come to plan their strategies. They may also be aware now of those who will not help them at all! They will no doubt have unearthed untold resources of creativity and imagination within the group, and if all has gone well they will have won the gift of an emerging group solidarity. But most of all, they will now be in the very strong position of knowing the situation well, and it will be out of this knowledge that their theological reflection can now be developed with clarity and power.

Notes

1 Useful Foundation Courses in both the arts and the social sciences are available from the Open University for those group members who want to be in a position to judge the material for themselves. I would, however, strongly advise against adults taking GCE or equivalent courses; these are designed primarily with children in mind.

2 Many frameworks are available. See, for example, that offered by Henriot in the chapter entitled 'Social Analysis: A Practical Methodology' in Joe Holland and Peter Henriot SJ, *Social Analysis: Linking Faith and Justice* (Orbis/The Center of Concern, 1983).

3 The 'small area statistics' are usually readily available, but local councils may be able to supply more relevant breakdowns of the local data.

4 See the fuller discussion in Robert J. Schreiter's *Constructing Local Theologies* (SCM, 1985).

5 For example, Community Change, Inc. has produced an *Institutional Racism Audit* for The General Theological Seminary, New York (1983).

6 Functionalism has been associated mainly with the work of Radcliffe-Brown and Malinowski. See, for example, Robert A. Manners and David Kaplan (eds), *Theory in Anthropology: A Source Book* (Routledge & Kegan Paul, 1969).

7 See Laurie Green, *Power to the Powerless* (Marshall Pickering, 1987). Available from Poplar Rectory, London E14 0EY.

5

Reflection

In the previous two chapters we have looked in more detail at what it means to experience and explore a community or an issue during the process of doing theology. Sinking ourselves into the experience in this committed way, and then the painstaking analysis involved in the exploration of the situation, takes time and energy. I have known one group where these first two phases of the theological enterprise took as long as two years, but others I know have had to condense the work into a matter of weeks. Nevertheless, we have to be aware throughout the process that it will be essential to move eventually into reflection upon all those findings and experiences. This is the next important phase of the Doing Theology Spiral. Let us glance again at the cyclic diagram in order to remind ourselves where we have got to on the spiral.

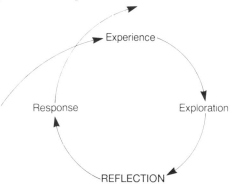

We noted earlier how easy it is for some theologians to get locked into reflection alone, without regard to the situation in life surrounding that reflection. But we must likewise guard against the other extreme: of becoming so immersed in the experience that we fail to reflect adequately. It is as if the Martha and Mary syndrome (Luke 10.38–42) overtakes some groups, and they become so taken with the business and activity of analysis that they cannot make the space and quietness for reflection and meditation upon what God is doing or suffering within the situation they are analysing. It may be that their fear of moving on to reflection is borne of a growing realisation of the immensity and complexity of the situation they are confronting. However, the reality is that in the process of theological reflection upon the situation, such fear of inadequacy and complexity should subside. This is because it is during this phase of the cycle that much light begins to dawn and this gives the group a handle on to the experience, which makes all the data and information much more manageable. The vision and the energy that is liberated during the process of the reflection phase is quite remarkable, and should be looked forward to by the group rather than shunned.

Challenge from the Christian tradition

It is important that the process of analysis should not have been thought of as a morbid dissection of the situation we are confronting, but, instead, as an attempt to paint a living and vibrant picture that has clarified and unified the perceptions of the situation rather than merely searched for pathology within it. Plenty of celebration should therefore have accompanied the exploration, as well as concern about the failings that have become evident in the community or issue. But it is the process of theological reflection that can now bring things into even clearer perspective, for if the exploration phase has become a little too clinical and analytical, our theological reflection will now broaden our horizons as we reflect upon that analysis in the light of faith.

The reflection phase can be such a positive experience because it is here that we attempt to look afresh at the situation we have experienced and explored, and begin to see within it the very presence of God. And where God is, there hope is also to be found. This presence is made ever more clear and transparent to us when we bring the story of the Christian community's past experiences of seeing God in the situation alongside the particular experience that we have now been exploring. I doubt, for example, whether any latter-day Jew or Christian who knows the story of Moses would be able to walk past a burning bush today without stopping to ponder whether there was something of godly importance in the experience. The Bible, church history, our experiences of worship, Eucharist, baptism, hymns, sacred music, and so many other things that go to form our great Christian heritage, will all hold up pointers to where God has been experienced in the past and how God may continue to be experienced today. If we plunge our-selves into this great heritage, just as we have plunged ourselves into the situation by experience and exploration, then we will develop a much clearer perception of God's presence and activity in the world – the world that God creates, sustains and cherishes. This is our hope as we now seek to reflect theologically in the doing theology cycle.

We must be careful at this stage not to be forced by an over-simplistic reading of the Doing Theology Spiral into thinking that having completed our exploration stage, reflection will never lead us back to a re-exploration of the experience. For, on the contrary, we are bound to find that as we bring biblical and liturgical insights to bear upon the matter, so we will have to go back, look again, and redefine what we understand to be the major problems and causes of the situation. But this time we will be looking more concertedly and self-consciously through the eyes of faith. We may find ourselves being led to redefine the problems completely in the light of our Christian heritage, and then on reflection, to ask what it is about that heritage that has led us so to redefine matters. The Christian heritage will help us to look at the world, and the world in turn will help us to look at the heritage. Each may at times be critical of the other, and we will have to use all our skill, sensitivity and wisdom to discern which of the two to use as our major inter-pretative tool in any given situation. This may not prove to be as easy as it sounds, but more of that later.

One thing that our reflection upon the Christian heritage will undoubtedly bring to the situation is a new awareness of contradictions within our experience.

Let me take the example of how the Bible can so often point up contradictions in society. Sitting in a leather binding on the bookshelf, the Bible creates no problems except that it attracts dust, but if we read and use it well, it asks profound critical questions of our human condition and becomes a subversive book. In pre-Reformation times, government agents were anxious lest the Bible shuld become available to ordinary people, and in Latin American countries the Bible has often been confiscated by right-wing governments because of the dangerous ideas the peasants find within it. In the Soviet Union, only since *perestroika* has the Bible been openly published for general purchase.

I have described elsewhere[1] how, during my ministry in Birmingham, I worked with a group of Christians who began a biblical study of the parables of Jesus, asking what made them such striking stories. They soon perceived that each parabolic story begins with a short account of a situation in life that seems to present no great challenges. But, then, usually towards the end of the story, there is a sudden change of gear, and the story whips round and challenges the hearers. For example, something may go very wrong for the hero who, after building bigger barns to store all his wealth, finds that his life is at an end and he cannot enjoy the fruit of his labour (Luke 12.16–21). Or, as in another example, the villain of the story, having proved himself an unjust steward, finds himself admired, even though he has used all sorts of questionable means to secure his own future. He finds that he is applauded for at least having the sense to realise how critical his predicament has been (Luke 16.1–8). Sometimes the whole situation in the parable changes, as, for example, when the farm-workers wake up to find that weeds have sprouted up in their newly sown crop (Matthew 13.24–30). Or the generosity of a character in the story passes all known bounds, as when the father welcomes the squandering rascal of a prodigal son back to his home with open arms (Luke 15.11–32). On every occasion, there is an unexpected twist in the tale of the parable – what the Birmingham group began to call 'God's Unexpected'. When that group then looked back at their locality with this Unexpected in mind, they saw with fresh eyes certain features of the social landscape which would have been totally unexpected before. They began to notice the hidden poverty, the generosity of those in need, and the now obvious injustices of the community. Then they looked back at the Bible and saw more and more evidence of God's Unexpected – in the birth of Jesus in a stable, in the death of God's Son as a criminal on a cross, the choice of lowly fishermen and prostitutes as Jesus' closest friends. As they looked back at the contradictions in their locality in the light of this, they began to appreciate that it was exactly these same lowly people whom Jesus, in the Gospels, had taken as his special friends. Yet they still do not seem welcome in the local church, and still get the worst deal and least respect in society. But most dangerous and subversive of all, the group began to feel the urge and the mandate upon them from the Bible stories to do something about the situation. So theological reflection on a situation can be a subversive activity when it begins to point up the contradictions in this manner and then spur a group to social action.

But it is not only the Bible that can do this. The same sort of challenge to our situation can also come from elsewhere in our Christian heritage. Some people have found on entering a beautiful church building that they have had to start asking questions about the ugliness of their own lives or the situation that surrounds them. Others have looked at Christian symbols like the crucifix and have been brought up sharp. Some have received Communion and been shocked to think how different the equal sharing of that action is from the unequal distribution of gifts in our own society. If we receive God's choice wine at the Eucharist and then refuse to give to others of our own luxury, it takes only a short time of reflection before we sense the contradiction of our actions. There will be many symbols, actions and stories from the Christian traditions of faith both within the Bible and without it, which will serve to challenge our contemporary experience, and this reflection phase gives us opportunity to discern those connections and contemplate them.

Why do theological reflection?

During this reflection phase we will be endeavouring to tease out the connections of meaning between, on the one hand, our contemporary situation as experienced and explored and, on the other hand, the great wealth of Christian history, teaching and faith – what I refer to in this book as the Christian faith traditions. So why do we seek to make these connections? First, immersing ourselves in these faith traditions helps us view our experience from the alternative perspective of the Divine. One aspect of this new perspective, which the Christian heritage brings to our contemporary scene, might for example be seen in the fact that in the incarnation God has been experienced by the Christian community in the holiness and otherness of the sufferer and the servant.[2] God seems therefore to see things, to hear things, from the point of view of the sufferer and of those most in need in society. This is a perspective that is rarely appreciated by us, but if we immerse ourselves in the traditions of the Christian faith then we can begin to make this way of viewing things our own, and we can begin to see things to which we were altogether blind before we opened ourselves to these faith traditions. Perhaps this opening of ourselves to God's perspective is something of what St Paul meant when he prayed that we might take on 'the mind of Christ' (1 Corinthians 2.16). But there are also other reasons why, in our theological reflection, we will wish to bring the insights of our Christian tradition to bear upon the findings of our experience and exploration, and so make the connections between that situation and our Christian heritage.

First, there is our wish to check out our contemporary thinking and action against the alternative authority. We are wanting to know whether we are telling the Jesus story or whether we are relating a different story altogether, perhaps one of our own making. We therefore check to see if there are connections between our own experience and the Christian experience through the ages as recorded for us in our great faith traditions. To do this we will need to come to terms with the problem of the tension between faithfulness to the text of the tradition on the one hand, and contemporary relevance on the other. If we can overcome this dilemma with integrity and find the connections between our Christian heritage and our contemporary scene, then this will reinforce our faith in our actions and give us the courage to continue.

Another reason for wanting to make these connections with our Christian past is that some of the faith traditions themselves will require checking against the authority of present experience and our understanding of God's present actions. A clear example of this is to be found in the church tradition of the infallibility of the Pope. Our particular denomination within the Church may not accept that tradition as it is commonly understood, and may hold the view that we cannot accept that doctrine as permissible because it does not stand the test of being checked against other traditions (maybe the biblical texts) and, more particularly, against our contemporary understandings of authority and validity.

Yet another reason for wanting to make these connections between faith and life is that it provides occasion for our God-given creative imagination to become inspired in the process of seeking what the traditions have to say to our situation. In this way, the creative spark has its chance to develop in us under the guidance of the Holy Spirit so that we are not simply thrust back into the dullness of an uncritical acceptance of either the tradition or the present situation. Theological reflection provides us with the creative double-edge of reason and imagination.

Finally, we are wanting to contradict those who argue that even for Christians it is not necessary to use 'God-talk' in relation to our contemporary situation because we have appropriate disciplines already to hand in the secular sphere. Our successful practice of the pursuit of meaning and relevant action using theological reflection proves them wrong. In bringing our Christian heritage into connection with our contemporary experience, we guard against a blinkered acceptance of the world. It is this blind affirmation that has hampered many Christians in the past and has led to their uncritical subservience to the injustice of social pragmatism. For while acknowledging that theology of itself does not contain the necessary tools to analyse the internal structures and causal relationships within society, we do maintain with all seriousness that it is only theology that can take the raw material unearthed by our exploration, and work with that material to look for the meaning of it and sense the relationship that the Transcendent has with it. This quest for the Divine is of course the prime motive of the whole exercise, so while the theological reflection may, according to our cyclical diagram, follow on after the experience and exploration phases, it only comes after in terms of methodology, whereas in terms of importance, it precedes them both. So even though we save theological reflection until this later stage of the cycle, we are not allowing the world to lead us by the nose, nor are we content to stop at analysis of the world, but we commit ourselves entirely to the importance of theological reflection, which now becomes possible by virtue of the preceding 'secular' analysis.[3] So we will be allowing ourselves the excitement and adventure of the quest for an undogmatic and unideological faith, by which I mean that we will not come at experience merely to lay upon it the prejudiced dogma of a bygone age, nor open our traditions to a simplistic scientism, but will bring our faith traditions and our felt experience together into a creative mix. This is what theological reflection is all about.

The connections that we will discover between our traditions and our present experience will be of various kinds. First, we may find that our intuition senses certain *similarities* between the faith traditions and the present issue. On the other hand, we may be provoked by the total *opposition* that we see between certain elements of, for example, the Gospels, and the situation. But thirdly, the connections between the traditions and our situation may initially come to us as quite unclear intuitive *hunches* or suspicions. We sense that something is 'on' between elements from each side of the spectrum and we feel that they must connect somehow, although we will need to take time to discover quite how.

In order to do theological reflection then, we have to develop methods of bringing into juxtaposition our present life experience and the treasures of our Christian heritage, to check one against the other, to let each talk to the other, to learn from the mix and to gain even more insight to add to the store of Christian heritage. However, it has long been recognised that we live in a world that must feel very different from the world in which the great traditional treasures of the faith were born. The Bible, the early Christian creeds, the sacramental and early liturgical life of the Church were all formed and developed in contexts very different from our own. Our modern world-view is so very different that making sense of what was in the minds of those who lived during those early Christian centuries is not always easy. When we first approach the Bible or the creeds we are apt to think all is well, for surely humankind has always been confronted with the same basic issues, and God is the same yesterday as today. Believing this is true, we can immediately be at one with the text. However, the scientific application of scholarly theology has slowly but surely convinced us otherwise, for it is far from easy for us to make the required leap across from our own culture to that of the first Christian centuries and to know the mind of the writers and the first hearers of the scriptural message. In fact, the more we investigate the gap, the more we realise the extent of the difference between our culture and theirs, and the improbability of a late twentieth-century person ever being able to comprehend how people thought and felt in those earlier days and cultures now so far off. And if we cannot fully comprehend the culture, then how can we comprehend an artefact or text that emanates from it? There seems to be a gap between ourselves and these treasures; a gap of time, of culture, of expectation and perception. If I try to straddle the gap I get myself into complex problems of integrity, for when I properly acknowledge myself to be a person from a scientific culture, then biblical talk about being inhabited by demons seems to be a violation of what I know about illness, microbes, genes and so on. If, on the other hand, I take models from the Bible to look at contemporary political issues, that would seem to do violence to the specificity of the biblical history. If for example I want to talk about the city, and use passages about the city from the Bible, I may be forgetting at my peril that in biblical times a city would have had a population only the size of one of our contemporary urban parishes. I stand in danger of overlaying the biblical material with all sorts of modern psychological and sociological paraphernalia that have no place in the original culture, and probably put me miles away from the intended meaning of the text. We are therefore presented with a problem: how can we make the leap, and interpret from one situation to another? This is what theology, in common with other disciplines, calls the problem of 'hermeneutics', the word hermeneutics meaning 'interpretation'. We will certainly need to return in a later chapter to some of the subtleties of the difficult issue of this 'hermeneutical gap', but suffice it here to say that our reflective task is to find some way of bridging this cultural gap and seeing connections between the Christian heritage on one side and our present experience on the other – to hear resonances, to ring bells, to sense similarities, to sense opposition, to build up a whole range of sensitivities to the

tradition so that we can draw upon it to check our present actions and understandings and see if our own story is part of the Jesus story, or not.

The liberation of the imagination

We will want to develop methods of reflection which of themselves do not rely
upon academic expertise, and this for two reasons. First, such an approach will
allow far more Christians to engage more fully in the theological endeavour; and
second, those who have allowed their studies to suffocate their imagination need a
chance to recover this side of themselves.

Our imagination has the facility to make leaps quite naturally, almost in a
playful way,[4] and this faculty can be nurtured in the Church in order to help us
across the hermeneutical gap. There will be a variety of ways of doing this, but the
underlying process of making connections will be largely the same. We do it by
drawing elements from one side of the gap, say from our own situation, and then
we draw something from the Church's heritage on the other side, which seems to
have a significant connection with that first element. The two things seem to fit
together in our minds in some imaginative way. Groups can be helped to appreciate what happens here by referring to another diagram. First of all we remind
ourselves that during our phases of experience and exploration we have attempted
to face up to the situation or issue that we have decided to study.

Facing the
situation

We have already looked intently at the situation before us and have tried to
perceive the important issues and factors within it. It is now, in this reflection
phase, that we look back at that experience from the perspective of the Christian
faith traditions of Bible, sacraments, Church and so on. The situation then looks
at the Christian tradition and perceives new things there. But likewise, the tradition looks at the situation and brings a critical edge to it. But as we watch the situation and the tradition confront one another so we notice fascinating things
happening.

It does not take us long to discover that the two faces that we have drawn, when
brought together, create a whole new factor – and the image of a candlestick
emerges from between the two faces as if to shed new light on the old faces. The
intuitive leap is made. The mind has been allowed to move into a new dimension
and to look at the meeting of experience and tradition from a whole new vantage
point. It is not simply the face of experience, nor simply the face of tradition, but as

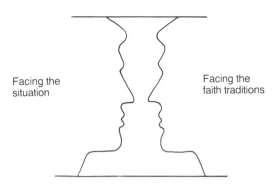

Facing the situation

Facing the faith traditions

they meet, we have a new light shining upon both and so this encounter illumi-nates whole new spheres of understanding. There is created here a new conscious-ness and a new-mindedness that are reminiscent of what is now spoken of by liberation theologians as 'conscientisation'.[5] But this new consciousness or new-mindedness is not so far removed in meaning from what our traditional word 'repentance' tries to express, and indeed in New Testament Greek the word *metanoia*, usually translated as 'repentance', could more literally be translated as 'new-mindedness' or 'change of mind'. As the face of the gospel looks upon our experiences, so there is for the disciple a new mind, a new way of looking, which is felt in the heart as well as the intellect, and demands change and response. So the encounter between the experience and the Christian heritage in our theological reflection is a moment of new-mindedness when the disciple is brought to a whole new awareness and very often a challenge to repentance.

As we each look at the two faces in the diagram, we may experience the fact that the brain makes the transition from seeing the two faces to seeing the image of a candlestick in a fraction of a second, and clicks instantaneously from one inter-pretation to the other. If we wish to study one of the perceptions more carefully, then we have to make a decision to hold one or other of the two perceived pictures in our mind's eye for longer than just the few seconds that the brain would allow, were it left to play intuitively with the two images. This disciplining of our mind allows for a more careful investigation of the alternative image to be made, before we hand control back to our imagination so that the first image may appear again. This same disciplining will also have to be a feature of our theological reflection, for we will often find ourselves intuitively coming upon all manner of snap connec-tions between the contemporary situation being explored and elements of the Christian tradition, but we will need a time of discipline when we check out those imaginative leaps to discover what they have to teach us and to discern which connections are appropriate and acceptable and which are not. Towards the end of this chapter, I will explain exactly how that happens.

Another example of how the imaginative connection is made can be found in the well-known story of the fall of the apple upon Newton's head. He had for long periods immersed himself in the complexities of mathematical physics, but only when the apple fell did his mind make the leap of discovery. We have many similar stories that record how these imaginative leaps of discovery are made time and again, when someone finds themselves comparing seemingly dissimilar factors which serve to prompt a new disclosure. And this new disclosure is often experienced and spoken of as a moment of revelation.[6]

How then are we to develop methods of allowing this same imaginative flair to operate in the theological arena? First we must acknowledge that to try to make intuitive connections between vast and rather unmanageable abstract ideas from each side of the hermeneutical gap would require extraordinary perception and erudition. The process is made easier however by the fact that during the experience and exploration phases we have already analysed these unmanageable themes into their much more manageable constituent parts. So we can make our theological connections at this more manageable level. This is precisely how Newton seems to have arrived at his moment of discovery, for he too had aready analysed in his mind the various elements of the problem of gravity, so that the fall of the apple related directly to what was already becoming clear in his mind. When we go through the painstaking process of analysis in the exploration phase of the theological cycle, we are doing the same thing – subdividing the data and making preliminary sense of them so that the imaginative connection can more easily be made with the elements from the traditions of faith.

But actually making the leap across the gap from all the analysed material about our situation into the Bible stories and the other traditions of the Christian faith, may not prove to be so spontaneous and easy even then. We may need help to do it. At its most straightforward, the process can be rather like the 'brainstorming' with which we are already acquainted. The group can take a word that has surfaced during the exploration as being a key word, and allow itself space to let its collective imagination come up with as many stories from the Bible as possible that seem to relate to it in any way at all. Maybe other elements from the Christian tradition are triggered too, such as passages from hymns or symbols from worship. Likewise, if we wished to start from the other side of the gap, say from the tradition of the Gospels, we might subdivide a particular Gospel into its stories, themes or characters, and then check across the gap to see if any connections come spontaneously to mind from within the situation that has been the object of our study. Using this 'brainstorming' technique, we can allow ourselves to note down without question the first things that come into our minds, and give our imagination full rein knowing that we will have time later to check to see which of the connections that have sprung to mind may be acceptable as authentic and valid connections to make.

At first, many groups will find this process rather difficult and will need the help of particular exercises designed to assist the imagination as it seeks to discover the connections across the hermeneutical gap. We will therefore take time in this chapter to look in detail at some aids to help the imagination in making this hermeneutical connection.

But before we do so, we would do well to stress that the hermeneutical gap may well be bridged, and the connection made, not only during the reflection phase but also during the active response phase. Jesus constantly challenged his audience to produce good fruit and so made it clear that we may know a person's truth and integrity by the quality of their fruitful actions. This leads us to suppose that it can also be in the area of action and response that the connections with the faith traditions can be made and that we can check to see if our lives are conforming to the Jesus story by seeing if the fruit of our actions pass the test. After all, Christians are called upon not so much to give assent to a set of propositions as to give their lives in active commitment to a person. So it is that we can sometimes find ourselves engaged in making connections with the Christian heritage through our practice, just as much as during our theological reflection.

Many who find making theological connections difficult, resort to the production of a list of likely biblical passages from which can be chosen a passage that relates to the theme or issue; but my hope would be that the theological group can learn to find more natural and incarnational ways of locating those elements within the treasure store of Christian tradition which resonate with the subject in hand. Whether it is appropriate to rely upon theological specialists to direct the group to the appropriate elements from the tradition is a question I will come back to later, but I am inclined to think that there is usually enough information and wisdom in most groups not to make this necessary, at least in the initial stages. The specialist may have his or her part to play later in the process, as we shall see.

Letting the faith traditions speak to experience

Over a period of years I have been building up a compendium of what I call 'set pieces' or 'ways in' to working with the Christian traditions, and I want to share some of them now. The reader may well know many of them, or may have come across different versions of the same ideas. I call them 'set pieces', as in soccer, because there must be an infinite variety of ways of playing them and developing them as the needs arise. There will also be many other approaches or 'ways in' that are not so contrived, but come quite naturally from the life of the group. A good theological enabler would always do well, however, to have a whole range of approaches readily available to use as the group needs arise. So here are a few, and a note of explanation with each. We start with some approaches to the use of the Bible.

A SELECTION OF 'SET PIECES'

Biblical approaches

1 First of all, some groups will find themselves impaired by thinking that they do not know enough about the Bible even to begin to make connections between the stories there and their contemporary scene. If this is the case, a *simple list approach* can help, whereby we ask the group to think, for example, of all the stories that they can remember about Jesus or all the stories that he told. As people name a story, it is written or, even better, drawn up, so that the memory is affirmed and reinforced. Most groups will be amazed to discover how much of the Bible they do in fact already know. They may then wish to *group* the stories into the ones that the members think relate in any way to the subject in hand – the issue that is the focus of their theological work. Grouping stories or memories of snippets from the Bible can in itself be a reinforcer of memory, and a great affirmer of the group life. Next, they may wish to list just particular stories, perhaps those that relate to certain actions or events in the life of Jesus, or they may try grouping stories as

they feel they relate especially to certain people, places, actions, the town, the countryside, or some headings that the group choose as appropriate to their issue.

If that doesn't work and the group is still anxious about its lack of biblical knowledge, then it may be helped by the use of a concordance. Within most groups there will be someone who is quite good at 'looking up', and the big concordances feel and look so much like telephone directories, and work in a similar way, that most groups are not intimidated by them at all. The concordance is simply a directory of biblical references listed in order, so that given a key word any number of references can be found in the Bible, both from the Old and New Testaments. There are many good concordances on the market, and even one produced on disc for a group with a home computer.[7]

2 Second, there are the well-known *checklist approaches*. One example is the 'Swedish Method' of Bible study, where the group is equipped with a list of pictures, the first being a question mark, which indicates that the group should at that point look for questions to ask of the text; then an arrow to prompt the group

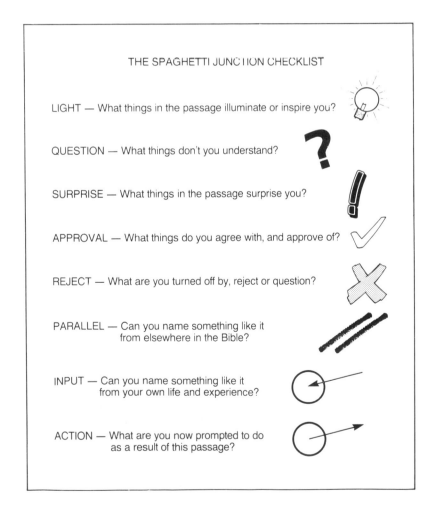

THE SPAGHETTI JUNCTION CHECKLIST

LIGHT — What things in the passage illuminate or inspire you?

QUESTION — What things don't you understand?

SURPRISE — What things in the passage surprise you?

APPROVAL — What things do you agree with, and approve of?

REJECT — What are you turned off by, reject or question?

PARALLEL — Can you name something like it
from elsewhere in the Bible?

INPUT — Can you name something like it
from your own life and experience?

ACTION — What are you now prompted to do
as a result of this passage?

to look for interesting new thoughts; and finally a torch, which represents any light that the group feels is thrown upon the issue by the text. There are many variations on that theme, but perhaps the one which was worked out in my last parish will be of use. We called it the 'Spaghetti Junction Method'. Each parishioner had a copy of the list on page 84 to keep in their Bible, and we used it often in groups.

3 *Using bibliodrama.* We may often have seen biblical stories acted by children in Sunday school, but adults can find that doing this themselves can bring things alive in vivid ways. We have already spoken of how drama and role-play can be used to bring alive aspects of the exploration phase of the Doing Theology Spiral, but now we can utilise similar methods as we get to know the biblical traditions and bring them alongside the situation.

First of all there is *dramatic reading.* This is drama at its simplest, but must be used with caution in groups who dislike reading. On Palm Sunday and Good Friday it is becoming customary to have a group read the gospel aloud in our churches, each main character having a reader and all joining in for the words said by the crowd. Many groups will therefore be familiar with this style, and it can easily be adapted for other times of the year and not just used during Holy Week.

Mime is a little more adventurous. One or more voices read the chosen story or text – or if we prefer, we can use a pre-recorded tape of the passage – then other group members act it out. Others may act as audience if they wish to. This can work very well if readers are carefully chosen beforehand so that non-readers are not embarrassed. After the miming, everyone, discusses the experience of how it was to read, to pretend to be a character, or to look at the happening.

Role-play is even more imaginative. The group work out who are the main characters or participants in the action of the Bible story, and then the roles are distributed. Some may act as the onlookers, others may group together as 'the Sadducees', 'Herod and his followers', or whatever else the story may require. Where the group has more members than there are characters in the story, a small number may choose one character to play together. As well as lending support to shy members, this sharing of characters can be very beneficial in getting people to understand the role they have chosen, for some time is always taken for getting into role before playing through the story. The story is acted through just as many times as seems helpful. I have heard of role-plays like this going on late into the evening in one very working-class parish where all sorts of non-church-goers also turn up at a neighbour's house to act out the Bible passages, and they will be all over the house and even sitting on the stairs, once the action of the story involves them. When the play is finished, everyone says their own name aloud to make sure all are out of the role they have just played and, as always, everyone then gets a chance to say what happened for them and what they feel they have learnt from the experience.

Then there is the *role interview.* This is where one or more of the group opts to play a character from the Bible and is then 'interviewed' in role by another group member. Others look on and then, after getting out of role, everyone discusses the experience. My most exciting experience of this method occurred when a man acted the part of Mary Magdalene. The group really pressed him about his feelings in that role and especially what, in the light of that, he now thought Jesus had to say about women. He could not believe what he found himself saying. It may not always be a biblical episode that is dramatised in this way of course, for I have seen this method used by a group to act out a period from church history, in which one member who had seen a film about Martin Luther was interviewed in that role by the whole group. They learnt a great deal from the story of the Reformation that evening.

Another approach is *character identification*. Each group member chooses a character in the biblical story with whom they feel they identify and then explains why. We can even do this without actually acting the play through, and this can be particularly beneficial for those who like to talk but are too embarrassed or frail to act.

Body sculpture is another method that is especially helpful for more immobile groups. Here, the story is performed by the group in one or a series of tableaux. Either the whole group act the story together, or else just a few act while the others look on. When the group feels it has captured the essence of a scene, it 'freezes' the motion for a few seconds to feel the sculpture. Remaining as still as they can, they themselves look round to see how their own body positions relate to the position of the others in the sculpted picture they have made. As always, discussion follows – and we have to give these discussions sufficient space and time, as it is such a pity to rush it. It is about right to allow two, three or even four times the amount of time for the discussion of these dramatic episodes as for the actual 'acting' itself.

And while speaking of drama, it is worth mentioning *street theatre*, for bibliodrama can be enacted on a very grand scale too. Some groups construct a mini Oberammergau in their local high street during Holy Week and call it 'The Way of the Cross'. It clearly has an evangelistic emphasis, but much is also learnt by the players themselves. I once took part in one of these events which was acted out on a reasonably small scale on the streets of a council estate with very few church members to speak of, but local people actually stepped out of their front doors to take up roles when they saw that we didn't have enough Roman soldiers or onlookers. They soon got into the action.

To role-play the part of *the receiving community* can also prove very helpful. For example, if the passage in question is taken from St Mark's Gospel, which we might presume was written with the Christian community of Rome in mind, then the group imagines itself as part of that early Roman Church and asks itself 'What can we in our situation learn from this passage?' or 'How will we use this passage in our Roman context of persecution, within non-Jewish surroundings?', and so on. Role-playing in this way can help the group appreciate how the evangelist has used the story in his Gospel.[8]

4 *Ringing bells with biblical themes*. Many groups, as we have already admitted, may not know individual Bible stories well; but most seem able to name the major themes of the Bible, so we have another method that starts from here. If we are working with the Old Testament, the themes named may include Exodus, Creation, Babylon, and so on. In the New Testament, the themes may include Incarnation, Parables, Disciple choosing, and so forth. The group writes up these themes on a wall chart and names a few examples of each of the themes just to make the words less abstract. In the next column on their chart the group then

writes up words that express for them the meaning of each biblical theme. So the technical word 'incarnation' will elicit more normal-sounding words like 'giving birth', 'getting down to earth', and so on. It is then possible for the group to think of examples from their exploration work where they have seen this same theme occurring. They may think, for example, that their Sunday school classes could do with being a lot more 'down to earth' if Jesus is going to be experienced there. They have thus connected between the major biblical theme of incarnation and their own experience of Sunday school work. The biblical theme word has rung bells in their experience and they are making the connection that may in time help them see the sacred in their ordinary experience. The chart may then be extended with more theme words and columns as the group requires. I have often used this method, which is developed from Dr John Vincent's work in Rochdale and Sheffield, and I include on page 88 a few columns of just such a chart which was produced by a group of Christian educators in Birmingham who were looking for theological connections between their work and the Bible.

A similar exercise can be done by referring to *biblical characters* rather than biblical themes. Here, particular biblical characters are chosen as the point of entry and their life stories, or whatever we know about the characters' activities, are put up on the wall chart. In the light of this, the group then considers its exploration of the theme at issue and whatever imaginative leaps can be made when the particular character is explored are charted up for all to share and discuss. It is also possible to run the same cross-referencing exercise for *biblical processes*, but in this case we first note that certain orders of events are repeated in the Bible, and these structured orders can be found to repeat elsewhere in our experience. Students in training for ordination are interested, for example, to note the order of events after Jesus' baptism. It becomes clear, on looking at the Bible, that immediately after his baptism and before he moves into public ministry, Jesus is taken off into the wilderness by the Spirit to think and pray about the shape of the ministry into which he is venturing. All sorts of temptations cross his path in the wilderness as he seeks to prepare himself. The Old Testament seems to follow a similar order, for as soon as the People of Israel pass through the waters of the Red Sea they too are thrust out into the wilderness to be tested and tempted before entering into their promised land and the ministry for which God has called them. The connection can then be made by those who are at present undergoing ordination training, for although they have heard the call and made the commitment, before they can go into their professional ministries they too have to be tested and trained in preparation for the task and role that lies ahead. They find the order of the process in the biblical record rings bells with their own experience, and this helps them to see where God is active in their training experience.

5 There are also some techniques we can use to enable groups *to move back into the spoken Bible*. Behind the printed text of Scripture there lies the spoken story, the early preaching and worship from which the text originated. One method by which a group can experience this is by moving themselves back into that oral tradition. The method essentially offers opportunity to learn the story or text off by heart as a group. This is done by first of all deciding as a group what the turning points of the chosen story are. Next, key words are selected that symbolise those

MAKING CONNECTIONS WITH BIBLICAL THEMES

The subject taken by the group in this example was adult education.

Gospel theme	Our own words	Other examples	Educational implications	Practical responses
Incarnation	Living alongside Hands on	St Francis Our own contexts	Not just theory Participation	Start from experience Commitment
Disciples	Groups, friends Very mixed	Our own team Local congregation	Not solitary All abilities	Questions and answers Conflict allowed
Miracles	Practical caring Signs of Kingdom Help marginalised	Shelter Oxfam Prayer group	Practice involved Meaning within Learner-centred	Practical needs met Empowers the weak Non-significant are valued
Parables	Everyday story but new meanings	Good films Poster captions	Ordinary happenings and Kingdom surprises	Create experiences which point to God's action
Sending	Try it yourself	On placement Apprenticeship	Allow learners active engagement	Not all talk but groups try it
Table fellowship	Feedback, support, and prayer	Annual assessment Team debrief	Support after experiences Team-building	Debrief experiences Clarify aims Affirm group
Sacraments	Material signs Pointers which interpret	Beauty of nature Commercial logo Traidcraft	Find symbol of the experience as a living resource	Not just words but signposts in action
Crucifixion	Total risk Identity with oppressed	Nelson Mandela Oscar Romero	Risk of injury and pain, risk life and our image	Expect trouble Engagement is risk Need awareness
Resurrection	Unexpected new life	Eastern bloc Wisdom of the elderly	Look where you don't expect it Who moved stone?	Don't give up! Be confident but don't take credit
Ascension	'Unless I go' Leader leaves	Childhood heroes fade away	Leader dispensable yet affirms	No dependency, learner takes responsibility

etc.

turning points. The group then gets used to telling the full story with only those key words as a prompt. When that is accomplished, even the key words are removed from view and the spoken story comes alive in the group once again, even after so many generations of being only words on a printed page. Then the group works towards discovering how to bring life to their telling of the story, in the same

way that actors would learn their parts and together would discuss which intona-
tions and gestures best go with the story as they understand it. This experience can
be a real eye opener. This approach can also be very helpful with groups that
prefer not to read, and indeed non-readers often prove to be better at this sort of
remembering of text than do those who read text all the time.

6 Another method of Bible study is for the enabler to come to the group with
prepared questions. Walter Wink offers a way of preparing questions that encourage
groups to dig beneath the more obvious elements of the Bible story and go deeper.[9]
His questions require group members to utilise aspects of their creative imagination through the use of dance, clay, pictures, song and so on, just as I hope we
ourselves may do in Bible study. But Wink has his participants expressing their
answers to questions about the text rather than simply acting out the story itself.
His questions first of all require the participants simply to read the text carefully –
for example, 'What does Jesus say to the woman?' But other questions will ask for
some creative and imaginative responses; for example, 'Who is the paralysed
person in you?' or 'What does Jesus say to this situation?'

7 The reflection phase offers ideal opportunity for the use of the *expressive arts* in
our spiral of doing theology. Painting or chalking pictures, working from television and video, slide shows, photographs, dance, cartoons, clay modelling,
murals, and so on, may all have their part to play. I once had a fascinating
experience in Germany where we were each given a lump of clay and asked to play
with it as we heard an account of the creation story being read. This was
accompanied by live music. Then we were asked to take the clay as God had in the
story, and mould something that represented what each of us treasured. I was
really surprised by the depth of expression and discovery that that engendered. I
have also seen pictures, tapestries and dance sequences that open up Bible themes
in remarkable ways. And of course our church buildings are absolutely full of
symbols and artistic representations of our faith which can be used to spark
connections with the situation that we have been exploring. Sometimes the group
can work from artistic expressions of the faith that have already been produced by
others, or they may do better to use these various media to express what they
themselves need to say.

We are lucky to be living at a time when there is being published a great wealth of
Bible study packs which take for granted a participatory and committed group
style. Many of these packs are ideally suited to our approach and can be taken and
developed as the needs of the group determine. I have painted a very broad picture
of some of the various styles of Bible study that could be of service to us in our theological reflection, but for more detailed description the interested reader may wish
to utilise the list of publications, packs, pamphlets and addresses that will be found
in the Bibliography at the back of this book. However, some words of caution must
be added, for any 'off the peg' study pack must carry the disadvantage that it
cannot really begin from where the group itself is, because it has been written by
people with a totally different set of experiences. Nor do many packs treat with
much seriousness the basic contemporary issues of class, gender and ethnicity, but

instead address the readers rather abstractly from the perspective of an isolated and interior psychology and without regard for being in a particular society. For this reason, Chris Peck, in his very helpful paper on Bible study packs, suggests that we describe them as 'participatory' Bible study rather than 'experiential', since there is rarely much clarity about which 'experience' is being reflected upon.[10] But despite these disadvantages, some of these packs are very fine pieces of work and can usefully be built into a programme of theological discovery by a group. The group can best keep reasonable control over such pre-packaged material by having a cardboard box in which such packs are kept and which is open for all participants to browse through. They can then draw from the box when they themselves feel a pack will serve their purposes – even if they have to rework the study guide considerably. Having a box like this also stops any one person having the power of a guru, which could derive from knowing the techniques and methods that others do not know. The box makes it open to all to be leader of the Bible study meetings.

Connections with other Christian treasures

We have been concentrating on various ways of making connections between our own situation and the biblical material, but these methods can equally be used with other areas of the Christian heritage of faith. We can, for example, utilise these same methods to make connections with our *worship experiences*. The sacraments, and the sacramental actions, the creeds, the hymns and canticles, can all be brought alongside the situation that concerns us, and theological connections can be made. Similarly, we can use these same methods to connect with the *lives of the saints* or theologians of the past and present – and to help us in this, magazines, television or video film will often give the group a sufficient amount of information about the character from which to work.

When the group becomes really adept at connection making, and feels confident, then it is possible to use similar 'ways in' by making connections with some of the major *doctrines of the Church*. We can look at some of the great themes of belief such as the nature of the Trinity, Creation, Evil, the Fall, Jesus, Church, Spirit, Kingdom, and so on. In each case we utilise all the techniques we used for the biblical material – analysing, listing, acting, painting and so forth – in order to reflect from this great heritage of the faith to see what these doctrines may tell us about the situation we are trying to face in our experience. There is a danger here, though, because there is evidence to show that even for the vast majority of church people the well-known and well-rehearsed theological words such as redeemer, reconciliation, or even salvation, can not often be translated into real meanings any longer, and most people can give no reasonable definition of what any of these words might actually mean.[11] It is necessary therefore to pick up on less intimidating words if we are going to express the truths of the faith effectively, and to do this we need to learn to become more adept at using home-grown words, images, pictures, songs, drawings and the like. If we do decide to work with these more abstract doctrinal words, we can sometimes usefully operate the same 'brainstorming' technique that we have used before, in order to break down these big theological concepts into smaller workable elements. The way it works, as I suggested earlier, is to ask the group to take time to play at word-association with the doctrine in question and write their ideas up on the wall chart. So, for example, from the abstract theological word 'creation', the group might brainstorm such words and phrases as 'making things, power, the image of God, the factory, clay, gardening', and so on. With these much more manageable words in view, the group feels less intimidated and well able to continue making its connections. My rule of thumb in theological workshops is that, whenever we find ourselves really stuck, the brainstorming technique should be considered, for it so very often proves productive.

An altogether different way into this reflection is to ask the group to consider the *indigenous theologies* that they are already living by and working with. They might be asked to reflect for example at greater depth upon the life lines that they were asked to draw when they first joined the group. Drawing a simple representation of their 'Life so Far', and then considering where in that life they have felt God to have been present, can be a stimulating way to unearth the theologies that people are already operating by. It is then possible to investigate the extent to which these indigenous theologies connect with the study in which the group is engaged.

In all this we must not underestimate the place of *prayer and meditation*. Quiet meditation together in the group while surrounded by all the explored information about the subject in hand can often bring to mind elements of the Christian tradition and heritage that resonate very strongly with the situation. Afro-Caribbean Christians are very gifted in coming up with elements from the Christian tradition that relate to the situation in hand, and it may well be because they are, by and large, a people of prayer. Periods of free worship in the group may also be opportunities for connections to be made between the situation under discussion and elements of the faith traditions. A member may catch herself or himself thinking about a Christian symbol, a line from a hymn or a service, a sermon they once heard, and so on. The key is to let the imagination have space in God's presence for connections to be made that later can be looked at more carefully and critically in order to see what it is that can legitimately be learnt from them. The books by Charles Elliott, Gerard Hughes, James Cone and others[12] may inspire groups to make up their own meditations and share them with the larger congregation in their Sunday worship. Others will find that hugging and touching or meditation through the five senses, can all be mind-expanding ways into the experience of prayer, as can the use of music, or indeed silence. Some find that the keeping of a spiritual journal (written or tape-recorded) or the making of an internal dialogue with an imagined figure can also allow theological insights to penetrate. Others have found the *reading of philosophy* or metaphysics a ready stimulus to more insight.

We see then that the possibilities are endless of how we might find ourselves making these spontaneous, imaginative connections between our explored experience and the great treasures of our Christian heritage.

Exploring our intuitions

As we work with the faith traditions in this way we begin to understand how dynamic they themselves are. The traditions of Bible, creeds, sacraments, Church and so on, are not static monoliths handed on in some pure and untouched form from generation to generation, but are changed in all sorts of ways as they pass from culture to culture, from community to community, from age to age. Once we have acknowledged the fact of this dynamism within the traditions, then we really are in a much better place from which to do theology. For once we have fully appreciated the contextual nature of the thoughts and ideologies that come to us within the traditions, then we understand that to start our theological work from anywhere but experience is in one sense quite impossible, since even our conventional 'learned theology' will have emanated from an experience rather than simply a disembodied revelation. With this notion of the fluidity of the tradition firmly in mind, let us recap for a moment so that we can be clearer about how it is proposed that the great variety of exercises and methods that I have just sketched might actually bear upon the situation which we have been experiencing and exploring in our cycle of theology. How do we do it in practice?

Before anything else, we do well in the group to use the set-piece exercises to skirmish around the heritage of the faith tradition in order to remind ourselves of its breadth and vitality. Just remembering that we have all the treasures of Bible, Church, worship, prayer, doctrine and so on, can be an enjoyable experience when some of the foregoing participatory methods are utilised. But then comes the time when the group looks back to the issue at hand and to its exploration. As it considers each element of the analysis in which it has been engaged, it frees its imagination to make those exciting leaps in order to see where the connections can be made. We expect these connections to occur where similarities or antagonisms are perceived between the explored issue and the traditions of faith. These imaginative leaps can be facilitated by any of the methods we have just surveyed, so that the issue is brought under the scrutiny and judgement of the faith traditions. For example, it will be remembered that towards the end of our analysis in the exploration phase, we teased out the 'dominant values' that seemed to be operating in the situation. We may have decided that in our specific situation the values that were predominant were money, growth and success. In this case, we would now take each value in turn and let it trigger in our imagination any elements from the traditions of our Christian faith that came to mind. We could do the same not only with these dominant values, but for each element and avenue of the exploration until a whole range of connections were made. Each time a Christian faith tradition is thus focused, we can utilise all the participative study methods to get right inside that Gospel story or Church doctrine or hymn or whatever, to tease out even further any other connections that might be made. But of course we will still want to go much further than this in discerning what the connections actually have to teach us.

So the imaginative leap is made – using all the methods described – and we intuitively suspect that there is something in a connection that our imagination has been inspired to see. The Holy Spirit is operative in the process of reflection

Reflection

AN INTUITION

upon the issue that we have explored, and intuitively suggests that a particular element in the tradition – an element from the Bible, sacraments, church history and so on – is somehow resonating with the experience in question and has something to teach us for today. So there emerges an *intuition* of what the tradition may hold. We might draw it in the following way.

The 'intuition' is an imaginative leap which sets up an interplay between the explored issue and the Christian faith tradition so that each is affected by the other. The question starts to arise then of how the tradition we have intuitively thought of may interpret today's experience and what indeed may be the appropriate interpretation from today of that part of the tradition. The intuition sets up a two-way challenge. The next task will be to check that the intuition is not an illusion which might be contradicted by all else that our Christian experience and God-given reason tells us. This checking-out phase can be called exploration, for it will require analysis and a search for meaning, using all appropriate disciplines and tools just as before. So our newly reflected diagram will emerge as follows.

During this new exploration phase, it will be necessary to check out all that we know about the particular tradition, be it a piece of biblical text, a happening in the history of the Church, a doctrine, a hymn, or whatever. We will need to explore its original context and we will endeavour to see how this part of the tradition fits in with all the other segments of the tradition by cross-referencing, analysis and careful appraisal, just as we did earlier when the issue itself was the object of our exploration. There are many academic theological tools at our disposal to help us with this part of the exercise, where the intention will be to explore the piece of the tradition so well that we come to a moment when we can venture to say that the intuition does or does not make some valid sense. So from this careful exploration of the original theological intuition there may well now emerge a 'new witness' from within the tradition that can speak afresh to the situation. Our diagram then begins to complete a fresh cycle, thus:

This new witness will have an authority for the issue we are exploring, and yet will also now be known to have integrity in relation to the whole Christian tradition. It can be put back into the reflective encounter with the issue and must now be taken not merely as a leap of the imagination, but as an authoritative new witness to how God has been experienced in the world. But before moving on to consider what may happen, let us pause to check more carefully what is going on in this secondary cycle as it occurs within the reflection phase of doing theology. An example may help.

I was once working with a group of inner-city Birmingham people who decided to take as their concern the issue of unemployment. It was a felt experience for the group and they wanted to explore unemployment theologically. They therefore set about the experience phase of the cycle by getting in touch with the feelings associated with the issue. Then, during their exploration of unemployment they amassed a great deal of information and evidence about the problem. When they felt ready, they began their reflection by brainstorming all sorts of Bible stories that they felt related to the issue. Of the many that were suggested, one stood out for them as being particularly significant, and this was the story of Jesus healing the lame man at the Sheep Pool, which they found recorded in St John's Gospel (John 5.1–18). The group had an *intuition* that there seemed to be in this story a picture of how Jesus relates to many of those who are powerless amid the structures of life, and they wanted to see if this Gospel story did indeed hold any insight into their predicament. So it was that the group felt that there was a resonance here between their unemployment experience and the story in the tradition, but as yet this was only an intuition, an imaginative leap as yet to be substantiated.

They therefore began to *explore* the tradition much more thoroughly. They discovered that the story details how those who wished to be healed had to be raced into the pool while the water was still bubbling, in order that the curative properties of the water could do their work. The man Jesus met, however, had not managed in all of thirty-eight years to get into the water, and so he had remained lame. The group saw in this man's predicament an exact parallel with how it feels to be the last in a long line waiting for a job, knowing that only the first in the queue really stands a chance of employment. After a period of long-term unemployment, the enthusiasm and hope begin to wane, just as it appeared to have done for the man by the pool. Jesus asked him a question that was so reminiscent of the question asked of the long-term unemployed – 'Do you really want to be healed?' 'Do you really want a job?' Jesus, however, ignored the rehearsed answer that the man had learnt to give, and cured him anyway, thus giving power to the unnoticed man waiting in the queue.

The group continued its exploration of the biblical passage and noted that the position that St John gives this particular story in his Gospel does indeed point towards the possibility that their understanding of the passage could be accepted as a correct interpretation. For example, the subsequent events in the story and Jesus' words to the cured man in private about his sin (verse 14) all pointed to the fact that Jesus appreciated that the man was held captive to societal structures in just this way. So the group felt more convinced that their interpretation of the passage was at least strong enough to warrant careful consideration. They thoughtfully considered such information as they could find about how the causes of illness were at that time understood, and what this investigation gleaned did indeed point to a clear relationship between the feelings and thoughts that surround unemployment nowadays and the ideas that were then current about illness. They checked to see that this reading of the story was not contradicted by all that they could find out from the Bible commentaries about the narrative and its original context. It was then possible for the group to take their findings as authoritative for them, as a new witness from the tradition. The new witness was that Jesus does seek to give power to unnoticed people waiting in the queue. It was this finding, this word, that they mixed in the crucible of reflection and from that mix there followed some fascinating responsive and faithful action on their part.[13]

So within the reflection phase of the Doing Theology Spiral we now discern a secondary cycle – a 'reflection' of the major cycle – which takes the intuitive leap and explores it carefully until it can be decided whether we have here an authoritative word from the tradition which can stand as a new witness to the situation we have been exploring. We can build this secondary cycle into the major one now and expand our understanding of the total process of doing theology. To see the whole expanded diagram is, I think, quite helpful at this point.

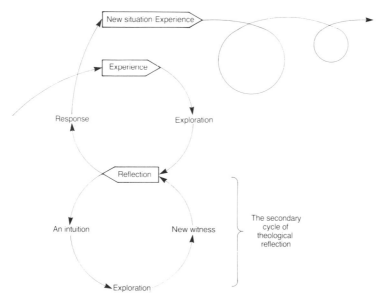

When we carefully check out the tradition by use of this secondary cycle of theological reflection, we are doing what conventional theologians have been doing for centuries, for they have been involved in a living process that, over the years, has added meanings and interpretations to the tradition in relation to each challenge and age through which the faith has journeyed. A series of theologies has been worked out in particular and distinct situations, but in the course of time they have been taken as authoritative beyond the situation for which they were originally intended. The true theologian then has the task of checking at each turn of experience, to see if each part of the tradition is really any longer authoritative for the new situation. Perhaps we can see more clearly now why it is that to equate the corpus of tradition with theology itself is really a major error, and only those who still see themselves as 'readers' of theology would understand it in that mistaken way. Theology is clearly a living process, not a fixed body of knowledge. This having been said there is nevertheless a great store of Christian theological

tradition which is the accumulation of centuries of reflection and contemplation by
Christians as they have tried to understand the ways of God and God's relationship with humanity. This store will include biblical studies, church history, and
many different theological sub-disciplines. For those readers who are not sure
about what these sub-divisions of conventional theology are, I have sketched out
something of the scope of these theological areas of study so that it can be seen
more clearly how they fit into and are used in the process of the secondary cycle of
theological investigation that we have just described. This description of the study
areas of conventional academic theology I have set out at the back of this book, in
the Appendix.

The key to the right use of this great wealth of theological tradition is that it
should always be used in the service of doing theology and never be allowed to
become either an end in itself or a world for itself. Those who become enticed by
the library may spend all their life moving round the secondary cycle of reflective
theology, never engaging with the major cycle which it is there to serve. Those
who specialise in this more academic endeavour should therefore be brought into
the service of the active mission of the Church so that their labours may be more
readily utilised, and the benefits of their work be evident in the praxis of theological action–reflection and fully inform the life of the Christian community. If
they allow themselves to be divorced from the community, then their labours will
be uninformed by experience; if the Church pushes them totally to one side, then
the present activity of the Christian community may not be informed by its own
past experience.

Focusing the vision

By this late stage in the reflection phase of the doing theology cycle, we are in a
position to let the new witness from the tradition of our faith address and confront
the issue that we have explored and analysed so carefully. There may in fact be a
whole range of elements in the tradition, from the Bible, the sacraments, the
Church, Christian hymns and so forth, which all seem to have something to say to
the situation. As they do, we will seek to probe the contemporary situation
critically to see where, in the light of all the theological work accomplished thus far,
the situation accords with God's will and where it does not. And it will be well if the
group can be as precise as possible in this discernment. As the group looks at the
situation in the light of faith it will have cause for celebration and cause for
anguish. There will be photographs, statistics and stories that are a great cause for
joy and celebration, but there will probably be other information and experience
that cause the group to weep concerning the situation with which they are
engaged.

Their joy and sorrow will be made all the more poignant by their discernment of
where God is present in the situation they have investigated. It is to be hoped that
they sense Father, Son and Holy Spirit actually within all that they have felt and
observed. But they must ask themselves what God is doing there and whether the
Almighty is triumphing or suffering within the situation. If they have not felt
God's presence in all that they have explored, then they must ask what it is that has

been stopping them from discerning that presence. Maybe they remain convinced that God simply is not there! The group will be helped in this quest for God's presence by referring back to their previous investigations as to what in the situation was felt to reinforce or destroy gospel teaching and values. They may already be able to sense at least the possibility of an opening up to God in the situation, or they may feel that this possibility is clouded over by frustration and injustice. When the group is ready, it will be able to draw up for itself on the wall chart a list of ten elements in the situation which are for them causes for real joy. These will be signs of God's grace and causes for celebration. When this is complete, another list is created alongside it of ten elements that are causes for sorrow in the situation. These in turn will be signs of humanity's sin, and causes for repentance and challenge.

At this point there is usually a felt need in the group for a time of meditation, and if one of the members has a gift in that area then the group will be helped by the creation of the right sort of atmosphere during which each of the Ten Sorrows and Ten Joys can be prayed through and taken to heart. Obviously, some groups may find that the rosary forms an ideal meditative framework for prayer at this critical point, but whatever style of prayer is found to be appropriate, after such an experience the group should be in the right frame of mind to dream a few dreams together of how things might be if God's will were truly done in the situation for the people involved. It is that vision or dream that can be given expression in words or, even better, in a big group poster or a banner. In whatever way the group finds most helpful, they give expression to that vision so that it can be referred to from time to time as they move into the struggle to respond faithfully in the situation. In some senses, this group vision is a focusing of the possibilities of the coming of the Kingdom of God around the issue that has been the group's concern and, despite its somewhat Utopian quality, the vision, like the Kingdom, will help the group to keep their eyes on their ultimate aim. The vision banner will always be ahead of their reality, like the pillar of cloud and fire in the Exodus wilderness, but it will still be an ultimate goal spurring them on to see God's will done.

Having a vision of the Kingdom so clearly expressed will help the group in other ways too. First, it will prevent them from limiting their responses to the merely personal concerns that individual members may have, however important they may be. Second, having the vision writ large like this reminds the group that the final goal is bigger than anything we can do of ourselves. We must guard against seeing ourselves as the saviours of the situation in which we are working but, on the contrary, we do well to remember always that we are just one facet of a wider reality and that the victory has already been won by another, through his passion and resurrection. Third, the vision prevents us from forgetting that our little endeavours are intended to play their part in a much bigger movement, and that we may have many unknown friends in the situation who are also working to see righteousness prevail. They may share our vision and be just as important players in the action as we are ourselves. Having the vision written up rather than hidden away inside our minds, makes it into something that anyone can share if they so choose, for it makes it a shared and public cause. The vision almost serves as a policy document for the group, from which can grow policies with purpose. This helps to ensure that the group's future strategies are more than vague shots into the dark.

Expressing the group vision in written, pictorial or banner form may not of course be the result of just one attempt. I have known groups add sections into their vision over a period of months, as they have gained more experience and as they have noticed omissions. It is good to check out the vision statement from time to time, to refer to it, and to ask sharp questions of it in the group in order to open up new avenues for adventurous responsive activity. The vision should be checked to see if it continues adequately to represent the group concerns for the poor and the downtrodden, for individuals as much as for structures, and so forth. The vision is not then a static thing but like all our theology, a developing and growing dynamic.

But the most important thing that expressing our vision can do for us is to inspire us to move forward now into the next phase of doing theology – the response phase.

Notes

1 Laurie Green, *Power to the Powerless: Theology Brought to Life* (Marshall Pickering, 1987). Available from Poplar Rectory, London E14 0EY.
2 See, for example, John 13 and Philippians 2.1-8.
3 See the further discussion of this issue in Chapter 7. Note also the words of Segundo: 'Any and every theological question begins with the human situation. Theology is "the second step"' (Juan Luis Segundo, *The Liberation of Theology* (Gill & Macmillan, 1987), p. 79).
4 Dr John J. Vincent uses the children's game of Snap as a model of this playfulness. See, for example, John D. Davies and John J. Vincent, *Mark at Work* (Bible Reading Fellowship, 1986), p. 15.
5 See, for example, Brian Wren, *Education for Justice* (SCM, 1977), pp. 80-9.
6 See Thomas Kuhn, *The Structure of Scientific Revolutions* (University of Chicago Press, 1962), especially pp. 110ff.; Arthur Koestler, *The Act of Creation* (Hutchinson, 1964, 1969; Pan Books, 1970).
7 For example, Cruden's Concordance, or Young's Concordance (both Lutterworth Press). The databased concordance is produced by Bible Society Software, 1989, and is called 'Bibliotec'. It utilises the Good News Bible and is IBM compatible.
8 Bishop John Davies has developed a number of such methods designed to reach back to the experience of the receiving communities. See especially the account in Ian M. Fraser's *Reinventing Theology as the People's Work* (USPG, n.d.), pp. 56f.
9 Walter Wink, *Transforming Bible Study* (SCM, 1981; new edn, Mowbray, 1990). Although Wink utilises his pre-set questions in a rather authoritarian manner, it is still possible for the group to formulate its own questions and then work from there in a similar way to that proposed by Wink.
10 Chris Peck, *Participatory Methods of Bible Study* (University of London, Department of Extra-Mural Studies, June 1988). A number of points made in this chapter are dependent upon Peck's admirable study.
11 cf. Geoffrey Ahern and Grace Davie, *Inner City God* (Hodder & Stoughton, 1987); also see *Views from the Pews*, a report of the Inter-Church Process of the BCC (BCC and CTS, 1986).
12 Charles Elliott, *Praying the Kingdom: Towards a Political Spirituality* (Darton, Longman and Todd, 1985); Gerard Hughes, *God of Surprises* (Darton, Longman and Todd, 1986); James Cone, *The Spirituals and the Blues: An Interpretation* (Seabury, 1975).
13 Green, *Power to the Powerless*, pp. 87ff.

6

Response

When, in the summer of 1963, Dr Martin Luther King preached his famous 'I have a Dream' sermon at the Washington Civil Rights rally, he described, to the quarter of a million who attended, his vision of a new America. It was an inspiring vision that was at once all-embracing and yet specific in its focus. King spoke both of a general well-being for a land where all were believed to be created equal, and he also spelt out in concrete terms exactly what that might mean. He gave vivid examples of his dream – 'that one day on the red hills of Georgia sons of former slaves and the sons of former slave owners will be able to sit down together at the table of brotherhood . . . I have a dream that my four little children will one day live in a nation where they will not be judged by the color of their skin but by the content of their character; I have a dream!' It was this dream and vision that had carried him through the harsh struggle of his campaigning for human rights in the United States, and it was a vision that, once shared, has proved an inspiration to countless men and women ever since.

We have suggested that the theological group gives expression to its dream, its vision, so that in its own way it too can capture something of the drive and inspiration that comes from sharing a commitment. The group by now will have struggled with the complexities of exploration and they will have brought to that analysis the visionary insights of the Christian heritage; and as these elements have been plunged together into the crucible, a clearer vision has emerged of how God's Kingdom might relate in concrete terms to the issue that has been their focus all along. But now that they have their dream, what will become of it?

The cycle of doing theology urges the group to move now from reflection into response and to make the action–reflection relationship complete by engagement once again in committed and informed action. Let us remind ourselves of how the cycle impels us now into action, by referring once again to the diagram.

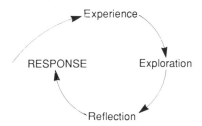

This style of theology is anything but inconclusive, and rather than leaving us to linger in our reflections, it drives us forward, like King's dream, into faithful response. It is of course in the very nature of praxis that this should be so, for the

praxis interrelationship of action and reflection is not only a feature of this particular way of understanding theology but is actually demanded of us by the
Christian faith itself. Faith has the dynamic quality of being at once both an
awareness of salvation and at the same time the courage and determination to act
faithfully. The life of Jesus is our ultimate example of an inextricable unity of meditative reflection and committed action, and praxis bids us emulate that style of
loving and living. As we have journeyed around the theological cycle of experience, exploration and reflection it has been necessary for action to play a relatively
minor role at times, even though we have attempted even then to make it part of
our 'experiential' style of operation. But now, as we move into the response phase
of our cycle, action comes once again very much to the fore. But this is not to say
that we now forget reflection altogether – for this would not be true to our praxis
style either. Some theologians have argued that we should substitute the new word
'orthopraxis' for the old word 'orthodoxy', to do justice to the belief that it is not
by the quality of our propositional beliefs that we are judged, but by the quality of
our faithful Christian action. It is important to remember, however, that it would
be foolhardy to engage in just any old action simply in order to prove ourselves
active Christians; we must engage in action of faithful quality. But how might we
judge that our action is of this standard if not by reflection and discernment? So we
need action and we need reflection, and the constant tension between the truth of
the faith and its faithful implementation must always be our concern. As much as
it is proper to say that faith cannot be reduced to action, we must also remember
that faith without works is dead.

What this means for us is that the business of moving from our dream or vision
into faithful response in this phase of the cycle will be a complex and difficult
business indeed! We will have to take into consideration a threefold tension. First,
as we have explained, there will be the tension between being active agents in
God's world and being reflective thinkers and meditators. Next will be the tension
that has been explored between the social analysis that we have made of the issue
and the insights and mandates that have come to us from the heritage of our faith
traditions. And third, we will have to juggle too with the tension between what we
would hope for and the constraints of our mortal predicament.[1] So, for example,
despite the enthusiasm of the group for their own vision, they may find themselves
confronted by the realities of a Church that may not altogether welcome their
commitment to faithful response. For when we look to the Church to be theologically committed to action in matters of justice, peace and community, we soon
become aware that many Christians do not expect this to be the Church's task at
all, but are, if anything, rather fearful of it. They may simply not realise that the
Church has a great deal more to offer than the solace of tea and sympathy,
however important and necessary they may sometimes be. For the Church carries
the promise of liberation, the promise of truth in action, and action in truth. It is
the privileged instrument of the incoming of the Kingdom of God in the world;
and to this great task its central act of worship bears witness, for even the
Eucharistic sacrament of the Church, in which Christians share week by week, is
not simply a personal thanksgiving nor merely a source of comfort, but it is a
communion, a shared action of the whole people of God, which proclaims God's
active involvement at every level of creation, in the here and now. This is

emphasised by the materials that are used in the action – bread and wine – symbols of all natural resources, of manufacture, distribution, social conflict and need. And it is emphasised again in the actions of the priest when he or she takes, blesses, breaks and shares the bread as symbol of our common need of sustenance, thanksgiving, sacrifice and shared ownership. It is for this reason that it is appropriate for the group doing theology to perform the Eucharist together as it moves into this response phase of the cycle, for it is especially in the Communion that the statement is made plain about the need for our theology to bear fruit in responsive sharing action. During the Holy Communion service we find ourselves praying 'Thy Kingdom come, Thy will be done on earth as it is in heaven; Give us this day our daily bread and forgive us our trespasses, as we forgive those who trespass against us.' We are called to share God's dream and participate in that vision through active concern for the Kingdom.

Knowing what is to be done

Being assured that such theological response is necessary, and having given clarity of expression to their vision, how is the group going to determine precisely what action should follow? It is to be hoped that some suggestions for action will aready have been made during the whole process of the cycle, and that as these have come up, so they will have been noted in order that they can now be considered more seriously in the light of all the exploration and reflection that has occurred. It may be, however, that the group intuitively knows what is to be done because the process of having to express their vision has moved them instinctively into action and response. For example, I remember once being in a group that had been concerned about the difficulties they were having in worshipping together when so many of their number were not aware that their use of exclusively male language was hurting other members of the community quite profoundly. The group therefore set time aside to consider the pain of some of its members. The experience was addressed, explored and reflected upon, but there was not enough time in the session to make any decisions about a group response. It was noticeable, however, that once the subject had been so carefully reflected upon, the participants were naturally far more aware of how their language damaged their relationships and how it was hurtful to others, and they spontaneously made efforts to be more caring in their speech. It is to be hoped that as we engage in the Doing Theology Spiral, so our lives will be changed and our instinctive behaviour transformed, simply through the heightening of awareness that the process offers. This will happen at a personal level, but, as in this example, the group may together find a new shared sensitivity also.

It may not always be possible however to act so spontaneously in discerning the appropriate response, and the group may find itself somewhat unclear as to what a correct outcome might be. If this is the case, then the careful analytical exploration that was undertaken earlier will now be very helpful, because it will be there that a number of clues will be found to the discernment of an appropriate response. For example, if during that earlier phase, the group had been able to specify what the dominant values were that were operating in the situation, then in the light of the later theological reflection, it should be possible to decide whether those values are the ones that a Christian group should reinforce or, on the other hand, seek to counter. The personalities and groups involved in the issue will also have been located during the exploration and again, in the light of the theological reflection and stated vision, the group may decide which they wish to support and which to question. During the exploration phase, the group will also have focused historical, geographical, social, economic, cultural and religious factors in the situation, and again, some of these factors will be found to conform to their vision and others must clearly be questioned in the light of it. So it is, that during the cycle the group will have become clearer in their own minds about what Christian principles they are going to act upon, and wherever they see forces for or against those principles, then that is where they may want to engage their own energies, either to support or to challenge.

As the group considers their earlier analysis and the material that they have gathered during the whole process of their theological work, they now try to discern what particular responses they may be able to make in the light of their faithful reflection. It is as if they are taking elements from their exploration of the issue and placing those into a crucible alongside elements that are coming to them from their theological reflection. Under the crucible, and energising it, is the inspiring flame of their vision, and from the mix they hope to tease out a number of possible responses that the group feel they might make to the issue. Some groups are helped to understand the process by drawing this simple picture of the crucible.[2]

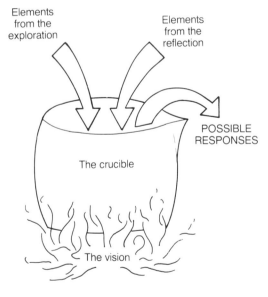

Elements from the exploration

Elements from the reflection

POSSIBLE RESPONSES

The crucible

The vision

From the crucible emerges a series of suggestions as to what the group might do as a consequence of all that they have learnt, and each of these suggestions can be carefully considered in order to determine which should become the agreed group response. But before this final decision is made, suggestions can be added into the mix that may have been thrown up from elsewhere – for example during the process of interviews, questionnaires, meetings, visits and the like, which were undertaken by the group during earlier phases of the cycle. Suggestions may come from the most unlikely sources, but at this early stage none should be discarded without question. A few brainstorming sessions by the group may raise even more suggestions for action, so that before long there is a range of possibilities on the table.

It is to be hoped that in this way the responses that are suggested will have arisen not from outside the situation but from deep within it; for so often in our society, action is imposed from above by those who do not necessarily know the situation intimately and will not have to live with the consequences. But the process envisaged here, and which is pictured in the image of the crucible, reinforces the importance of our incarnational principle of engagement and allows ideas for response to arise from the situation itself and from those who are most intimately engaged within it. Above all, it is a method by which we seek to discern God's presence incarnated within the situation, and the suggested responses will in some senses be attempts to join in that activity of the Divine, engaging in those same suffering or celebratory activities of God who is already operative within the situation.

It is sometimes asked why it might not be possible and easier to engage immediately in intuitive action quite independently of the demanding work involved in the process of the theological cycle. Would it not be just as satisfactory to put aside the complexities and demands of theological exploration and reflection and get straight to the action? While we are not in the least wanting to deflect any Christian group from the importance of engagement, it also has to be said that the Church is rather too good at engaging in a wealth of activity that appears to be for activity's sake alone. Many parish churches overwhelm themselves with actions, meetings and projects that are not necessarily directed by careful theological reflection, and may in fact be a squandering of energies and resources rather than a faithful commitment to engage incarnationally with God in the world. Commitment is the adventure of faithful action, but engaging in any old action can be the outcome of frenzied excitability or frustration, deriving from an inner anxiety about needing to be useful rather than an adventurous risk based upon a determination to engage in Kingdom issues. We are not called to fritter our lives away but to risk them faithfully – and the cycle gives our action this quality.

Responses can be so diverse that it is almost impossible to give examples here without seeming to exclude other possible ideas which in the right circumstances could be just as important and creative. But for the sake of clarity and in order to prompt the reader to appreciate how broad the spectrum of responses can be, let me offer a brief survey of the sort of responses that may be likely to surface.

Sometimes there occurs within the group a *new attitude* or determination to behave differently in certain situations as they may arise, and this in itself may become an appropriate theological response. An obvious example of this was found within the group just referred to, which became aware of the hurt their exclusively male language was causing. Some groups may likewise find that their awareness of racism is so heightened in following the cycle that that heightened awareness in itself becomes their response. Some may find that their theological work gives them a new attitude to their own sense of identity and this enables them to have a better regard for themselves in future; and where self-esteem or confidence has been under attack because of social circumstances, such a response can be highly significant. Sometimes the whole group is so moved by new aware- ness that they feel led to make a more concerted response still by making a *group resolve* – not to eat meat perhaps, or to challenge racism or snobbery wherever they find it existing in groups, meetings or relationships.

Responses may occur at quite a personal level too within the group, one member perhaps finding herself able to make an important life decision, as Freda did in our earlier example. Taking *personal responsibility* in this way may lead group members to seek a job change, to begin visiting an elderly relative again, or maybe to take more initiative in relationships at work or in the family, and so on. On the other hand, many groups will want to engage in more concerted group activity such as the *setting up of a project*. Maybe there is a need for a youth club, Sunday school, women's refuge, law centre or some other major initiative, which the group feels prompted to undertake together. As well as the setting up of clubs and amenities, such projects may become more politically ambitious and a community initiative may present itself from the crucible as the essential response to a local community problem such as dirty streets, lack of play space, or inattentive local councillors. Some groups organise high-profile projects in order to influence political or community decisions, while others will find themselves engaging in more traditional, maintenance-orientated pastoral support projects such as meals- on-wheels or playgroup work. On the other hand, rather than initiating new projects, the group may choose to make *joining an organisation* their theological response. By active participation in a group such as Friends of the Earth, Shelter, a trade union, or a charity, the group may feel that it is adding its weight to an endeavour that already shares something of its vision and is trying to bring that dream to fruition in the situation. Sometimes the response takes on more of an *educational* flavour, and the group determines to share some of its learning and concern with the wider community or congregation. Part of the response that the Leprosy Mission knitting group made was to set up a small exhibition of their learning in the entrance hall of their church, and other groups may try to spread the word about their concern even wider and see awareness-raising in the local schools or street markets as their contribution to the issue that concerns them.

Some responses will have more to do with the *restructuring of present activities* than the introduction of new projects. It may be that it becomes clear during the theo- logical cycle that the time has come for renewal in the worship at their church, or maybe the style of Church Council meeting that they have been used to requires remodelling in the light of their theological discoveries. New baptism or evangelism policies, the presence of more lay leadership in the local church, the revamping of the local playgroup programme or more emphasis on community care at the local residents' association, may each present themselves as viable restructuring-type responses. On the other hand, it may be that the theological group is so surprised and delighted by what they discover during the exploration phase of the cycle, that their response is the *celebration* of all that is good in the situation, by means of parties, banner-making, worship and praise, and the reinforcement and affirmation of all the good qualities that they see emerging.

And so our list could continue. We could document the activities of those groups who might choose to set up residential *communities*; those who decide to *move house* to a location alongside the poor; those who decide to stay where they are in order to be a sign of the continuing presence of God in the locality where they are set. Other groups have engaged in *symbolic actions*, others have responded in *prayer*, while others may even decide to stand in local council *elections*. But whatever the response may be, it will have derived not so much from a commitment to strict agendas or complex project management, as from a determination to stay with their vision of the Kingdom in that place and remain flexible and open to the moving of the Spirit in the situation in which the group has immersed itself.

It is at this point that most groups will find themselves having to choose one response from among a number of alternatives that have come to light during the process of all their theological work. The crucible may have presented them with a range of varying possibilities, but before a choice can be made, there will need to be some clarity as to the criteria by which to judge between the possibilities on offer, and this is not always as straightforward as it may seem.

Criteria for selection

The difficulty about choice arises from the fact that behind the decision as to which response to select will be an assumption about what it is that is the ultimate purpose of the theological endeavour. For having worked steadily around the cycle, the group will now be at the point where their own predispositions about the ultimate goal of the exercise will come very much to the fore. If they see theology as a reinforcer of the status quo, it will be at this point of decision about action that that predisposition will be most evident. If a participant has a much more radical purpose in mind, then once again that will evidence itself in the sort of active response they will now prefer. So, to ask ourselves what we consider to be the essential purpose of theology is neither an abstract nor merely a utilitarian question but an issue, the outcome of which will determine our future direction.

I have tried to make plain from the very first that I see the purpose of theology not merely as study for study's sake; let me now be more constructive than that by saying that I judge the purpose of the theological enterprise to be contemplative, instructive and transformative. First then, theology's purpose is to offer a means by which we may even more nearly find that knowledge of God for which the soul longs. By describing this as its *contemplative purpose* I am not wishing to register it as a turning away from the world, nor as an inactive wallowing in solitude. I do, though, want to emphasise that through the doing of theology we are given an opportunity for discerning the presence and activity of God more readily and adoring God within that discernment. But as important as this purpose is, it is not to be taken alone or it will degenerate into a self-indulgent escape from Christian responsibility. It is important, then, to recognise the second purpose of theology, its *instructional purpose*, as something of a balance to the first.

In the very act of discerning God's presence we are offered opportunity to learn more about God's nature and action, and this knowledge in turn is edifying and builds us up into human beings who are even more aware of God's will and the world's destiny. This can be instructive in encouraging us to become better people, more sensitive to the complexities and pitfalls of our own human nature,

and more attuned to God's hopes for us. Theology can help us in all this, but
having brought us thus far, it can do more than instruct us – it can become a
channel for the committed action that should be the outcome of this new awareness. As if to crown its contemplative and instructive purposes, theology has as its
essential aim the transformation of the present so that it may conform to the hopes
and yearnings of the Kingdom of God. Thus theology helps us discern the
presence of God and to learn whatever we may from that encounter, but its third,
transformative purpose takes up from there and offers us opportunities of working
with God's saving intention in the transformation of ourselves and of society, as is
God's desire. But all that I have said thus far about theology's purpose could still
pass as a conservative description if it were not for the fact that the transformation
we speak of is to be understood structurally and politically as well as at the level of
the individual. For God's transforming action is accomplished through love, and
love does not limit itself to individuals but has concern for the whole ecology, the
structures of geography, history, economics, culture, society, and religion –
precisely those structures with which we had to concern ourselves in our exploration phase in order that we could understand the context that surrounds and
contains us. When Christ is transfigured on the mountain (Mark 9.2–8), he is
joined by Moses and Elijah, representatives of the whole religious, legal and
prophetic structure of the Jewish nation. The transformation that theology invites
us into is likewise a political, social and personal transfiguration, and certainly not
an apolitical or disembodied one.[3]

But to speak of political as well as personal transformation is an undoubted
threat to many, for while a change in the structures of international trade for
example may be good news for the people of the Third World, this same change is
going to mean discomfort for those of us in the West, just as the healing of lepers
on the Sabbath proved disconcerting for the healthy amongst Jesus' contemporaries. What is good news for a leper may look like frightening transformation for
those who have always been concerned for their own well-being rather than that of
others, and this is why God's bias to the poor may appear on the surface as bad
news for those of us who are rich. But it only appears that way from our own
limited and self-concerned perspective. From God's perspective it's good news for
us too, but it will take considerable awareness on our part to recognise that. So
theology's essential purpose is transformation and that will inevitably be
uncomfortable for many who have much to lose.

But as we venture towards active response there will also be the added fear that
we may make mistakes and our responses may lead us not into transformation for
the better, but transformation into something even worse. To counter this fear,
Jesus gives us his parable story of the unjust steward who, when confronted with
the moment of crisis, is applauded for having made some significant response even
though it turned out to be a rather questionable one (Luke 16.1–8). We are called
upon to take the risk of joining in Christ's transformation of ourselves and of
society, even given that we may fail him. ' 'Tis better to have loved and lost than
never to have lost at all.'[4]

Theology's transformative purpose is to be glimpsed in the earlier stages of the
enterprise, but is perhaps most evident in this response phase of the cycle for it is
here that the group must give itself to active engagement and make its own mark
on history. For in past ages theology's concerns have taken theologians into such

issues as justification, or the challenge of the scientific method, but today the theologian will have to give an active account of how Christians can live and operate faithfully in a world that rarely conforms to the demands of the Kingdom of God. It is from this basis that the theological group must confront the many possibilities for action which have emanated from the mix of exploration and theological reflection, and choose from among them which response to make their own.

Having thus clarified the ultimate purpose of the whole exercise, it now becomes possible on that basis to formulate a number of concrete questions which will enable the group to single out from the many possibilities which response to opt for.

1 *Importance and viability*

To begin with, the group must determine how important its members believe each of the possibilities to be. They will have to be convinced that the response they select conforms to their vision in some worthwhile and important way, but on the other hand they must set against that the viability of the suggestion, for they will need to choose something that is at least manageable for them. It will be necessary for the group to remember that they will not be able to fulfil all the aspirations of their Kingdom vision in just one response, and their action will always in some regard be only provisional. But this should not discourage them, for even the project that we call 'the Christian Church' can only be provisional in relation to the vision that is the Kingdom of God. The group's aim may have to be on a very small scale, but the group members should not allow themselves to feel downhearted about this. They may for example be a group of elderly patients in a nursing home who have begun a Doing Theology group and they may find themselves limited by their lack of resources and capacities, even though their vision is clear. There are two things in our Christian traditions that give considerable reassurance in this situation. First, Jesus teaches that the widow's mite is still a worthy contribution to the work of the Kingdom (Luke 21.1–41), for it is both a significant example to others and, in its own right, is a sign of the presence of God's Kingdom. Second, it must be appreciated that a very small beginning can put a theological group into an altogether different situation, a new experience, from which new and perhaps even larger things in turn may come. That small group who decided that their response was to have a small knitting club for Leprosy Mission, ended up leading a service of worship on the theme of creation for the whole church congregation and, in addition, found ways of including the housebound in their membership. There must be untold examples of the proverb coming true – that from small acorns great oaks do grow. Even more can be expected of the mustard seed (Mark 4.30–32).

2 *Who is it for?*

The group must next ask themselves what their own role might be within each of the possible responses. Will the group be operating *instead* of those who are experiencing the situation, will they be acting *with* them, or will they be functioning *as participants* themselves in the midst of those who are primarily affected by the issue? Our intention must always be to make sure that people are not being taken over by others, but that they increasingly become the responsible agents or subjects of their own lives.[5] In other words, they are the ones who must be allowed to make their own decisions in their own way about their own lives and situations. Any hint of paternalism on the group's part, however well intentioned, will only make the group feel better at the expense of those they seek to serve.

3 At what level does the response operate?

The group must also be careful, when selecting its response, to determine the levels at which each possible project might operate. It is important not to get into actions that are only going to deal with symptoms and never address the basic causes of them. Prevention is always better than cure, but if the project never allows the group to tackle prevention, then it may turn out to be reinforcing the problem by administering anodynes where major social surgery is called for.

Of the suggestions that the group has before it, there will be some that aim more consciously at personal concerns, while others will relate more directly to group or community concerns. Others may highlight the issue at regional, national or even international level. If the group can settle upon a response in which the issue is focused at a whole number of levels, this will enable a fuller appreciation of the wider implications of the issue and help all to see the nature of the underlying problems more clearly than ever before.

4 Who will be involved?

During the exploration phase of the cycle, the group may have made contact with groups other than themselves that are also involved in the issue or community, and the chosen project should be a cause for the building of alliances with such groups wherever possible. The response should therefore be ecumenical wherever feasible, should not duplicate work that is already being done, and should ensure that all who want to help have opportunity to be appropriately involved.

5 What does it seem to achieve?

There must be at least some clarity about what the response is intended to achieve and for whose benefit. As the group scrutinises each possible response, it must therefore ask, if the response proves to be successful, who stands to gain or lose by it? Would the action reinforce the things about which the group is joyful and challenge those things in the situation that give cause for anger, or would it give out all the wrong messages? For example, would the project encourage liberation and discourage dependency, or would it do quite the opposite?

6 Will the response preach the gospel?

In all these questions there is the same underlying concern that the response should be a witness to the transcendent God in the midst, and to the reality of salvation for all creation. In some small way, the chosen project should then point to the conversion and transformation of some pressures of injustice or lack of love, and thus become a living witness to the group's vision of the Kingdom in that place.

Eventually, through this process of questioning, prioritising and elimination, one or two manageable responses are fixed upon by the group. This moment can be a very important one in the group's life, and it is worth while taking time aside for thankful celebration together with meditative affirmation.

Aims and strategies

Having decided upon a response, the next stage in the process is to determine what actually has to be done at ground level to see it fulfilled. If the response is to be in the nature of a major project, then it may be very helpful to interview those who already have experience in the field, although their advice will need to be checked against the particular vision to which the group itself is working. For example, the group may need to discuss the vexing question of 'means and ends' in order to determine whether certain actions would or would not be ethically acceptable in the pursuit of their goal. From whom, for example, are they going to accept financial help if it means sacrificing some of the integrity of the project in order to keep it financially viable?

Prayer and sensitive discussion should help the group over such difficulties, so that they get to the point where they can specify with some clarity what precisely it is that they wish to see happen. Different methods and frameworks are available to help groups plan their action, but I usually find that groups work well if they make a simple list of their various practical aims; that is, what they hope their response is going to achieve. They can then append to each of these aims the phrase 'by means of . . .' and then complete the sentence with a particular strategy which they hope will achieve each aim. This can all be made up into chart form and put up in a prominent position in the group room so that all the participants have before them an agreed framework for action. An example may prove helpful at this point.

I was once involved with a group that had taken as its concern the issue of homelessness on the streets of their city. After working round the cycle of doing theology, they decided upon a manageable response in relation to just five homeless young people with whom they had become acquainted. Their chart of aims and strategies looked like this:

Issue: **Homelessness in the city**

Response: **To set up a home for five young people**

Aims and Strategies

1 Aim: To get youngsters off the street.
   Strategy: By means of setting up a house in Woburn Road as a home for five young people.

2 Aim: To give security and attention to the youngsters.
   Strategy: By means of two of our adults living in and the rest taking constant interest in the home.

3 Aim: To get to know more about the problem of homelessness.
   Strategy: By means of listening to the youngsters.

4 Aim: To prompt the local authority to have more care for homeless youngsters.
   Strategy: By bringing what we learn to the attention of local councillors and officers.

5 Aim: To be aware of God's presence with the youngsters.
   Strategy: By doing the whole thing sensitively as an intentionally Christian group.

Naming practical steps

Again, if an ambitious project-type response has be selected, then it will be necessary at this stage to see what practical steps have to be taken in order to accomplish each of the stated strategies. One simple way to determine the practical steps that will be required is to utilise a technique that I have described elsewhere,[6] known as the Hopes and Fears diagram, which has often helped groups who are not used to strategic planning.

   The group first draws a large chart similar in design to a rugby football goal or capital letter H. The left-hand upright represents where they are now, while the right-hand upright represents where they might be in one year's time. Above the horizontal cross-bar are written all the good things or 'best hopes', and below the cross-bar, all the bad things or 'worst fears'. At each of the four corners of the diagram the group writes up how it feels. So at the top left there will appear all those things that are presently the case and that feel good to the group. But below and to the left will be written all those present things that the group does not want to see remain. They can then move to the right-hand side of the goal post and at the top write up how they suspect things might be in one year's time if all were to go wonderfully well with their project. Below will be written all their worst night-

HOPES AND FEARS

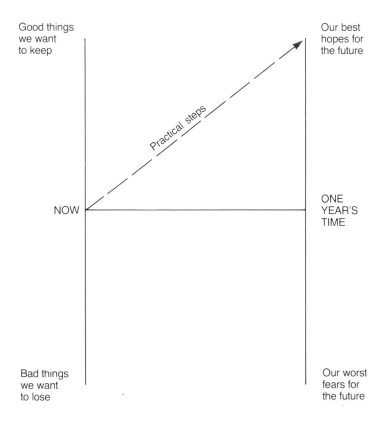

mares about what could go wrong. So, for example, if a youth-club project were being planned, then one of the many dreams that may be listed on the diagram might be the hope that the club should be full each evening, while below that will be recorded the fear that no youngsters might come, and so on.

A dotted line is now drawn to run from 'where we are now' at the left of the diagram up to join our best hopes for the future at the top right of the chart. Along this line are written up as many suggestions as possible, which, if followed up, may help to ensure that that dream is attained and the nightmare avoided. In the example about the youth club's concern about numbers, suggestions may include 'advertise well', 'go to the schools and inform youngsters there', 'have posters printed', 'ask youngsters what programme they would support', and so on. In this way the planning begins to take shape in the mind of the group, and members opt to take responsibility for each aspect of the strategy.

We can draw such a diagram for each of our aims and as answers are called out in the group, so they are charted up on to the diagrams.

A second well-known approach to planning practical steps in the group is to use a simple 'force field analysis'. Here, we look to each aim and strategy in turn and list first the factors that may prevent that being achieved, and then those factors that will encourage its achievement. We then work out together in the group ways of reinforcing the encouraging factors and discouraging the preventative factors. A third and very simple method of working out the practical steps is by the use of a large wall calendar. The framework this offers enables the group to draft out what needs to be done, in what order and by whom, so that each aim and strategy may be achieved efficiently. Each group will discover its own preferred way of planning aims, strategies and practical steps, but when all this is done it will still be time to take a deep breath and move to action!

Implementation

It is not easy to express how much more exciting it can be to engage in action that is the outcome of theological investigation, rather than merely to be activist for its own sake. It is also exhilarating to be engaged in theology that has practical action at its heart, rather than theological reflection that hangs back from practical engagement. Doing theology is not just a theory for the feeble-hearted, but demands the practical living out of the implications by committed, faithful disciples. The challenge is daunting, but the outcome is usually inspiring to observe. For as they begin to engage in responsive action, so the group learns to mobilise resources of people and funding, to set up management structures, bombard the media about members' concern, wage diplomatic offensives and encourage volunteers. So much is gained from this practical experience that can never be gained from theory, and so often ordinary members of the group prove to be far more adept at wise implementation than do the more learned members. If the group has never engaged in anything like this before, then things are never the same again! But this is just as much the case for those who engage in responses that are not so project-orientated; because, even though the action in which they engage may be familiar to them, after having had the experience of working round the theological cycle, they find themselves undertaking the response with a new awareness and with the inspiration of knowing that their action is intimately related to their vision of the Kingdom.

Dealing with our fears

It has to be said, though, that many people are fearful of engaging in this phase of the cycle of doing theology, because they are aware that it may lead them into activities that expect too much of them or else challenge them politically. However, there are ways of helping participants overcome these fears so that they may more adventurously confront the challenge of doing theology. For example, one simple rule of thumb for a group for whom this is a brand-new exercise, is to start with very small, manageable responses and only to develop bigger and more demanding projects as time goes on. In this way, the group slowly but surely gains confidence in itself and its abilities, and does so at a steady and manageable pace. One of my greatest personal delights is that so many people tell me that through their years in the groups, they have found themselves able to undertake all sorts of tasks very successfully, even though when they first joined their group they would have been quite frightened by any new challenge. But this is only achieved if participants are given the opportunity and time to gain confidence. The groups must not be rushed.

There are a number of other factors and strategies that help to build the confidence of the group and encourage participants to risk a little more of their potential. The first is the simple and obvious strength of friendship and group solidarity which is developed as time goes on. The group learns to work together in many ways even before they have to venture out into responsive action, by which time they know one another well and have learnt how best to support one another. Another helpful way to build confidence is to have the group visit other projects together so that they can see what other groups have managed to achieve. It is very usual that groups return from such investigative visits full of ideas and much encouraged. A third great asset, ideal for allaying fear of action in the group, is the great treasure store of parables that Jesus told to his disciples. So very many of them seem to have been specially designed to allay similar fears among his first followers. For those who fear that the challenge will be too great for them there are stories about faith the size of a grain of mustard seed, and about mountains being flung into the sea. For those who prefer to hide their talents away, there is the story of the lamp on the lamp stand; and for those who fear that their project may not succeed, there is the parable of the sower, who goes out to sow even though he knows that not all his efforts will yield a hundredfold. He tells them to be light, salt and leaven in the lump, rather than to opt for an inactive faith. And most important of all is Jesus' challenge, that if we really wish to gain everything we have to be prepared to risk it all. 'If you really wish to save your life, you must lose it' (Matthew 10.39). It cannot be foolhardy to risk a life you must surely lose in order to gain something that cannot be taken away.

Continuing round the spiral

We must always remember that our theological work is not completed when we implement our response. For this new activity should move us into a new situation which will itself require exploration and reflection. As we plan the response, it is therefore all to the good if we can structure into the programme an element that demands we continue around the spiral and not end things there. So often in church activities, the outcome of planning is an action that is never evaluated, nor ever thought about again in terms of how well it may have achieved its theological aims. We never have a chance to reflect upon what has been learnt from the experience. One way in which we may ensure that reflective activity runs along-side our responsive activity is to split our response into two separate but inter-relating elements. One element will have as its primary purpose the active implementation of the project, while the other element will be designed to offer opportunity for further reflection upon the response. The way that this was accom-plished in the project for the five homeless youngsters just described, was by the setting up of a group that would run alongside the project and learn constantly from it, thus ensuring that there would be no way in which the project could con-tinue without engaging in a constant interrelationship of action and reflection. This allowed the cycle of doing theology to continue as a spiral, moving constantly forward as an exercise in theological action–reflection praxis.

Operating in this way offers adequate opportunity for the evaluation of the work by the reflective group, but it is also to be hoped that as the spiral is continued, there is retained a constant celebratory flavour in the whole enterprise. Celebration within the context of worship is of especial significance in any group that is doing theology together, and worship is often the occasion too for marking a turning point in the work. When a project is about to commence, it is very good if those who are going to have special responsibilities within it are commissioned during worship for the work that lies ahead of them and are assured of the support and encouragement of the prayers of the others. Time and again I have heard it said in such groups that despite the difficult and painful issues that a group has tried to address, there has been so very much to celebrate and give thanks for.

Having taken the last four chapters to present a more detailed description of the Doing Theology Spiral, I have run the risk of giving the impression that the whole exercise may be too complex and wide-ranging to be manageable. It has to be said, however, that describing a process is usually a recipe for making even a straight-forward task sound rather too complicated or boring. If I were to describe on paper how I would tie a shoelace, I could soon have the reader giving up in desperation. In order to describe what is for many an enjoyable and free-flowing process, I have taken it step by step, and in a rather more systematised and slow-motion fashion than would be natural. I hope that this has proved helpful in providing clarity, but when a group becomes well practised in the art of doing theology, it is my experience that it can eventually turn into a much more free and spontaneous activity, like the natural stream of our consciousness.

It may be, however, that a group already feels able to do theology in a much more natural way without the need of all this descriptive analysis. While that is commendable, care must still be taken by such a group that all the phases of the cycle are being adequately covered and that basic elements are not missing. It is, after all, usually easier to go spontaneously wrong than spontaneously right, and I do believe that theology is so extremely important that it demands rigour and care. For while I have argued for a way of doing theology that is rather different from the more conventional academic understanding of the subject, my anxiety about theology being too academic a discipline does not in any way mean that I believe it should be sloppy or lack excellence of procedure. When it is done well and incorporates reflection and responses that are vitally committed to the group's vision of the Kingdom of God, then doing theology proves itself to be one of God's wonderful gifts to the faithful community. Like Martin Luther King's dream, it takes up a vital strand of our experience and breathes into it new insight, new courage and new life in the Spirit.

Notes

1 This threefold tension is described in diagrammatic form by Clodovis Boff in *Theology and Praxis: Epistemological Foundations* (Orbis, 1987), p. 172.
2 The crucible picture is developed from an idea from the Urban Theology Unit, Sheffield.
3 Immediately after receiving the Nobel Peace Prize in Norway in 1964, Martin Luther King addressed a meeting in Harlem, explaining that he felt that he had had a trans-figuring experience – he had been on the mountain top – but he felt now that he had to return to the valleys to see his dream fulfilled. From that point on, King's work was addressed at a new level. He became more concerned about the institutionalised urban poverty of the northern black ghettos and his mind turned to more political and structural programmes. This forms a fascinating parallel with St Luke's Gospel where, immediately after the transfiguration, Jesus sets his eyes on Jerusalem, the centre of the political and religious structures of his contemporary society, and he travels to his destiny.
4 Samuel Butler, *The Way of All Flesh*, section 77.
5 Human beings must become the agents or subjects of their own history. Paulo Freire argues this strongly in *Pedagogy of the Oppressed* (Penguin, 1972), chapters 3 and 4. Brian Wren, in *Education for Justice* (SCM, 1977), begins his whole argument from the issue of subject–object relationships (pp. 2–8).
6 Laurie Green, *Power to the Powerless* (Marshall Pickering, 1987), pp. 62–4. (Available from Poplar Rectory, London E14 0EY.)

7

Challenging implications

At the beginning of this book I questioned whether our conventional under-standings of the nature of theology were adequate, and suggested that the time was ripe for the discovery of a new way of being theologians together that would no longer be solely dependent upon those who have academic gifts to share. I have therefore offered a style of doing theology that has been largely developed along-side those who have alternative gifts to offer, and I have taken time to describe some of the details of this more action-orientated theological method. In this chapter I will consider first a few problems that surround this alternative approach to doing theology, and then begin to make an assessment of whether or not it really addresses some of the problems that I considered in earlier chapters. After that, it will be helpful to consider what place the specialist theologian now has, given this approach, and how we may be looking for a new collaborative theologian to emerge. And if that be the case, consideration will also have to be given to how the Church may be able to find and train such people.

First, then, we turn our attention to a rather thorny issue – an issue that many who engage in this 'experiential' approach to theology prefer to sidestep com-pletely. In an earlier chapter, I touched upon the problem of how we might legiti-mately translate something from one culture into another without gross distortion, and this problem does, I think, warrant more careful consideration at this point.

The problem of hermeneutics

Perhaps the best way to express the problem is to recount an experience I had some years ago when attending a conference on Practical Pastoral Theology in Manchester. I had put my name down for a workshop on 'bibliodrama', which is that technique of Bible study already described that attempts to bring our dramatic gifts of self-expression to the study of the biblical text. After an intro-duction, we were asked to try our hand at the real thing and to choose characters from the story of 'Jesus stilling the Storm at Sea' (Mark 4.35–41) in order that we might act out the experience of those characters as the Bible story unfolded. Coming from a long line of merchant seamen, I thought I would try my hand as one of the fishermen. We talked through the roles carefully, in twos and threes, before acting out the episode. We fishermen decided that we would pit all our skill, courage and seamanship in an attempt to keep our Lord from drowning. We felt that, as fishermen, we would know from years of experience that sometimes the sea, for all our endeavours, might overpower our flimsy little craft. Nevertheless, we would bring all our skill and strength to the attempt.

And so we acted out our story – Jesus sleeping despite the gales, and we labouring hard with all our heart in a valiant effort to save him. But then someone in the action woke him up. He stood and, with a mere gesture of the hand, stilled the raging sea. We fishermen had expected to feel overwhelmed with gratitude and admiration at what he had done, but instead we were amazed to find ourselves really upset. For, at a stroke, Jesus had made our skills redundant and had by implication made us redundant too. The only thing we had to offer was our seamanship, and he did not seem to need it. In fact, he was better off without us. We felt that next time we'd let him walk, and we told him so! It was not at all the response we had expected of ourselves.

We were so nonplussed by the experience that we really did not know what on earth to make of it. A simple piece of bibliodrama had hit us sharply with feelings, ideas and actions that seemed to have no place in the original text. We had been asked to get ourselves into role, act it out and feel our responses, and so we did. But our responses turned out to be altogether different from what we had anticipated and we were left feeling far from comfortable.

However, that episode does help to pinpoint our current problem, for what we had done to the text through our bibliodrama was to 'psychologise' it in a very twentieth-century way. We had tried to begin from our personal feelings as fishermen and had worked from there into the text, but our twentieth-century feelings proved to be at odds with what originally appears to have been the intention of the text. Now, at the heart of this problem lies our quest for the importance of contextuality, the problem being: Should our own context or should that of the original writer take precedence in our interpretation? When first we approach a text, for example as Sunday school children, we approach it quite naturally, and naïvely jump happily from our own culture into the culture of the text, quite unaware that the first-century Palestinian culture that surrounded the original text may have been quite different from our own. But, as children, if the two cultures are all at odds one with another, that is of no consequence. We recognise the passage simply as a good story and we make of it whatever we fancy, in a whole-heartedly subjective fashion. And as children we do just the same with the texts of the Sunday service and the hymns. On this basis, a child is quite happy to name its cross-eyed teddy bear Lee, as a result of hearing the phrase 'Glad-ly, the Cross I'd bear'. We happily laugh at such a mistaken interpretation of the original, as the child has sought to make contemporary sense out of it, but should that child grow up and go to a theological college, she or he will begin the studies required by historical criticism and slowly but surely it will begin to dawn that there is an immense contextual difference between the original text and our own situation. The more we learn, the more we might begin to feel that only the highly skilled Aramaic-speaking theological anthropologist can even begin to get over the cultural hurdles that stand between us and the original meaning of the text![1] Now, I have to admit that I actually enjoy reading such scholarly work and admire the intellectual devotions and rigour of such specialists, but the outcome of their science is to make any self-respecting preacher very wary indeed about assuming to know what the writer of any scriptural passage may have possibly meant when it was first written. And if the theologically trained preacher, after spending a good proportion of each week in tough scholarship, has only a very slim chance of understanding what the linguists, cultural anthropologists and textual critics have to say, and thus just have an inkling of the original meaning, then where on earth does that leave a busy parish priest or a group of lay folk, who simply do not have the time for such an exhausting exercise?

This then is the hermeneutical problem – the problem of interpreting one cultural text within its context, and thence applying it to other cultural contexts and other cultural texts. Even the Aramaic specialist may come to the conclusion that the task is impossible. The adoption by the Church, over the last century, of scientifically orientated scriptural analysis,[2] has in fact led most preachers to learn something of the intricacies of that complex science when at college, but then, when confronted by a congregation, they have thrown their college notes into the waste-paper basket in desperation, closed their eyes, crossed their fingers, and got on with preaching from the heart. Many have felt that however scientifically honest that method of theological analysis was at college, it is a style of theology that has eclipsed their abilities. They have therefore had to give up trying, and have reluctantly, and not without a tinge of guilt, given up the quest, and have adopted a pre-scientific approach to the text and to theology.

However, this has encouraged many a congregation to think that Christians have to live their lives as if 'out of time', and refuse to acknowledge as valid the culture in which we are now set. While in church, we have to pretend that our modern scientific findings are fallacious or totally inadequate and revert to pre-scientific notions of the factual accuracy of the biblical text for all time. We will find ourselves beginning to believe in demons and to speak of nature miracles, but will somehow manage to draw ourselves back from the altogether absurd by simply omitting to speak of a biblical flat earth or 'waters above the heavens'. But once we adopt this style of approach to the problem, we begin to tread a very difficult path, having arbitrarily to choose the parts of the biblical culture we like and disregard other parts in favour of the more up-to-date scientific and technological culture in which we are incarnated.

An alternative response, which some twentieth-century Christians find themselves making to the hermeneutical problem, is to erect what I might call a 'rainbow of faith' across the cultural gap; by this, I mean that they adopt a preparedness to take all on trust without recourse to reason or any other verification, relying rather on a simple and emotional 'assent'. They speak as if God has provided Christians with the hermeneutical problem as a test of faith, wishing from us only blind and unreasoning submission. Surprisingly, this approach can convince some quite intelligent people for considerable periods of time, but it is an approach that is probably more Islamic in style than Christian.

I am glad to say, however, that some scholars argue[3] that there are already certain lines across the hermeneutical gap between our cultures that do allow us to make at least some connections, in all reasonableness, between our contemporary experience and our Christian heritage of treasured traditions.

The first life-line across the gap is *language*. For all its complexity, the biblical text, or any other text for that matter, cannot mean just anything we like, and there are some notable successes in the history of our scientific attempt to get at what some of the original meanings might have been. Our tools for translation are getting better all the time. We have in the Appendix to this book outlined some of the tools that the scholars will bring to the interpretation of the text, and although those tools may still need many more refinements, they do sometimes offer real insight.

The second hopeful life-line is offered to us by the fact that the texts are, after all, pieces of *literature*, and as such depend upon understood conventions which writers and readers have always taken for granted. They did then and we do now. There are certain styles of writing that are appropriate to certain circumstances; for example, there will be different styles for worship, cinema scripts, newspaper columns or medical reports. Within each 'genre' or writing style, there will be conventional phrases, structures of writing, and innuendos, all of which will be perfectly well understood by the people who are conversant with that style and know for which purpose the material has been written. If, however, we take a text originally meant for a song and drop it into the hands of a person expecting a medical report, then, when they read the words 'I'm forever blowing bubbles', they may be completely bemused until they become aware of the 'genre mistake' that they have made. So it is that scholars of literature can discern from the structures of the text at least something of its original meaning and context.

Third, we also have the disciplines of *spirituality* to help us bridge the hermeneutical gap between our contemporary context and the original meaning of our Christian traditions. Sometimes we are surprised to find that some of the rather archaic language can mean quite a lot to our 'spiritual ears' if they have been trained in the school of prayer. We do share this very basic and profound Christian experience with those first-century writers, and worship and meditation can build some bridges into the past at a deep level. Jungian analysis is helping us to understand how this linking may function,[4] but the method is still open to the charge of 'subjectivity', a theme that we will return to in a moment.

Fourth, there is no doubt that the volume and integrity of our store of *historical information* are becoming greater all the time. We are, for example, discovering new data about the cultures of biblical times almost every day through the recent sociological studies that are being made of the period.[5] There is no doubt that our understandings of the New Testament epistles, for example, are considerably expanded by knowing more about what was going on in Corinth at the time that the Corinthian epistles were written. And it is that sort of hard information that can help to prevent us from getting our biblical role-plays into a frightful historical mess.

Some scholars will maintain that *tradition itself* is of the nature of a seamless robe which stretches across the hermeneutical chasm from one culture to the next. Original texts, on this reckoning, have been interpreted repeatedly through the ages so that these accretions of meaning have become part of the community's understanding of what the original text revealed. Thus, by immersing ourselves in the tradition as it presently stands we are merely playing our part within a living and developing organism which reveals today as vividly and accurately as it did in first-century Palestine. As I will make clear later, I have much time for this understanding of the nature of tradition, but those who go on from here to argue that the text is thereby, sufficiently at one with our present context to be able directly to determine how we should act and think within our contemporary situation are forgetting that during the last forty to sixty years human history has undergone a radical shift. This shift has been evidenced in terms both of the speed of change and in the technological revolution that has overwhelmed us, and all this has resulted in the final severance of any continuous line of applicable tradition that once may have existed. And even if we could agree that such dogmatic tradition was ever intended to dominate our present contextual predicament, that would be tantamount to arguing that Christians should be ruled by nostalgia. On the other hand, the vast majority of modern people will know almost nothing of this tradition, let alone invest it with this degree of uncriticised authority. Over the last few decades this secure stand of tradition has had the rug of accelerating history pulled from under it.

Some Christians find that a study of *church history* allows a tentative line to be stretched across the cultural chasm that divides us from our traditions. This too is certainly so, but a scientific approach to the history and politics of past church life must be distinguished from the use of the Church's traditions themselves as some kind of infallible and authoritative interpreter of the early texts. We have to realise that bringing one part of the text to interpret another part of the text is not the same as trying to understand the contexts from which both texts derive. Such a resort to the authority of the tradition may form a spider's thread, but never a bridge across the gap that divides us from our founding documents.

It may be of course that on hearing all this we cannot really see what the problem is about and we are happy to come innocently to the text and just let it 'speak to us' in the here and now, without all these difficulties getting in our way. If that is so for us, then it may be that we are consciously or unconsciously following the lead of some hermeneuticists who approach the question from a rather different viewpoint. Following in the steps of scholars like Ricoeur and Schweizer,[6] we may feel that a text once inscribed takes on a life of its own and that the writer knew full well that we would not have any way of knowing what was in his or her own mind at the time of writing. The writer was prepared to let it go at that, hoping that we would be inspired by it none the less. After it is 'released' from its original context, a text accrues to itself 'surplus meaning', and so the interpretations through the ages become as fascinatingly a part of the meaning of the text as that which was originally intended. This approach has more recently won great acclaim in theology and has allowed the traditional stories to live for themselves. It has also allowed theology to enter into the realms of modelling, drawing, or role-playing the biblical text from the perspective of our own culture and experience. This understanding of the matter assumes that there can be no interpretation of a biblical text that is absolutely faithful to its original meaning while at the same time being totally relevant to our modern context. In the face of that challenge, the approach opts for contemporary relevance rather than faithfulness to its original meaning, on the reasonable assumption that the person who originally released the text to be read knew that that was how it would have to be.

If we should choose to follow this approach and opt for subjective relevance – as so many unwittingly do in any case – it would be important to be aware of its inherent dangers as well as its benefits. The dangers of this 'story telling' approach to theology are brought home to us in the old admonition 'Don't tell stories!' And the reason that stories have not always been trusted is that there is not necessarily any immediate way of verifying whether or not a story is based on any objective truth. The problem therefore becomes one of authority, for if we are to interpret our traditions of faith in this subjective fashion, who is to say that there is any objective truth in any of the interpretations? Who will be able to say to the Afrikaner Church 'No, your racist interpretation of the text is false!' They will be able to reply 'But this interpretation is right for us'. As the old saying has it, 'Everyone will be their own Pope'.

I am not sure where this leaves us. I cannot, in the light of all this, adopt the conventional theological stance of asking groups to be quiet while I pretend to be the scholarly know-all. I cannot do it because first, it would be ridiculously authoritarian, and second, I cannot pretend to *have* all the latest historical–critical material at my fingertips; and even if I did have it to hand, there is nothing to guarantee that it would make the text more understandable. For if I really know my stuff I may have to admit that all my additional, scholarly, contextual information makes the text even less comprehensible to the modern mind, for now I will have reason to know just how very different things were then from how they are today. I therefore *of necessity* must opt to go largely with Ricoeur and other such scholars and let the text trigger in my own experiences certain resonances, knowing that the outcome will be new every time. I will build in as many checks and balances as possible from the scientific work done by the theological scholars, but I must make of the Bible an imaginative contemporary tool rather than an interesting but irrelevant archaeological dig. This is the essence of the approach I have detailed in this book, although I have also tried in the Doing Theology Spiral to build into the process ways in which our theological endeavours can benefit from the historical–critical methods of scientific scholarship. I have chosen a method that asks us to 'brainstorm' and 'let bells ring' and allow elements from the tradition to 'connect' with our present explored experience. But I have also asked of the conventional disciplines of theology that they help to check out what our inspired intuitions may offer us. And maybe this is, after all, what the Holy Spirit intends, for then I, the new reader (or role-player for that matter), will be placed by the text at a new crossroads, and made *to make a decision now* in the context of my own culture, and play my part in writing the next page in the text of the good news. I thereby become a gospeller myself and a living carrier of the tradition rather than merely a recipient of it. And, after all, did not the writers of the biblical text write with this intention? Surely the evangelists did not merely write in order to record an archive about Jesus, but to present to the readers and hearers a fresh moment, a contemporary challenge, and a new yearning.[7]

The question of authority

This debate, however, simply leads us back into the issue of authority, for the question still remains: How do we know whether we have read into the text what we prefer to see there rather than what is in fact there? For it may be that in the process of all our experiential and incarnational theology, we have been cavalier with the text, ignoring its integrity and its original meaning. In biblical scholarship our usual intention is to be guided *out from* the text to an intepreted understanding, whereas the methods we are espousing run the risk of allowing us to read *into* the text from our own subjectivity certain material and authority that is not actually there. However, let us consider for a moment how it is that even after close scrutiny, we never seem to castigate the New Testament evangelists for delighting in a quite cavalier use of the Hebrew Scriptures for precisely these purposes. If we look at St Matthew's Gospel for example, the writer seems knowingly to take certain Old Testament passages way beyond their *original* intention. This indeed has been the tradition of Jewish exegetes for thousands of years. I believe with St Matthew and so many other of the New Testament writers that it is quite legitimate for us to be led in this way from old biblical passages into new discoveries, but I would then take care not to give anyone the impression that our new discovery is *the* meaning of the original passage. We arc not at liberty to read back into the passage and claim some sort of 'biblical authority' for our findings. Some readers, even those who are exponents of so-called 'experiential Bible study', may find all this rather disconcerting, but I really do think that there is no permissible alternative. This is not to say, though, that the Bible or other parts of our faith tradition are of little service to us, nor to imply that they lack authority or divine inspiration. As we shall see, it is quite the reverse.

Let us now return to a consideration of my experience of acting out the story of the stilling of the storm on the lake, for the outcome of the experience is quite significant. What happened was that the unexpected responses of those of us who were acting as fishermen in fact led the whole group into an intensely helpful discussion about the nature of miracle, and the question of whether miracles plunge us back into the chaos from which God at creation initially saved us. That discussion was fascinating and extremely helpful to all who took part, but we could not legitimately have then taken the Scripture as some sort of authorisation for our findings, because although the actors' anger at Jesus was, in the context of that Manchester conference, perfectly authentic, the fishermen's anger was not actually in the original text. What this participative approach to theology does for us therefore is not to make it legitimate to pretend that things are in the text that really are not, but it makes us take a fresh look at the way in which we can claim the biblical texts to be relevant and 'authoritative'.

We must presume from all that has gone before, that the biblical writers were, like us, engaged in a dynamic and creative exercise. They too were selecting from the living stories that were carried within their community of faith, and drawing ideas from them which seemed authentic for the situation and context in which they lived and into which they wrote. But they, like us, had certain safety nets under them to save them straying too far into total subjectivity. They, like us, did not do their theology in isolation from the group, but were themselves members of the fellowship of faith, and no doubt that fellowship restrained them if they seemed to be straying too far from the community's shared understandings. It is exactly the same for us, as we too are kept more objective by our membership of the fellowship of faith. And what is objectivity after all, except a collection of subjective observations and interpretations? But saying this is not to denigrate objectivity, but it is to take very seriously the fact that humanity only knows things through experience of them, and therefore the subjective element must always be quite fundamental in any human knowing. I would argue therefore that it is the collective solidarity of the believing group that in the end is the element that makes all the difference. And we can add to that a safety net that the New Testament evangelists did not have, and that is the modern tool of historical criticism and scientific, sceptical scholarship. For it is this that can sometimes help us to hear more accurately the collected subjectivities of the Christian community over the centuries, thus bringing even more so-called 'objectivity' to our experience.[8]

We are constantly brought back to the knotty issue of authority, sometimes preferring that our present experience should be given authority to shape our response to the Christian heritage, and at other times feeling that the heritage should shape our response to present experiences. Often, even the tradition itself vacillates, at one time coming down on the side of revealed tradition, and then at another time opting for the primacy of contemporary experience. Thus it was that Israel was sometimes called to faithfulness by the events of current history when by total indulgence in the tradition, they had been blinding themselves to what was all around them; but at other times they were brought back sharply by the prophets to the heritage because they had allowed themselves to be uncritical of the circumstances that surrounded them.

The cycle of doing theology is sometimes accused of allowing the world primacy over Scripture by virtue of the fact that it is the contextual situation that is experienced and explored prior to the reflection phase when those resultant findings are brought into confrontation with the Christian traditions. Surely, it is argued, the Christian should let the Bible set the agenda so that the world can be conformed to its mandates. In response to this concern, it is first of all necessary to remember that God is in the world as well as in the Bible, and is to be found there and obeyed there. This is how it was possible for Christians to live faithfully in Christ even before the New Testament texts were available to them, and it allows us to look to God in the world just as much as it allows us to seek God in the Bible.

Second, we do need to recognise that Jesus was quite antagonistic to those of his contemporaries who chose to take their lead from the traditions and Scripture rather than let the Scriptures interpret the current situation. He is recorded as having called the Pharisees hypocrites (Matthew 15.7) precisely for this reason, for according to the evangelists they had blinded themselves to the suffering needs of their fellows by seeking uncritically to superimpose the scriptural traditions upon what God was actually crying out to them in their national and community life.[9]

Third, our cyclic diagram does in fact acknowledge that even the most determinedly 'objective' observer of the experience will interpret it according to their preconceived system of values and meanings. This is why our diagram has a line leading *into* experience as well as out of it. This too is why during the experience phase of the cycle we allow time for the participants to share their stories, their preconceptions about the issue, and their indigenous theologies and philosophies. But it is nevertheless true that my hope is that conventional theology should stand back from the exploration phase as much as possible so that the secular disciplines, like sociology, may be allowed to do what theology cannot do – analyse the causal relationships within the issue or situation. Theological reflection is *then* able to look for transcendent presence and meaning – a task that those secular disciplines simply cannot perform. So we are acknowledging that different disciplines are given to us by God to do different things. For example, I would not attempt to use the discipline of psychology to mend a motorcycle, nor do I wish theology to describe the internal workings of local government's social services department

– but, once it has been described by the appropriate discipline, I do then expect theology to understand it and interpret it! So the doing theology diagram acknowledges the prior order of other disciplines over theology – we acknowledge that authority – but we affirm the prime function and authority of theology when it comes to the more important task of helping to discern God's presence with us in our experience.[10] So I am in no way seeking to imply that the Scriptures have no authority for us, nor that they are necessarily lacking in historical veracity; but I do maintain that the nature of their authoritative use has to be substantially reformulated if we are to be true to how God works in the world.

In the model of doing theology that I have proposed, there will be many different groups operating at all sorts of levels, each working out its own local theology as dictated by its experience of the encounter between its situation and the explored faith traditions. A profusion of groups would inevitably lead to a proliferation of theological insights, and I would take that resultant diversity and plurality as an indicator of life and growth within the Church. Such an array would represent the great variety of gifts and functions that there are within the body of Christ and would be a sign of the abundant diversity of the grace of God active in Christ's Church. This diversity usually causes great anxiety, however, among those who have a concern to see the Church as a controlling and monolithic institution. So, as if the question about biblical authority were not already difficult enough, this whole issue now begins to turn itself into a somewhat political question and requires us to frame the question of biblical authority thus: 'Who is it in the Church who should have the power to decide what the Bible means for today?'

Who should do theology?

Now surely the people who are best placed to do theology, and to tell the Church what our Scriptures mean for us today, are those who know God best. But the old Latin tag tells us that 'God is known in proportion as he is loved', not in proportion to the number of books we have read nor according to the validity of our ordination. Neither the theological specialist nor the ordained can claim special access into the love of God, since we can only presume that God communicates on the same terms with all. The professional theologian and the cleric will bring particular and very important skills alongside those of others, but no one access, however carefully researched or authorised, can of right claim precedence over other forms of access to an appreciation of God's love, nature or will. Each person will have a different way into God and God will have a specific way in to them. The power to decide the agenda for the Church should therefore be in the hands of the whole Christian community acting together and incorporating into its deliberations the special experiences of many different types of Christian people.

This calls for an 'every member ministry' or 'lay apostolate', which is not to say that the laity should share the vicar's ministry, but that the authentic collaborative ministries of the laity should be affirmed and incorporated into the very fibre of the Church's life. The thrust of the lay apostolate and every-member ministry campaigns reminds us that there can be no Christian who does not have a vocation, and no church that does not have a ministry. So also, it should prompt us to realise that there can be no Christian group that does not have a responsibility to be theological. Vocation, ministry and theology – all belong to all of the people of God. Yet we also affirm that in pursuance of each of these responsibilities there may well be specialists around who help to promote these aspects of Christian life. In the theological sphere there should be those who immerse themselves in the Christian faith traditions – some seeing themselves primarily as 'technicians' who encounter the complexities of the texts, the histories, languages and so on, using all the scientific critical tools at their disposal. But while we might think of their task as a preliminary to doing theology – an excavation or archaeology, if you like – there will also be many more who engage with these traditions only sufficiently to become adept in providing to theological groups in the field a ready access to the traditions. These bridge builders will need to have a number of special skills and a great deal of sensitivity. I suggest that we call these enablers 'People's Theologians',[11] and that their task might be sevenfold.

The People's Theologians

I would suggest that first and foremost these people's theologians must know at all times that they are primarily *members of the community* that is committed to God's will to transform our history in accordance with the reign of God. They must never be allowed to drift away from the concrete realities of the Christian Church in mission. They must never consider themselves in any way superior to other members of the community, nor in any sense the gurus of the local theological groups. There has been a tendency both in human relationships training (growth groups) and in participative Bible study for specialists to make great claims for themselves and their expertise, and the people's theologians will be under the same pressure to claim kudos and status. But they are only there as servants and equal members in the mission. Next, the people's theologians must know themselves to be finally *accountable to the local groups* who are doing theology. The task of the people's theologians will never be to guide the groups into certain actions or to try to dominate the groups in any way, especially by means of intellectual prowess. They will have a clear responsibility to provide to the groups such materials and expertise as they are asked for, but not to go beyond that brief. In order to fulfil this role, the people's theologians will need to be *soaked in the tradition* sufficiently to be able to draw upon it liberally and to know what the more 'technical theologians' are saying about it. If they have imbibed the fruits of theological scholarship, they will be better able to question the groups and check them if they feel they have wandered on to questionable ground. But the people's theologians will never have the final judgement in anything, for that must always remain with the group itself. They will have a responsibility to be servants of the Christian faith tradition and not controllers of it. Fourth, while working within and as members of the groups, the people's theologians will have a role somewhat akin to the *animator* in community work, whose task is to provide exercises and opportunities for the groups to feel their own power and to make their own decisions. This will call for all the skills of the adult educator and a deep spirituality to go with it in order that the animator should not get carried away on an 'expertise' trip. It will be the responsibility of the whole group to help the people's theologian to cope with the temptations of such specialised skills. These group and adult education skills will be put at the service of the group, so that they can operate with the traditions and with their own experience in an exciting and creative way. The use of bibliodrama, expressive arts, charting, brainstorming and so much more – all these will be part and parcel of the repertoire. Fifth, the people's theologian can help the group to keep a more *level head* if they find themselves being carried off into an over-emotional or over-sentimental simplicity of interpretation of the faith. Their job will be to try to crystallise for the group in more creatively hard-headed ways, what it is that the group is excited and energised by. There is no wish here to clinicalise the enthusiasms of the group, but simply to keep the group to the task of faithful theology rather than an indulgence in a sloppy lack of clarity, bite and action. Sixth, the people's theologians must have *integrity among the poor* and be acceptable to them. We might say that such theologians need more street credibility than restaurant presence, for there is always a temptation for specialists to react in class-determined ways. The acquisition of integrity in this area will very often require an option for downward social mobility on their part, and a preparedness to learn the language of the downtrodden – if it is not already their mother tongue. Only then will the people's theologians be able properly to communicate with members of groups who find themselves in those situations. Finally, the people's theologians must affirm the theological responsibilities and *abilities of the groups* and never allow a group or its members to hand the theological task to others. The group participants, after all, will be just as enamoured of the conventional understanding of what theology is as anyone else, and will not easily see themselves as theologians. It is in the nature of oppression that the oppressed begin to think in the same categories as the oppressors, and so group members will themselves believe what they have been told for so long – that they are not academic enough to handle theology. So the people's theologian must be constantly vigilant lest he or she be considered by participants as the only theologian in the group. Each and every group member will be bringing specific gifts to the shared theological task – so they will all be theologians together.

All these points suggest that even given the democratic and collaborative style of theology that I have proposed, there is indeed a place for the specialist, the middle person, or people's theologian, but that person must be aware of the scope *and* the important limitations and temptations of his or her role.

The problem of resources

There seems, though, to be a dearth in the Church of those fitted for the role of people's theologian. Most of the men and women who would like to try are too class-bound, or else are not particularly skilled in bringing the tradition together with political and social realities. Others do have these skills, but are at present too far removed from the action. However, there are some initiatives that are trying to redress the balance. Centres such as the Urban Theology Unit in Sheffield, the soon to be opened Simon of Cyrene Institute for black Christian studies in Wandsworth, the Women in Theology groups, the Aston Training Scheme and some of the Urban and Rural training projects, together come part of the way to fulfilling the Church's desperate need for this sort of resource. The Roman Catholic Church in Britain is giving a lead to other denominations and is pushing ahead quite vigorously,[12] but more resources are required if we are going to equip the whole Church with the right kind of expertise and personnel. I certainly would not want this movement of people's theologians to become clericalised, and would hope that some of the present participants on basic lay-training courses may feel the call to take this commitment seriously and move into 'doing theology groups' at local or issue level. Those of us who are ordained might be in a good position for some of our number to opt for this particular ministry too, but if this is the case it will require, I suspect, a significant 'conversion' experience among many of our clergy. The skill of enabling theology to be 'done' rather than merely 'read' has not been taught by many of our colleges as yet. However, some colleges and courses, I am glad to say, are now beginning to move into training their students to work with adults in fostering reflection and action, but again it has to be said that only a tiny handful of our tutors at theological colleges would ever claim to be highly skilled in these adult educational group skills; thus it is very difficult for them to train others in their use. Essentially the difficulty seems to be that colleges train their students to have a leadership message and function, whereas the best people's theologians will be trained primarily to be effective, enabling listeners. Neither is the sort of commitment to the marginalised that would be needed to function well in this role as evident in our colleges and courses as perhaps it might be. Some courageous experiments are entertained by these institutions, but the essential soul of much of our theological training remains inevitably confined within the classroom of privilege.

But having said all this, we must remember above all that although theology has been professionalised in these institutions, it is really a gift to all God's people, and my focusing here upon these so-called theological specialists may tempt us to forget that our overriding concern is not for any 'expert' at all, but rather the expertise of the group working together from their own God-given experience. In fact, this theological process can be worked adequately with no such expert on hand at all, if need be.

An assessment

Before concluding this chapter, I would like to make a brief reference to the six theological insights which, in the first chapter, were felt to be important preliminary markers for the style of doing theology that should be developed in the Church. I referred to them as the 'tent pegs' which, once firmly secured, would help us erect a proper model of doing theology. I think it would be helpful now to check to see if those markers have held fast during the development of the intervening chapters.

First, we may remember that I voiced a concern that full *salvation includes liberation*; I would hope that we have developed a style of theology which has as its constant reference not merely knowledge for its own sake, but the transformation of society so that it should conform more to our vision of what the Kingdom of God truly is and will be. This liberation is what gives the group its cause to celebrate.

Second, we stressed that *all theology has context*. Our theological style has based itself on the assumption that 'God is with us', and that we can therefore look at our context as a starting point for discerning and understanding God's activity and nature. The proper definition of the word 'context' is not merely 'the surroundings', but 'the thing and its surroundings taken together' and the transformation that we seek as we do theology is that which takes us and our society seriously. This more ambitious way of doing theology gives an account of itself in flesh-and-blood terms.

The third of our 'tent pegs' asked us to remember that *theology should include action*, and I would hope that although it has been primarily in the response phase of the Doing Theology Spiral that action has been to the fore, nevertheless, throughout each phase of the cycle the group will have felt active and vital parti-cipation in a moving and dynamic adventure.

Fourth, we noted in the first chapter the crucial nature of *the question of power*. Our cycle of theology is intended to involve all participants in a collaborative endeavour where leadership is shared within the group and where the transforma-tion that it encourages bids people take charge of their own lives and history, rather than be manipulated by the powerful. Even the simple matter of acknow-ledging themselves as theologians is a powerful liberation for many Christians.

The fifth 'tent peg' consists of a stress on *God's special concern for the oppressed*, and this has certainly been the focus of much of the theological method we have developed here. My experience is that it is possible for any group to journey around the cycle and do theology, but the outcome is less vibrant and gospel-orientated if the perspective of 'those who are heavy laden' is absent. Without that, it is difficult to hear the gospel clearly, hard to understand what is happening in society, and an uphill battle to sustain a courageous witnessing spirituality.

And it is this last 'tent peg', a *witnessing spirituality*, that is so crucial to the whole of what has gone before. Because of this, I am going to spend a little time in our final chapter in deeper consideration of this style of spirituality that is so fundamental to the doing of theology.

Notes

1 In fact, even the possibility of unearthing the original words of Jesus is hotly argued. See, for example, Eric Franklin, *How the Critics can Help* (SCM, 1982). See also note 6 below.

2 Reference to the first section of the Appendix will indicate something of the style of this scientifically orientated approach to biblical analysis.

3 In the argument that follows, I am indebted to Professor Frances Young's short lecture on the subject, delivered at Birmingham University, on 10 November 1984.

4 See, for example, Christopher Bryant, *Jung and the Christian Way* (Darton, Longman and Todd, 1983).

5 See Norman Gottwald, *The Tribes of Yahweh* (Orbis, 1979); Derek Tidball, *An Introduction to the Sociology of the New Testament* (Paternoster, 1983); and Howard Clark Kee, *Christian Origins in Sociological Perspective* (SCM, 1980).

6 The opening chapters of *Jesus* by Edward Schweizer (SCM, 1971) give a simple and clear indication of this style of approach which respects the integrity of the text and at the same time allows the Spirit ready access to our interpretative process through our concerns for present issues. See also Paul Ricoeur, *Essays on Biblical Interpretation* (Fortress Press, 1980).

7 See the introductory pages of John D. Davies and John J. Vincent, *Mark at Work* (Bible Reading Fellowship, 1986).

8 The difficulty is compounded when we remember that it can also be the prophetic minority group, going against the collective mind, that can sometimes put the community back on course. Where then is our collective objectivity, in the community or in the prophet?

9   The biblical account of Jesus' arguments with the Pharisees is rather at odds with what
    we now know about what the Pharisees taught and stood for. The point is still
    important in relation to our understanding of Jesus' meaning, however, and is
    carefully argued by Juan Luis Segundo in *The Liberation of Theology* (Gill & Macmillan,
    1987).

10 'The ultimate reason why theology *follows* social analysis is that the understanding of
    the sense of a fact can be satisfactorily effectuated only on the basis of an explication of
    the fact in question from a point of departure in its internal, ''profane'' structure. . . .
    It will take everything as a reading text to be deciphered in accord with the ''syntax'' of
    faith' (Clodovis Boff, *Theology and Praxis: Epistemological Foundations* (Orbis, 1987),
    pp. 85–6).

11 Such enablers may be referred to as 'pastoral theologians' in the literature and practice
    of Latin American liberation theology, but the word 'pastoral' is a specialist Roman
    Catholic word and may not be understood by others. Perhaps also, it is not very
    relevant to our heavily urbanised communities. See, for example, Michael Taylor's
    fine paper in *Putting Theology to Work*, ed. Derek Winter (British Council of Churches,
    1980), pp. 17ff.

12 For information, contact Maggie Pickup at Saltley Trust, Grays Court, 3 Nursery
    Road, Birmingham B15 3JX; Fr Ed O'Connell, St Columban's, Widney Manor
    Road, Knowle, Solihull B93 9AB; Mildred Neville, CAFOD, 2 Romero Close,
    Stockwell Road, London SW9 9TY.

8

Spirituality: the risks of conversion

A holy spirituality might be understood to mean that state of affairs whereby people become so open to the transforming touch of God in their total experience that other people become hungry for God when in their company. By this reckoning, spirituality itself is not so much a thing as a way of being and doing. I believe that encouragement to follow this liberating path to a fuller spirituality must be part and parcel of the theological enterprise and, in my submission, the quest cannot even be called theology without this spiritual dimension being present. At one time, all Christian theology was regarded as spiritual theology, for any theology worthy of the name was understood to be a reasoned attempt on the part of the faithful to understand the meaning of our encounter with God in our life journey. When taken in this way, spirituality was not considered as it sometimes is today, as a particular 'application' of theological understanding, but rather as a major element of theology itself. The earliest-recorded Christian theologies were all 'spiritual' theologies of one sort or another, and it was not until the birth of the universities in the later Middle Ages that the divorce between theology and spirituality really took place.[1] Students at the universities found themselves not so much under the spiritual authority of the local bishop or novice master, on the old monastic pattern, but now were in classes and seminars supervised by academic teachers who were supported by guilds quite independent of the bishops. This brought a welcome rigour and scientific thoroughness to the discipline of theology, but it also ushered in a new era of separation between the theologians and the witnessing Christian communities, and thus theology was allowed to distance itself from its own roots – roots that had until then been nurtured in that same spiritual hunger for encounter with God. But it is only when the whole theological enterprise remains rooted in this spiritual encounter that we can truly say that theology is being 'done' and not merely 'read'. As always, theology must be rooted in experience – experience of the Spirit of God.

I have repeatedly stressed that theology is best done when the experience we focus our theology upon is deeply felt. A peripheral issue in which the group is hardly interested will not engender the same degree of insight, whereas an issue to which the group feels a great deal of commitment will offer opportunity for the making of vibrant theology and hence transformation. Put another way, it is only by taking as our focus a situation or an issue that encounters us that we are likely to be focusing upon a sacramental encounter with the presence of the transendent God within our experience. When this happens, theology renders opportunity for us to come face to face with the Spirit of God. I find it helpful therefore to think of spirituality as the adventure engendered by the question 'Where do we find God?', and we can find God, we can experience this spiritual encounter not merely in one or other phase of the cycle but at the very heart of the whole enterprise.

The Bible teaches us to be prepared for challenge and transformation whenever we are thus encountered by the Spirit of God. In the Hebrew Scriptures, for example, it is the Spirit that inspires the prophets to proclaim the liberating word of God's active judgement (cf. Micah 3.8; Isaiah 63.11 and 14). In the New Testament Jesus makes constant reference to the Spirit's relationship with the incoming Kingdom of God where liberation, love and justice reign (cf. John 3.5; Matthew 12.28; Luke 4.14–19). As one scholar puts it, 'God is not idle but active, engaged in redemption, and the language which speaks of this engagement is the language of "Spirit".'[2] The Spirit of God, according to our biblical traditions, comes upon people and transforms them in order that they may rise above their normal capacities in the struggle for liberation. The Spirit thus opens up human history so that it becomes available to all sorts of new possibilities of transformation through the steadfast love of the Father and the grace of the Lord Jesus. It is this encounter with God's Holy Spirit that is experienced by the theological group as they journey round the spiral of theology, and find themselves thus 'inspired' to engage with the Holy Trinity in the transformation of their experience. When we are touched by the Holy Spirit of God in this way, then we sense it as the liberating and awe-inspiring invitation into a courageous and witnessing spirituality.

If we are to attempt to understand this encounter with the Divine, it may be helpful to remember that our tradition teaches us to look out for at least two major strands within that experience. The first strand is what we have lately learnt to call liberation, and the second strand has to do with celebration – the thanksgiving that has always been a major emphasis of the 'Eucharistic community'.[3] So, for example, when God speaks to Moses at the burning bush, God's command has these two facets: 'Let my people go, so that they can hold a feast in my honour in the desert' (Exodus 5.1). The call is both to freedom – 'Let my people go' – and celebration – 'a feast in my honour'. It is a vocation to liberation and celebration, an awareness of the need for freedom into full saving liberation and, at the same time, the celebration of the nearness of our holy God's presence and reign. In like manner, engaging the Doing Theology Spiral is, I believe, an opportunity for a spiritual encounter with the Divine, and so the group may experience both a yearning for the freedom for captives with all the struggle and repentance that that involves, and at the same time the group may wish to celebrate the promise of that freedom with feasting, fun, games, adoration and thanksgiving. One of the many things that our fellowship with the oppressed will teach us is that it is indeed possible to experience this celebration within the striving for liberation and to find joy even within such struggle. In doing theology we too can experience something of that openness to the Spirit's presence as she[4] challenges us to celebrate the vision and the victory even amidst the pain. Let us then consider how it is that doing theology in this open and transforming way can engage us in the sorrows and pain of the struggle, and at the same time allow us to experience the joyous celebration of the children of God. First let us turn our attention to how it might be said that there is pain and struggle in the process of the Doing Theology Spiral.

Theology demands self-sacrifice

My experience is that there is always struggle involved in committed theological activity, but that it is within that struggle that we do in fact encounter the Divine. First, the cyclic process we have described expects there to be *a committed involvement* and confrontation with an issue experienced in real life and this can sometimes be quite frightening. In addition, it will demand thorough honesty about who it is that benefits and who suffers in that situation, whatever it may be, and it is this honest reflection that invariably demands of the group a repentance, and a courageous determination to act as a consequence. At the same time, despite all our committed action, there will remain the realisation that of ourselves we are unable to solve the great problems that underpin the issues confronting us. The realisation that we as yet participate in the Kingdom of God only through our powerlessness can be a cause of great anguish and frustration. The disappointment, the fears of honesty and inadequacy, and the realisation of being so small and powerless amid such crushing problems, can all be very painful when the reality of it strikes home.

Related to this is a second anguish or disappointment to which our theological method introduces us. We have frequently had to come to the conclusion during the course of this study that *theology can only be provisional*, that there can be no easy answers, and no authoritative body of theological knowledge to which we can lightly turn. Answers do appear from time to time after rigorous engagement and hard work in the group, but even then it is abundantly clear that they are tentative answers that can serve us only provisionally. Tomorrow will require new answers because the world and God will already have moved on to new things. This living with provisionality has always been part of the Christian experience,[5] but such uncertainty is not often what people come to church for. They come, and we also may come, in order to have some unambiguous certainties in which to trust 'amidst the changes and chances of this fleeting life'. Yet our exploration into the nature of theology has led us to see that the only truth in which we dare trust is a dynamic and therefore changing process. We should have known this already of course from Einstein's remarkable discovery that things still make sense even though everything is in a state of relativity. We should have known it too from the Christian doctrine of God as Trinity, which speaks of God as a unity of dynamically interrelating persons rather than one static immovable force. But we human beings do not like to 'let go and let God', and instead we cry out for firm answers and simple explanations. Jesus, though, offered his followers no simplistic answers to their problems, but instead taught them to ask their own questions and become creative learners, learning on the road the appropriate ways of loving and living on the threshold of the Kingdom. The freedom and liberation that God brings is a freedom into the desert of provisionality so that our questioning may be completed in faith.[6]

It is clear from all that has gone before that the style of theology that I am espousing expects the clergy to relinquish the hold they have upon theology, that it may be 'reinvented as the people's work'.[7] This collaborative style demands a spiritual *sacrifice of status* by the ordained, who have in the past appropriated to themselves the theology that is more properly the property of the whole people of

God. They have kept theology to themselves partly because of their wish to have a professional body of knowledge to call their own, which in some degree makes up for the power and status that they have steadily had to relinquish over the course of the last three centuries.[8] As the clergy have pretended to this ownership of theological expertise, so also the laity have felt that to engage in theology at parish level would be to trespass upon the priest's property. In the process, the fine word 'laity', which originally meant the whole 'people' of God, has now come to signify those who have little to no knowledge of a subject – especially theology. The cyclic mode of theology that I have described in this book requires a revolution in this old regime, and this will cause undoubted pain and struggle. The democratisation of theology will not come easily, and many of the old guard will jealously hang on to what has been for them a mark of their professionalism; others may fear that if theology is given to the laity, they will 'get it all wrong'. The laity for their part may themselves lack courage to wrest theology from those who will not easily share it. But wherever there is a Christian will on both sides, theology can become a vital spark for the whole Church once again, although even those who forge ahead in this way will still feel the pain that comes of sacrificing their power to others and giving up their prestige and claim to ownership. This will require a gentle and yet courageous spirituality all around.

There is yet a fourth anguish into which the cycle of doing theology may press us, and this is the pain of *downward mobility*. The current political glorification of upward mobility is very difficult to square with St Paul's hope for us that we should pattern ourselves after the mind of Christ, who 'emptied himself, taking the form of a servant' and 'being found in human form he humbled himself'.[9] Just as the incarnation gave Christ a way into the experience of the heavy laden, so we too must practise that solidarity in our theological endeavours. He invited his first disciples to make that 'journey downward',[10] and so he may also expect that downward social mobility of certain of his present-day disciples who have perhaps been born into those strata of society that blind them to the experience of God's heavy laden. But such downward mobility will require of us the learning of the languages of the people, and especially the language of the streets, so that we may properly participate in and learn from the experience of those who are at the margins. So it was that when the great theologian Martin Luther was preparing to translate the Old Testament into German in 1524, he first stood in the market-place in Wittenberg for two weeks in all weathers just listening silently to the peasants as they went about their business. He did this so that he could use the people's language and not his own in his translation of the sacred text. To do any other would have wrecked his theological quest. The poor today know the language of the streets, and it is precisely this language that is appropriate to the expression of much of the theology of the New Testament, even though it is not the language often used by today's Western Church. Jesus himself seems to have practised this downward social mobility as he sought to express the more profound truths of God, and it would seem to me that the people's theologian must follow this same path if he or she is to find ways of putting tradition at the service of the servants of God today. This is a lesson that has been well learnt in Latin America and Asia, where even professional theologians have moved into the slums to live with the peasants; it is happening too in some of our own inner cities and Urban

Priority Areas. In this way, new profound theologies are being developed for the liberation of us all. Living with the poor has been a cause for great rejoicing, but when taken seriously it also proves to be a painful and unromantic experience.

We have considered just a few aspects of the pain and sacrifice that may be expected of those who engage in our model of theology – and many more could be added for those who face up to the more stringent and violent issues of our society such as racism, employment victimisation, and so on. But a witnessing spirituality will give courage and confidence amid the struggle, and will open the group to thanksgiving even amid the anguish. It is this whole spiritual style, as well as the method, that will create what I have termed a 'new way of being theologians'.

Celebration within the struggle

Our emphasis upon the concerns and the problems of the world should not blind us to the beauties of its potential and to the joys of the present playfulness of creation. Whenever I see a painting of Mary with the Christ child and see in the child's hand an orb symbolising the world, I am reminded of Moltmann's words, 'Not Atlas carries the burdens of the world on his shoulders, but the child is holding the globe in his hands.'[11] For God has created the world not of necessity, but for sheer joy and companionship. Even the strictest Puritans had to admit that humanity's 'chief end' is not to work and be useful but 'to glorify God and enjoy Him for ever'.[12] So it is that theology is more than a tool or a method, but is a joy in itself – a celebration of God and a free play with ideas and actions in response to encountering God within our experience. The Doing Theology Spiral is not offered only in order that it should be useful, but that it may allow us a new way of being theologians, and groups who do theology in this way soon discover the joy and fun of the adventure at each phase of the cycle. It is a joy, sometimes a joy best expressed by tears, which can give glory to God even amid the struggle and anguish of oppression. This is movingly expressed in a letter sent by an Argentinian Christian prisoner to her Christian comrades: 'Every time I am threatened by bitterness or anguish I feel the presence of God and all of you supporting me, and then I want only to rejoice.'[13]

It is as if theology itself had to undergo a Copernican revolution and stop beginning its every endeavour by asking questions about sin, evil and the Fall, and instead have us start where God starts, with creative joy. It is, after all, love, joy and peace that are the fruits of the Spirit, and to encourage such fruit the Church does not do well always to make its prime focus the sin and guilt of its adherents. Our theological group must indulge in thanksgiving and celebration by making their central focus the glory and wonder of God, and from this all manner of good thing will come. Primarily, this joyous atmosphere will give the group a little glimpse of heaven and a reminder of why they struggle to see the Kingdom of Heaven on earth. But such laughter and joy will also be a liberation in itself, for it will guard against Christian obedience becoming a legalistic subservience to rules, and it will turn obedience into a free and happy disposition. Joy and laughter will also unite the group in a strong solidarity, a solidarity of equals, where the normal hierarchies are suspended amid merry festivity and where all are welcomed and unrestrained. This open community can welcome people from all classes, all ages and both sexes, since celebration is the ideal vehicle for enjoying the company of others very different from ourselves. The celebrating group affirms many gifts too, for cookery, dance, song, drama, poetry, dress, all manner of talent and gifted-ness, come together to make the joy of the party and the thanksgiving. And to cap it all, the laughter of the community has a mysterious power to convert fear into courage; for it is fear and worry that keep us subservient and immobile, but we are no longer so afraid if we sing and laugh together. With Jesus as Lord of the Dance, his disciples can become as little children even while engaged so warily in the struggles with the powers of darkness. Such a joyous transformation of perception can be ours if our reflections and responses speak of Christ, and not of self-indulgent concern. It is often noted by black people in Britain, for example, that the last thing that they need or want from their white brothers and sisters is a wallowing in guilt for past atrocities and discriminations, but what is required is a positive and rejoicing commitment to a new way for the future. A spirituality that is at once repentant and also Eucharistically thankful will get us over this heap of indulgent guilt and move us into liberative action.

The sort of theology I have been describing will help us to do all this by encouraging us into the selflessness of the struggle, and at the same time by inviting us to the celebration of the Kingdom. But we must nevertheless be vigilant, for even this style of doing theology can be used to manipulate, evade and paralyse if it lacks an open-eyed prayerfulness at its heart. We must therefore put ourselves at God's disposal alongside the downtrodden so that we may learn from them the spirituality of joy amid sorrow and at the same time find a holiness that guards against subtly using or manipulating the downtrodden to our own ends. Living and working with groups who feel oppressed by others will require tremendous self-discipline if we are not to become either domineering or patron-ising. For example, it would be so tempting to try to push a theologically active group along a path that was not truly their own, or encourage them to work at a pace that was inappropriate. We must therefore have a sturdy openness to God's patience. Such self-discipline is a holiness, a spirituality, a giving of the self to others that allows, at the same time, acknowledgement, respect and celebration of oneself as an equal and gifted child of God.

The celebration of holiness

But lest I be misunderstood, let me explain that the holiness that must be at the heart of this spiritual theology is not the sort of naïve otherworldly monasticism that has so often been mistaken for holiness. It is rather an informed and socially astute wisdom which is totally given over to service of God's loving will in the world. Since our encounter with the Divine will occur within our experience of God's world, we will therefore need to develop an astute discernment so that we can distinguish God's sacramental presence within our experience from the selfish pretence that much of our experience will also contain. An example may serve to clarify the nature of this spiritual discernment.

It will for example require a depth of holy spirituality to respond to the challenge of the search for personal identity in our modern anonymous cities. For, in the modern urban crowd, the fight for the recognition of our own identity has to be balanced against the dangers of too much self-disclosure in an essentially hostile environment. It is to this end that we dress and 'perform' in the city according to certain group norms, in order to make sufficient statement about ourselves, but be still safely guarded. In the city we will see a whole theatre of surfaces being played out as people from different groups, ages and social backgrounds display their allegiances and concerns by means of the clothes, mannerisms and badges they wear.[14] These are the signs by which the urban person learns to discern who can be trusted, and who it would be best to keep clear of! It seems that this is the only way to survive the pressures of the overcrowded city. But when these surface expressions of identity become so important, then the command to love my neighbour as myself becomes a far more complex enterprise than ever before. For, in the contemporary city I have to ask the question, 'Who is my neighbour, when even my neighbour is no longer sure who he or she is?' (cf. Luke 10.29). The question of identity is a deeply spiritual one, which will require a spiritual discernment that turns anguish to joy by affording ways to enjoy the company of another even when that other initially is so nervous about their own identity as to fear any contact that goes beyond the merely superficial. The spiritual witness will be able to help the other sense that they are in fact made in God's image and that their identity is none other than a child of God. The spiritual witness will be an essential presence in the modern city.

Such spirituality at the heart of the theological enterprise will make our doing of theology into an opportunity for addressing the Divine presence within the contemporary situation, hearing the challenge and responding in courage and humility. So the essential and pivotal question of spirituality is 'Where do we meet the Divine?' And it is this very question that becomes the essential question for those who would 'do' theology.

Where do we meet the Divine?

For some years now I have been living with an old rabbinic story that continues to fascinate and intrigue me, and I suspect that it will help us to appreciate the subtle mystery with which this question tries to grapple.[15]

A man was going from village to village, everywhere asking the same question: 'Where can I find God?' He journeyed from rabbi to rabbi, and nowhere was he satisfied with the answers he received, so he would quickly pack his bags and hurry on to the next village. Some of the rabbis replied, 'Pray, my son, and you will surely find him.' But the man tried to pray and knew that he could not. And some replied, 'Study, my child, and you shall find him.' But the more he read, the more confused he became, and the further he seemed from God. And some replied, 'Forget your quest, my child, God is within you.' But the man tried to find God within himself, and failed.

One day the man arrived, very wearily, at a very small village set in the middle of an enormous forest. He went up to a woman who was minding some chickens, and she asked whom he could be seeking in such a small place; however, she did not seem surprised when he told her that he was looking for God. She showed him to the rabbi's house. When he went in, the rabbi was studying, so he waited a moment; but he was impatient to be off to the next village if he could not be satisfied, so he interrupted, 'Rabbi, how do I find God?' The rabbi paused, and the man wondered which of the many answers he had already received he might be told this time. But the rabbi simply said, 'You have come to the right place, my child. God is in this village. Why don't you stay a few days? You might meet him!' The man was puzzled. He did not understand what the rabbi could mean. But the answer was unusual, and so he stayed. For two or three days, he strode round and round, asking all the villagers where God was that morning, but they would only smile, and ask him to have a meal with them. Gradually, he got to know them and even helped with some of the village work. Every now and then he would see the rabbi by chance, and the rabbi would ask him, 'Have you met God yet, my son?' And the man would smile, and sometimes he understood, and sometimes he did not understand. For months he stayed in the village, and then for years. He became part of the village and shared all its life. He went with the men to the synagogue on Fridays and prayed with the rest of them, and sometimes he knew why he prayed, and sometimes he did not. And sometimes he really said prayers, and sometimes he only said words. And then he would return with one of the men for a Friday night meal, and when they talked about God, he was always assured that God was in the village, though he wasn't quite sure where or when he could be found. Gradually, too, he began to believe that God was in the village, though he wasn't quite sure where. He knew, however, that sometimes he had met God.

One day, for the first time, the rabbi came to him and said, 'You have met God now, have you not?' And the man said, 'Thank you, Rabbi, I think I have. But I am not sure where I met him, or how, or when. And why is he in this village only?' So the rabbi replied 'God is not a person, my child, nor a thing. You cannot meet him in that way. When you came to our village, you were so worried by your question that you could not recognise an answer when you heard it. Nor could you recognise God when you met him, because you were not really looking for him. Now you have stopped pressuring and persecuting God, you have found him, and now you can return to your own town if you wish.' So the man went back to his own town, and God went with him. And the man enjoyed studying and praying, and he knew that God was within himself and within other people. And other people knew it too, and sometimes they would ask him, 'Where can we find God?' And the man would always answer, 'You have come to the right spot, God is in this place. Why don't you stop a while? You might meet him.'

This story intrigues me because it gives some clues to our search for an incarnational spirituality by addressing that crucial question for theology: Where do we meet God? In our cyclic model of doing theology we have attempted to pay due attention to the here and now, the contextual situation in which God has placed us, and this paying of attention to context is not merely some methodological trick of theology but nothing less than a journey into God. For calm committed reflection in the community of believers, surrounded by worship, celebration and work is a way to meet God, and must be at the very heart of our theological life. Over the years, my own involvement in the Doing Theology Spiral has brought home to me a number of ways in which God is to be encountered within the theological process, and it may be helpful to offer just a few of those ways here.

First, it is very evident to me that *we meet God in the oppressed*, poor and heavy laden. Many times I have had to acknowledge during the process that the growing concern for the poor that comes of following round the theological cycle is more than just a social concern. In the parable of the sheep and the goats, which is recorded for us in St Matthew's Gospel, Christ actually locates himself in the body of the oppressed. He does not simply enjoin us to be of service to the poor as a moral outcome of following a just God, but he states quite plainly that it is *in them* that he himself is to be met. 'In as much as you did it to one of these, you did it to me' (Matthew 25.40). This is not altogether surprising if we look at his life, his teaching and his death, which each in their turn point out again God's intention to be present with the poor. Time and again, when we are living with the poor, they will smile and say they know God to be in there among them, although they are not sure exactly when or where he can be found.

Second, working with the Doing Theology Spiral has reinforced in me the conviction that *God is to be found in servanthood*. For an ordained person such as myself, engagement with this sort of theological group requires a profound conversion to a new style of relationship with one's fellow Christians. During my university and college training in England, I was seduced into thinking that I was learning a whole system of theological 'answers' which I could then impart to 'my' laity when ordained. I now realise that my experience of God is so partial that I need to be a fellow learner with God's laity so that together we may discern God's presence and God's will. I now also try to distinguish clearly between what it is to have 'expertise' and what it is to be an 'expert'. The first makes one a servant; the second, a trapped status seeker.

For all of us, clergy and laity alike, experiencing theology as an active adventure, as the spiral bids us, helps us all to appreciate our own reliance upon the presence of God's Spirit with us. Rather than restricting our theological discussion to comfortable areas, as some conventional theology does, our engagement with the harsh issues of life in God's presence has made us only too aware of how critical the hour is and how inadequate we would be if left alone without God's ever-present grace. A truer appreciation of the signs of the times allows us to know more fully that God's Spirit is with us.

Third, I am now much more aware of how I meet *God in the situation*. I think this can only really happen when we are no longer chained to the past by our faith traditions, but we use that heritage as a springboard into new discernment and vision. Again, an example may help. Christians often speak of finding God in nature, but for those who are separated from the countryside, this can sound very remote and rather romantic. By starting from where we are, however, many of us are encouraged to find God in our own experience rather than going outside it to appreciate God's presence. For example, my membership of theological groups has enabled me to regain what I had as a city child – what I might call an urban sacramentalism. Engaging the spiral of doing theology requires me to look at my own experience, even of marginalisation, and seek for God there. In this way, so many things have become sacraments of God's presence for me once again, just as they were for me as a young cockney lad finding God for the first time in the East End. As I now drive home at night along the urban motorway I wonder at the city and its red glowing furnaces and floodlighting. I feel there the majesty, energy and power of God and our solidarity with that creativity in a wonderful sense of belonging with God in the fascinating experiment of industrial production. I am delighted by a sense of wonder that we have been given the gifts to work with such complexity and find comradeship, worth and identity in the endeavour. When I stroll round the city centre I am impressed by the Council House where so many men and women have over the years worked through their political parties to devote their lives to getting our city right, working the democratic process in order to help all its citizens. I walk into the centres of banking and commerce, and am astonished at the attempt to create the 'good life'. The expertise and the vigour of wealth creation are amazing. And the service industries that support a city are for me another place to see sacraments of God's presence. Hospitals, shops, sewers, dustbin collection – are all gifts in their fascinating complexity. And with each and every one of these gifts I sense too the challenge, the anguish, even the terror when we get it wrong. When industry becomes unjust, when political parties seek their own aggrandisement, when wealth is created for only the few, when social services are badly resourced, then I can still feel God within it all, but this time yearning and suffering with his children. Working the Doing Theology Spiral has helped me once again to feel spiritual resources flowing up from the pavement – God's presence, even in my own urban situation.

Fourth, the theological cycle makes us address *the issues*, and here is yet another opportunity of finding God. Racism, ageism, sexism, politics, housing – challenging and burning issues such as these take on a new spiritual dimension when we put them alongside our Christian traditions. We may, for example, look at the tradition of the Magnificat (Luke 1.46–55), in which Mary sings of how she, the lowly handmaid, can now sense God's just presence in her life. 'He has scattered the proud in their conceit. He has filled the hungry with good things and the rich he has sent away empty.' We can sing the Magnificat and, with Mary, begin to sense God's presence with us in the challenge of our own situation. The difficulty is usually that conventional theology, while agreeing with Mary in theory that God 'puts down the mighty from their seat', has in practice wanted it to happen so gently that the mighty would not even feel the bump![16] But participation in the divine transformation of the issues of society offers us an experience of the profound immanent closeness of God, for here God is truly Mary's incarnate Immanuel – 'God with us'.

Fifth, the theological cycle helps the theologian to *critique the traditions* of theology by what is learnt of God from other experience. Jesus consistently held the Torah Law traditions of the Hebrew Scriptures up to the light of the suffering world, accepted the critique of the present and broke the law accordingly.[17] As we seek to let this happen, we too will find that the old traditional wineskins will no longer contain the new wine, but new wineskins will have to be fashioned in order that God's presence may be perceived even more impressively (Matthew 9.17). The moment when we appreciate that the traditions of the Sabbath were made for human beings and not the other way around often proves to be the very moment at which God's presence is felt most dramatically. So, for example, experience of the pain of those who suffer under the masculine slant of our English language leads us in the theological cycle to an exploration of that old wineskin, the English language, to find that it is largely pagan in origin and not essentially a Christian language at all. We then turn to reflect on its need for redemption and realise that our male-oriented theological language has blinded us to many of God's other more feminine attributes. It is not easy of course to take our mother tongue and acknowledge its limitations and prejudices in this way, because our language is so obviously part of who we are, but our openness to God in our theological work will demand that we look at it again with repentance and a new spiritual perspective rather than holding fast to our old pagan language as if it were an acceptable means of addressing God. But the real fascination of it all is that as we engage in this struggle to find ways in which our language can be redrafted according to gospel principles, so we find that we are in fact undertaking a spiritual journey in which we are confronted by the presence of the Divine. God is in the struggle.

And finally, doing theology also helps us to meet God by offering us a new appreciation of the *spiritual and sacramental nature of the whole of our lives*. When we look at the tradition of the three religious vows of chastity, poverty and obedience we perceive that the saints of the monasteries were attempting to treat as spiritual the three basic issues of contemporary life – sex, money and power. For what were these three vows if not an honest attempt to make an offering of their money, their sexuality and their power to their creator? We may feel that some of those monks and nuns adopted too austere an attitude to life, but they nevertheless saw these basic matters of sex, money and power very much as spiritual concerns. Following in that perceptive tradition, modern-day religious have a great deal to teach us about seeing spirituality as a complete and very physical commitment. We can meet God even in the hard-edged questions of sex, money and power – and not only through abstinence either! Doing theology from experience helps us to meet God in the spiritual sacraments of our everyday lives.

A courageous spirituality is a gift of God to the committed worshipping community, and I have to witness to the fact that Christian groups who take up this challenge of actively doing theology have noticed that their worship has come alive in a remarkable way. Their Eucharist is no longer merely a re-enactment of a liturgical rite nor a priest-orientated activity, but it becomes a clear participation in God's present action. For in these communities one becomes aware that the issues of race, gender, age, health and so on begin to be perceived aright as 'spiritual' issues, and therefore become the focus of the community's prayer and sacramental action. When, in the Eucharist, the words 'do this in remembrance of me' are restated, there is an awareness that Jesus is not simply referring to the community's need to share bread and wine together, but he is imploring his disciples to engage themselves in the committed and transforming actions in the world of which the Eucharistic actions are yet sacramental signs.[18] When he says 'do this', he is telling us to re-enact the loving self-sacrifice and challenging actions of his life. In this way the community's theology, shot through by worship and prayer, becomes as it should be, a wrestling, an active struggling, with an awareness of God's suffering and rejoicing presence in the world. This will be the active spiritual stuff of the new theology.

The practice of prayer

When Jesus speaks of the nature and art of prayer he refers back to a style long venerated in Jewish spiritual tradition – the tradition of argument and debate with God. We are told in the Book of Genesis of how the patriarch Jacob struggled and fought with God at the stream of Jabbok (Genesis 32.23–32). Likewise, the wisdom of the Book of Job is not to be found in the 'happy ever after' sections in its first and last chapters, but in the spiritual struggle and anguish within the relationship of Job with his maker. Similarly, the prophets continually rail against God, demanding, begging that he might act powerfully in history on their behalf. And this tradition of faithful argumentation continued even into the camps of the holocaust. It is reported that theological trials were held at Buchenwald, Auschwitz and other concentration camps when God was put on trial by the prisoners and found guilty of callous injustice regarding his gassed and tortured people. But after the trials, the prisoners gathered together once again in a minyan or prayer quorum, to worship and pray to God as before.[19] This totally faithful discipleship is echoed in the New Testament in many passages. Jesus despairs of God on the cross as he cries 'Why hast thou forsaken me?' (Mark 15.34). He pleads with God in the Garden of Gethsemane until his sweat is like drops of blood (Luke 22.44). He teaches his disciples to ask, seek and question God in sure faith that they will receive, find, and the door shall be opened to them (Luke 11.9–13). Life's agonising is part and parcel of prayer, and should not be separated from it as if the moment of prayer were too holy a place to allow our real concerns to surface. To bring our whole self before God in prayer is to bring our agonies and sorrows as well as our adoration and joys. It is for this reason that the thorny issues and tangled problems, which crystallise during the spiral of theology, can and should become the raw material of our prayer life. We will often find ourselves bemused and confused amid the questions that we encounter on our way round the cycle, and we will need the inspiration of the Holy Spirit if we are to rise above our own inabilities to understand them.

Each phase of the cycle of theology, if taken seriously, will be an attempt to live faithfully in the world without blinkers on; and having its own discreet integrity, each phase must be developed fully in its own right, and this will require prayer, spiritual sensitivity and courage. So, as the group first confronts the theme in the experience phase and when it then teases out the theme in the exploration phase, all that will be a form of prayer, so that it will be difficult to discern just where prayer begins and where theology ends, since they will be incorporated into the very fibres of a seamless robe of praxis. And yet it is right that there should also be intentionally focused moments of God-centred meditation, prayer and praise in order that the group may better discern how it is that the everyday aspects of doing theology can also become prayer. Special moments of worship serve to show us the presence of God in our whole lives; the sacrament of prayer helps us to perceive the sacramental Presence everywhere.

Since spirituality is a practical matter, it may be helpful here to talk once again in very practical terms, and to take a moment to describe a method of group prayer that I learnt from José Marins, a Brazilian priest of great insight and integrity. José works within Basic Christian Communities, which is a movement of ordinary Christians who are intent on the transformation of their society to conform with the reign of God.[20] The style of group prayer that he describes is very reminiscent of our cycle of doing theology, even to the extent that it has a diagram to go with it! But its essential purpose is to focus upon the Spirit's transforming presence within our experience. It is a frame of reference for prayer rather than a blueprint to be adhered to in every respect, but I find it very illuminating because it offers a way of putting prayer at the very heart of our Doing Theology Spiral.

First, this prayer method has to be understood as an integral part of the life of the theology group or community, and not as an interruption of the normal processes of the group's life. So it is natural for the group to start into its time of prayer by having some extended period of conversation together about the happenings in the life of the community with which the group identifies. The conversation must be about the ordinary but important events of life that touch the group members. It may be that there has been a recent bereavement or the community has some difficult challenge to face. Maybe one of the group has a particular worry or something to celebrate, and they are helped by sharing that with the group. The theme or issue that is the current focus of their cycle of theology may very well be crystallised by one or more of these stories or events. Time is taken to come to a fuller appreciation of the situation, event or person that the group has taken as a focus for its prayer by allowing a free exchange of experiences and exploration of those experiences. This first period of the meeting José speaks of as the 'Word about Realities'. When some time has been taken to talk like this in a natural way about these concrete realities, the group then moves to the part of the process called the 'Word of God'.

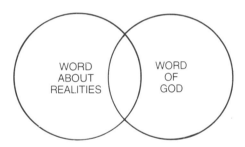

It is at this point in the process that the group searches its memory for anything within the Christian traditions of Bible, church, hymns, psalms and Christian stories, that resonates with the experience that has been described. How similar this sounds to what we have called 'reflection' in our Doing Theology Spiral. The peasants who are normally members of José's groups are mostly illiterate and thus they cannot read any biblical texts, but they will at this stage share stories and feelings about Jesus that often turn out to be scripturally rooted, although probably not precise. If they cannot find a word explicitly about Jesus, then they talk of what they feel to be Christian values. José is aware that certain stories, especially parables, are told time and again by members of his groups, and the intention is that the word of God that is selected should have some sort of relationship in their minds and hearts with what has been discussed already in the first phase of the meeting which they called the 'Word about Realities'. The Bible story or hymn or whatever has come to them from the Christian traditions is told not just once, but a few times, so that it becomes their own possession. As a certain word or phrase from the story, hymn or psalm is experienced as especially pertinent to their concern, so that word or phrase is repeated just a few times quite meditatively around the group. Then in silence the group lets this word or phrase 'echo' in their hearts and minds. Those who wish to make a brief comment may do so, although this is done prayerfully and is not intended to develop into a discussion or Bible study.

The third element in this prayer process is what José calls 'Our Word'. This is the moment, well on in the meeting, when the group may break into more common and traditional ways of praying in order to give some expression to the feelings, hopes and fears that have been generated during the meeting. Spoken prayers and the singing of appropriate hymns, chants or choruses may follow, together with any other expression with which the group feels at ease. José draws a diagram of three connecting circles to represent the process to his groups, and then he draws across the diagram two long lines in the shape of a cross.

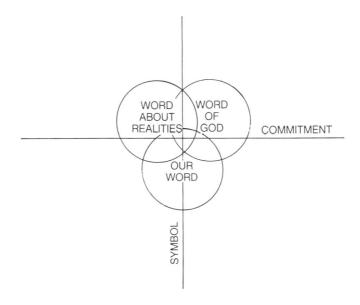

The first of the two lines is the line of commitment. This is drawn to represent the time that is now taken during the prayer gathering to determine what action or commitment should follow from their experience together. How similar this is to the response phase of our own cyclic diagram. The second line is to remind the group to fasten upon a simple symbol to represent the prayer session and their resultant commitment. It may be a simple knot in a handkerchief, or something more thought provoking like a seed or a cross. Each group member tries to keep that symbol by them until the group meets again; this is to remind them of the content of the session, but also to act as a symbol of their fellowship and shared commitment.

The whole process of the prayer meeting may be completed within the space of an hour or it may be much longer. It may stand in its own right or it may become just one element within one of the group's regular theology meetings. This simple spiritual exercise combines many features of the cyclic style of doing theology that I have described, and it serves to put the prayer of the community right at the centre of the enterprise. Prayer like this can be critical, questioning and struggling, and it helps the group doing theology to remember that the theology they are creating is a spiritual theology, intended to help them become adept at seeing heaven on earth, the breaking in of the Kingdom even amid the thorny issues and concerns of their life.

Pushing back the boundaries

To speak of theology and spirituality in the way that I have done is essentially to claim that God is at the heart of all our experience and that the old distinction between the sacred and the secular really does no justice to God's intimate concern for all creation. God is not only concerned with, and to be found in, religion. This may sound a very mild and obvious statement, but in fact it is a subversive and dangerous claim. For if the curtain that divided holy things from secular things in the Jerusalem Temple really was torn from top to bottom at the death of Christ (Matthew 27.51), then the conclusion that we must draw is that Christ died not only for a holy religion, nor even for the Church, but for the whole world. But the Church has not found it easy to be accepting of such breadth in God's generosity, and instead has wanted to claim God as its own private possession. Its theology has therefore tended in the past to be inward looking, keeping itself to itself, and it has not been allowed into the hands of those who are engaged at the margins of society.

My concern all along in this book has been to expand our thinking about the nature of theology, to break it out from its exclusivist trimmings, release it from those who believe that they are its guardians, and allow it across the boundaries and into the hands of common folk. To enable this to happen, though, theology itself has to be transformed because in its present mode it is unsharable. But my wish to democratise theology derives from an even deeper concern that those who want to guard and contain God within a certain sort of theology are in fact trying to put limits upon God's grace and generosity. Our meeting with the Divine, as experienced in the Doing Theology Spiral, makes us profoundly aware that exclusivity is not in God's nature and therefore should have no part in our faith.[21] For although God is specific, God does not raise barriers against being met. So while the Christian Church quite rightly must emphasise its distinct heritage and particularity, it should not sponsor an exclusivism that cuts itself off from others or puts barriers up to guard itself and its theology from the world.

The Church as a privileged instrument of the Kingdom

While acknowledging that the Church has a mission that will sometimes require that it should stand over against prevailing cultures and be prophetic of them, nevertheless one of the tasks of its mission will undoubtedly be to search out and pinpoint those signs of the reign of God that exist *within* the culture in which it finds itself placed. The Church must therefore be prepared to move forward, pushing out its boundaries, intent on finding God already at work in the world into which it is moving. Our doing of theology teaches the Church to push back the boundaries of its expectation and look for God even where we might least expect to find the Divine presence. For the gospel should teach the Church to search for what we have earlier called 'God's Unexpected'. The element of surprise that is manifest in Christ's birth in a stable is to be experienced time and again in so many of the manifestations of his gracious love, and as evangelists of the gospel of love we must push back boundaries, and look in the most unexpected places till we find God's steadfast love already at work there. Our missionary task is to witness to that love in action and join it there wherever and whenever we may find opportunity.

For while the Christian Church will quite rightly need to stand and be counted, resisting all attempts to merge it into the backcloth of prevailing trends, at present it runs the risk that, in the process of trying to proclaim the distinguishing features of its own identity, it will arrogantly dispense with the servant role that its founder modelled for it and restrict its theology by tying it up in the shrouds of past eras.

Let me indicate by means of a Latin American word picture what this model of theology may mean for the Church.[22] In the picture, the Church is represented by a wonderful family car. It belongs to a family who live in a lovely town house with a large garage attached, and in the garage the family keep their very splendid car. Every day the father of the family goes with two of his well-behaved children to inspect the car, cleaning its wheel-rims, waxing the bonnet, inspecting the oil gauge, even polishing the interior upholstery. But such a lovely car, the family are convinced, should never be taken on to the dangerous and dirty road. And for that reason the car is kept snug and dry in the garage, and the family think it best to come and observe it there instead of bringing it out into the open. Each Sunday the whole family pack their sandwiches and go out to the garage and sit together in the car. They eat their meal together there and sing very lovely and sentimental songs about journeys, roadway dangers and the beauties of the car. Sometimes things get so emotional that the family cry together a little because they are very nice people and love their car. They love it so much that once or twice a year the family invite all their neighbours to come along to a special gathering in the garage. The neighbours especially enjoy all the present giving that accompanies these big annual festivals. The family are very pleasant people, much loved and respected by all their friends and neighbours. But the fact remains of course that the neighbours know that the family is insane. The car has never been out of the garage. It is a great pity, but everyone knows that the family has gone mad.

The Church is a vehicle, a precious vehicle, but in one sense, at least, only a means to an end. It is important because it has as its reason for existence, as its abiding reference point, the Kingdom or Reign of God, and that reason for its existence is to be found out there on the dangerous road. The Church is a sacrament, a participatory sacrament of what happens when the Reign of God determines our lives. When the institutional Church gives itself to this transforming focus, then it is a precious and privileged instrument of the Kingdom; but if it denies this referent, then the institutional Church may be very far from being the true Church at all. It will be playing games in garages rather than venturing out to be what it should be. God's concern is for the whole danger-ous world, and especially all who suffer there, and action–reflection theology engages the Church in that divine concern. It is therefore inexcusable that the Church should be as self-concerned about the strictness of its exclusive boundaries and its own well-being as it sometimes appears to be. When the Church sings the hymn that makes the claim for itself that it was 'for her life he died', it is telling only part of the story. Christ died primarily to reconcile the whole world to God – and as part of that transformation the Church exists as a ready sign of that reconciliation. But it is right to say that it too stands in need of salvation and liberation, for it fails so often to fulfil its destiny.

And yet we its children are proud to acknowledge that the Church is that community which carries the liberating story of Jesus. It is the fellowship that seeks to live by that realisation and invites its millions of members to struggle to open themselves and the world to God's transforming presence. It is an instrument of the Kingdom that is engaged at every level of society in God's world so that it is there, ready to see God's present activity and work with it. And this sacramental foretaste of the Kingdom may be more than merely what we can see on the surface – for it is ever possible and probable that the true Church includes more than the institution that we normally recognise and call 'Church'. The boundaries of the true Church may prove to be incalculable and far beyond our limited horizons.

Popular belief and the Christian Church

I do not wish to minimalise the problems involved in so-called folk religion, but it always fascinates me to talk with those who do not go to church and to hear from them how they too have quite special experiences of God which they find hard to express. And of this great number there are a large proportion who feel the power and importance of Jesus in their lives, but do not for one moment believe that the institutional Church manages to be a vehicle for the expression of what they have been touched by. For in some of these cases God has clearly spoken to them in the language of their own culture, a language that the local church is a long way from learning. If we were of a mind to work our way round the cycle, and do theology with such people, we might be surprised to discover how God is already active in their experience, just as God is active in our own. We would have much to learn one from another about the gospel and about our human experience of God's steadfast love, and about the nature and function of the Church.

In Christian mission strategies of the distant past it seems to have been quite permissible to take even the vaguest semblance of Christian faith and 'christen' it. No doubt our Easter and Christmas holy days derive many of their symbols from pagan religions, but Christians took pagan festivals and christened them with new significance. We are happy to keep Sunday special not because we still worship the sun, but because we have taken what was there in the pagan indigenous culture and by christening it, we have let it speak of God. Would it not therefore be possible to reach back into this missional tradition and christen once again? And this christening does not have to be of an imperialist and patronising nature if the right active theology and witnessing spirituality undergird it, but it can become rather a gift for the better expression of an experience of God who is already present, but incognito. It may be that the institutional Churches have gone so far along the road of exclusivism in recent years that they would find it extremely difficult now to respond in this way to the new missional situation, and yet it remains true in Britain that a lot of people are still open to hearing the Christian faith proclaimed,[23] and are prepared to allow the Christian witness an avenue into their spiritual hearts. Many are delighted to be given an opportunity by the Church to express their home-grown spirituality in more cogent form, and this, after all, is one of the first and most fundamental step of evangelism – convincing people of the very presence of God. However, if we continue to reject this good will towards us, as we do with so many of our Church-centred policies, then it will be left for a different kind of Church to emerge and to take the mission forward. Perhaps small Christian cell groups doing their theology together, immersed in their local contexts, may even yet prove to be for the Church a bridgehead back into this vast harvest which stands ready waiting in the fields.

So we and all your children shall be free [24]

In the Acts of the Apostles we learn that it was the Jewish St Peter who first recognised that the non-Jewish Cornelius and his fellow Gentiles were also being inspired by the Holy Spirit (Acts 10). At first sight we are apt to read this story as an account of the conversion of the first Gentiles, but in view of all that has been said about our own need to push back the boundaries, we are prompted to wonder whether in fact the story is rather an account of the conversion of Peter himself to a more expansive appreciation of the Kingdom than his Jewish compatriots in the early Church could ever have envisioned. Today's Church needs this conversion to an awareness of God's expansive activity if its life, its witness and its theology are to be fearlessly true to the liberating gospel of Christ.

Jesus overcomes our need to put others at the margins so as to bolster our own status, by taking the very margins themselves as the centre of his new regime, the Reign of God. On many counts it may well have appeared foolhardy of me to argue that theology should be liberated from the hands of scholars and put into the possession of the whole people of God, including the unschooled and even the unchurched; but it is because of what I see God doing in Jesus that I believe our horizons can be broadened this far, and the boundaries pushed back so that all may be included. In the Gospels, we see Jesus time and again helping ordinary people to examine their own surroundings and situations so as to encounter there the Spirit of God within their experience. If we can transform theology so that it may help ordinary people to do a similar thing together, then it will be a transforming and spiritually potent theology indeed.

Notes

1 The history of the divorce between theology and spirituality is discussed by Gustavo Gutiérrez in *We Drink From Our Own Wells: The Spiritual Journey of a People* (SCM, 1984), and *A Theology of Liberation* (SCM/Orbis, 1974), especially chapter 1.
2 Timothy Gorringe, *Redeeming Time: Atonement through Education* (Darton, Longman and Todd, 1986), p. 87.
3 The word 'Eucharist' derives from the Greek 'to give thanks'.
4 I use the feminine of the third person of the Trinity, as I use the masculine of the first, as a symbolic way of emphasising the tradition of real personhood inherent in the Godhead. The Hebrew language talks of the Holy Spirit of God as feminine and we may suppose that Jesus would have used this style himself of the Spirit and the qualities that derive from her. The Greek translated that style into its own neuter word and the English has in its turn chosen to translate that into the masculine, and uses masculine pronouns to speak of the Spirit. This subtle shift of emphasis deserves to be questioned.

5 See, for example, Hebrews 11.1ff., 'Only faith can guarantee the blessings that we hope for, or prove the existence of realities that are unseen.'

6 I am not here thinking so much of the Vale of Soulmaking, as the experience akin to the desert experience of Exodus and of Jesus' own temptations in the wilderness. cf. the work of Harry Williams, *The True Wilderness* (Penguin, 1968) and *True Resurrection* (Fount, 1983) and the as yet unpublished Cadbury Lectures of Juan Luis Segundo.

7 See Ian M. Fraser, *Reinventing Theology as the People's Work* (printed by USPG and updated, recently republished by the Iona Community).

8 See the fascinating historical study by Anthony Russell, *The Clerical Profession* (SPCK, 1980). It is interesting to note that such lay theologians as we do have in our universities can still feel heavily marginalised by the Church at large.

9 *Alternative Service Book* (CBF, Church of England, 1980), p. 85. Based on Philippians 2.6–11.

10 Mark 10.28 etc. See John Vincent, *Radical Jesus* (Marshall Pickering, 1986), especially section 20.

11 Jürgen Moltmann, 'The First Liberated Men in Creation' in *Theology and Joy* (SCM, 1973), p. 40.

12 Quoted from *The Westminster Catechism, 1647.*

13 Gutiérrez, *We Drink From Our Own Wells*, quoted on p. 119. A letter dated 8 August 1975, Argentina, in *Praxis de martirio ayer y hoy* (Bogotá, CEPLA, 1977), p. 29.

14 See Jonathan Raban, *Soft City* (Collins, 1974).

15 I have made many unsuccessful attempts to trace the origin of this story. It reads like many a Hasidic story, but one typed script had the name Jeffrey Newman appended.

16 This phrase has been attributed to the wit of Stewart Headlam. See F. G. Bettany, *Stewart Headlam: A Biography* (1926).

17 See, for example, Luke 6.

18 For a full explication of this notion, see Gorringe, *Redeeming Time*, p. 157.

19 Elie Wiesel, *Souls on Fire* (1974; Penguin, 1984), p. 111, and see the unpublished doctoral thesis by Jeni Parsons, 'Modern Jewish Attempts at Theodicy, with Particular Reference to the Holocaust', Cambridge University, 1990.

20 See for example José Marins, T. M. Trevisan and Carolee Chanona, *The Church from the Roots* (CAFOD, 1989). See also Leonardo Boff, *Ecclesiogenesis: The Base Communities Reinvent the Church* (Orbis/ Collins, 1986). For contacts in Britain, write to Maggie Pickup at The Saltley Trust, Grays Court, 3 Nursery Road, Birmingham B15 3JX.

21 When Jesus is described in St John's Gospel as saying 'No one can come to the Father except through me', he is not trying to limit our horizons, but to expand them. He is not keeping out those who have never heard of Jesus, but he is explaining how total is his own presence in the world – 'I am the Way, the Truth and the Life'. All those who come to the Father will one day realise that they have done so through the Spirit of Christ, even though they were not to know that at the time (John 14.6).

22 Again I am indebted to Fr José Marins from Brazil for the word picture.

23 David Winter's book, *Battered Bride* (Monarch, 1988), details the significant findings of the BBC's Broadcasting Research Survey.

24 Paragraph 52 of the Rite A Eucharist in the *Alternative Service Book 1980* (CBF, Church of England, 1980), p. 144.

Appendix

A survey of sub-disciplines usually considered to be the content of academic or conventional theology

Some readers may be unaware of the extent and diversity of the sub-disciplines that are to be included in 'theology' as conventionally understood, and for clarity's sake I present here what can only be an outline sketch of what we might find in the syllabus of a theological college or course. I believe that these sub-disciplines can be brought to the service of the style of theology that is described in the body of this book, but the radical shift of emphasis which is there proposed may well demand the reorientation of some of the theological work surveyed below.

1 Biblical studies

The Bible is rightly recognised as an authoritative foundation document of the Christian faith, and in order to understand it better the scholars look intently at the Bible and bring to bear upon it many tools of discovery. The word 'criticism' is often used in this connection to indicate that the scholars' attitude will be one of exploration and digging down to find the truth. There is a whole range of approaches that lead into the overall discipline of biblical criticism, and I attempt below to sketch something of the landscape.

A Getting the right biblical text at which to look

(i) **Textual criticism** We have no biblical text actually from the hand of the authors. The oldest Old Testament fragment that so far has been discovered is from the third century BC, and the earliest New Testament manuscript is a fragment of St John's Gospel, dating from the second century AD. Many minor alterations were made either intentionally or unintentionally by copyists, and this means that although we have lots of copies to choose from, each fragment or manuscript may present a text that is slightly different from the next. Textual criticism tries to determine which variants are the most authentic or reliable. This is the arduous business of the textual scholar and is sometimes called 'lower' criticism.

(ii) **Translating the language** The Old Testament, or to use a better term, the Hebrew Scriptures, are written in the old Semitic language, Hebrew. The New Testament is written in a particular type of Greek, Koine Greek. Jesus probably knew both these languages, but his mother tongue was almost certainly

Aramaic, a Syrian Semitic language similar to Hebrew in many respects. The grammatical critic will attempt to recreate the thought forms and linguistic frame of reference that the original writers may have been using when the texts were written. This will help us to understand a little more what the text may have originally meant. It is notoriously difficult, however, to capture the feelings and thoughts of one language by translating it into another, especially when ordinary words are used in special 'theological' ways by the original authors. The use of lexicons, dictionaries, biblical wordbooks and concordances will help us to gain some insight into the meanings of particular words, but the linguistic critic will also need to search after the ways in which words worked together syntactically in the original languages. Even if we begin to appreciate all the nuances of the Greek New Testament, we will then need to get back to an understanding of what Jesus may have meant in his own Aramaic tongue. And it is not simply a matter of literal substitution of an English word for a Greek or Aramaic one, for each language has its own conceptual system and is a world in its own right. So the academic theologian will need a thorough grounding in the original languages of our Scriptures in order to get over some of these initial hurdles.

B Getting behind the text

(i) Historical criticism   Nothing in the Bible was written in a vacuum, but each book and each passage within it came out of a particular historical context. If we are to understand what was written in the Bible, we must investigate what was going on around the authors at the time. The scholars will therefore need to know the cultural background and the expectations of the original audience if they are to help us understand it. The second concern that the historical critic will have is to help us to appreciate the historical background of the events and stories actually described in the text itself. In all this, Bible atlases and geographies will help us locate the happenings, while contemporary manuscripts from other religions and cultures will provide helpful parallels, and archaeological digs and sociological analysis will also provide a certain degree of background information.

(ii) Tradition criticism   Behind many of the written sources that were used by the writers or editors, lay long traditions of story telling, worship forms, hymns, songs and so on. These oral sources also had a history of development within the community that cherished them, and the way in which these oral traditions grew and how they were crystallised into the forms that have come down to us, has to be understood by the scholars.

(iii) Source criticism   Biblical writers used written sources as well as the oral traditions of the people, and to such an extent that some biblical writers are better described as editors than authors. When they took written sources to work from, they made certain decisions about the incorporation of this material into their work. The scholar looks at these written sources and enquires about their origins and the processes of this incorporation. We sometimes also refer to it as 'higher' criticism.

C Asking how the text was used

(i) Form criticism   This sub-discipline classifies the literature into types or genres, and then associates those genres with the social realities that would have pertained at the time of their composition. The psalms were among the first of the biblical writings to receive this sort of attention, but in the New Testament too, the text divides into all sorts of genres. In the Gospels alone, there are miracle stories, pronouncement stories, parables, birth stories and so on. If scholars should find that a particular section of text seems to have its origin in worship, or in preaching, or in early Christian instruction classes, it will be easier to understand what the words themselves were trying to say.

(ii) **Redaction criticism**   Once the other disciplines have reconstructed the pre-history of each section of text or oral tradition, the redaction critic can then set about discovering why these separate sections were sewn together in a particular way to form a coherent whole. As each author made their editorial decisions, so he or she must have utilised certain criteria that guided their choice of material and determined how they were to position each section within the framework of the whole text. To find out the nature of these criteria and of the process of editing, scholars study and explore the background, cultural expectations and situations of each editor (redactor) or editorial group. The redactor will have had his or her message to get across, and the way in which the stories and sections are used will help us discern the redactor's own message and theological insights.

(iii) **Literary criticism**   This title can be used in a very wide sense, but we may use it here to specify those critics who concern themselves particularly with the way in which the various editors or authors have structured the work that they have produced. This discipline is very similar to redaction criticism, but it concentrates on matters of style, rhetoric and structure, and looks upon the Gospel or biblical book more as a work of art, using those approaches to the work that we might find operating upon Shakespeare's plays or Milton's poems in the world of artistic literary criticism. The shape of the whole work and the literary style of the author figure large in this type of interpretation, and philosophical structuralism is often strongly related to the discipline.

(iv) **Canonical criticism**   Many early books, gospels and writings that we still have, were not eventually included in the Bible, and the choice of what to include gave the Bible the shape it has today. The Bible is now more than just the sum of its parts, and one book is often taken to interpret another. One is felt to reflect another and often there is cross-referencing and quotation within the Bible as a whole. This final literary form of the whole text has prompted certain interpretations through the ages, and the Church has invested authority in each book of the Bible only in so far as it takes its rightful place within the whole. This has to be firmly understood and studied by the scholars if we are to appreciate how the texts have been interpreted by the Church through the centuries. The word 'canon', by the way, means Church 'rule' about which writings are included and which omitted.

(v) **Reliability**   Most of the biblical investigation that we have outlined above can be undertaken without asking whether or not we are getting to the 'truth'. However, when it is realised that in the New Testament, for example, the Acts and St Paul's letters differ in what they say happened at the Jerusalem Council, or when we discover that Matthew's description of the Pharisees at the time of Christ is inaccurate, or when we find varying accounts in the Old Testament of certain historical happenings, we are bound to want to ask where the truth lies, now that we are beginning to see the text in a clearer light. By bringing the insights of all the biblical sub-disciplines together, we may find ourselves making sense of some of these complexities. We will then have to make choices about whether we are to read the text as symbolical or as historical, and in what sense we might do either. It is at this point that we realise that God does not seem to have handed revelation to us on a plate in the Bible, but God has presented us with something that demands that we bring our reasoned critique, integrity and faith to bear upon the material in order to understand it.

2 *Church history*

The people of God have experienced God's presence through the ages, even amid the tough realities of politics and the rise and fall of civilisations. An appreciation of this story must form an integral part of the process of conventional theology. It was particularly the early centuries of our Church's history that saw the development of central Christian beliefs, Church organisation and worship; and for an understanding of the forms that are recognisable today, those early years must be scrutinised as accurately and perceptively as possible. Especially important to those early Christians were those groups who had very different understandings from their own about the nature of Jesus and his relationship with God and with humanity. In Jesus, was God just pretending to know what it is like to be human, or was Jesus so much a man that really he was not God at all? Scholars study what the Church did about these early doctrinal deviations, and they help us realise that a lot of those old heresies are not dead but are around within the Church, even today.

There have been many great turning points in the long history of the Christian Church, the most notable being the great schisms and reformation periods that sent the world into such turmoil. An understanding of the causes and disputes that led to these upheavals will help us appreciate the intricacies of the questions that were at issue, and will also lead to a more reasoned appreciation of the nature of the Church as it is today. We may even be led to a concern to work for more acceptance and understanding between denominations once something of the history is better understood. Church history will also focus more recent events, trends and personalities in the life of the Church so that we can more readily appreciate current features and issues that demand our faithful attention.

A very careful study of cultural, political and economic factors through the ages will help us to understand the story of our Christian Church; and by knowing what has gone before, we will be in a better position to understand the present and plan for the future.

3 *Christian doctrine*

It is within this discipline that we seek to live by faith and at the same time submit that faith to all the rigours of critical, rational scrutiny. Here we seek to 'systematise' the major themes of our faith, like the nature of the Trinity, the personhood of Christ, the nature of salvation or redemption, and work out in detail what we really do believe about each of them. We then see if they make sense separately and together.

The problem that we immediately encounter here is the problem of authority, for in some quarters of the Church it was strongly feared that this critical approach to such sacred matters was at least dangerous if not blasphemous. The Roman Catholic Church has feared that independent minds may mislead the faithful if human reason be brought to bear upon some of the teachings of their Church. Pre-Vatican II Catholics tried to get around the problem by differentiating 'dogma' (unquestionable fact as expounded by Church authority) and 'theology' (tentative critique based upon those facts). In this way it was made clear what was 'authoritative' and what was not, and the Church hierarchy could still determine for the faithful those dogmatic aspects of Church doctrine which, in their opinion, were simply not open to theological question. A similar approach has been used by some evangelicals to shield certain matters of belief from over-critical scrutiny. They have taken their lead from such thinkers as Karl Barth, who stressed that God cannot be the object of human inspection but is rather the Subject which gifts us with such revelation as God chooses. In this way Barth can say, like the Roman hierarchy, that there are revealed 'givens' from which we can move into theology, but which themselves are not to be questioned. The problem with such approaches as these is not simply that they are discordant with that enquiring spirit that has given birth to our culture, but also that there seem to be such profound disagreements among Christians about what is included within this dogmatic, unquestionable revelation and what is not. Doctrinal studies try to find a way through this impasse by applying the criteria of reason, biblical authority, inner coherence and so on.

4 *Philosophy of religion*

In the thirteenth century, Thomas Aquinas argued brilliantly that reason was the gift from God that provided a firm substructure and validating principle upon which revelation could then build. He therefore set about constructing what he felt to be sound rational arguments for the existence of God. Anselm had argued earlier that if we define 'God' as the ultimate thing that we can conceive, then some such must exist – whatever its attributes might turn out to consist of. That argument has always proved a difficult one to feel convinced by. An easier notion was Aquinas's thought that since everything is caused by something else, surely there must have been a first cause which started everything off, this cause being not only chronologically before all else but also logically prior to all else. Another approach of his was to look at how the reasonableness of creation required a designer. But such arguments lead in turn to other philosophical problems, for many feel that these so-called 'proofs' leave us with the difficult job of explaining why evil and sin could exist if our world is derived from such a wonderful designer. Or again, even centuries later, Pascal commented that all this rational argument gives the impression that God is rather cold and aloof and he felt that there was a clear difference between the warm God of Abraham, Isaac and Jacob, and the clinical God described by the philosophers. Sometimes, again, when thinkers have sought for 'proofs' of God's existence and have investigated the precise nature of miracles and so on, philosophy has seemed to be presumptuous, as if reason were asking God for credentials! – the human sin of pride. In response, the philosophers of religion have tried to do justice to an understanding of the warmth, vulnerability and relatedness of God and they themselves have lately been more tentative than arrogant about their claims; for despite the importance of reason in theology, it does have its obvious limitations.

Some philosophers and spiritual thinkers have suggested that in order to do justice to the holiness and otherness of God, it is therefore best to speak only of what God obviously is not. This is the Via Negativa or Negative Way. Other philosophers believe, however, that there is much that we still feel pressed to claim about God that is positive. We usually do this by using our language in a special way rather than to be content to say nothing at all. We may for example use analogy or symbolism, while others will find it best to use the language of story or myth about God, a myth being an imaginative story where a community expresses, and so is better able to come to terms with, some underlying truth or characteristic of its life in relation to God.

Philosophy of religion will help us therefore to understand *what* we are doing when we talk about God, and will help us do that with the integrity of reason.

5 *Ethics*

Human beings are constantly called upon to make moral decisions, to distinguish what they consider to be right and wrong and to act upon those decisions in particular circumstances. Christians are often understood to be under certain moral obligations to act in a 'Christian' manner in personal relationships and in society, but can such specifically Christian virtues, values and policies actually be formulated and agreed? Such will be the concerns of the ethicist. It is possible to discern within the Hebrew Scriptures and the New Testament certain frameworks of ethical decision-making which may or may not be felt to have application or relevance to present ethical issues. Words such as sin, grace and forgiveness will have such biblical roots, but have been variously interpreted and understood during the intervening centuries of Christian ethical study. Some major theologians of the past such as Augustine, Calvin and Luther have played substantial roles in the history and development of the discipline and scholars will also study their work.

But Christians are not the only human beings confronted by ethical challenges, and so the ethicist will investigate secular concepts such as goodness, value, duty and so on, and the work of secular philosophers or theologians of other faiths will also be considered in order to see what their explorations have revealed.

This sub-discipline attempts to be more than theoretical and generalised, and often addresses specific issues in great and urgent detail in order to understand the complexities and implications of our ethical decision-making in such areas as law and justice, war and peace, medicine, industrial and ethnic relations, marriage, sexuality and so forth.

6 *Liturgy*

Worship is such a central feature of Christian faith that the study of worship and liturgy will occur within many of the sub-disciplines we have described; but especially for those academic theologians who play an active part in Christian religion, the study of liturgy itself and the meaning and acts of worship will warrant specialised attention. It is often remarked by scholars that it is worship that precedes doctrine and theology, since human beings naturally set about giving praise, adoration and devotion to God before they formulate why it is that they are doing so. The historical development of worship, its shape, particular practices and deeper meanings, will all be of great concern to the liturgist, who will attempt to make some sense of the immense variety of different styles and understandings of worship, both formal and informal.

There is a growing concern that worship, although a natural human function, is no longer a vibrant and vital experience for many in our contemporary cultures, and much revision and reformulation is at present occurring. The liturgist will play an important part in helping the Church to stay true to its liturgical traditions while at the same time giving contemporary expression to its faith in rite, ritual and worship.

7 *Spiritual theology*

Many human beings seek a relationship of some sort with the divine ground of their being and an understanding and description of the varieties of this activity has been variously termed mystical theology, spirituality or spiritual theology. This relationship with God influences in turn the way we live our lives and it also influences some styles of society, especially in the eastern and southern hemispheres. This sub-discipline may therefore find itself ranging quite widely in its attempt to understand both the nature and the implications of prayer. There are many 'schools' or styles of prayer, often with great teachers or saints of the past figuring in each. There are great classics of spirituality to be read and assimilated but, more important still, scholars will attempt to move deeper themselves into understanding how it might be that humankind finds itself able to come close to God and finds itself accepted there.

8 *Other theological disciplines*

Within conventional theology there will be a range of other sub-disciplines of a slightly more practical nature, and these may include some of the following.

Pastoralia is the careful study of how to minister in a given circumstance. In the past this has predominantly featured the one-to-one relationship of counselling, but now there is a little more emphasis on how social groups work and on the nature of societies. The more advanced colleges may even expect students to study the major schools of depth psychology, group and relationship analysis, together with the works of Marx, Keynes, Weber and other major observers of society. Each of these secular disciplines will be viewed in terms of its Christian integrity and utility, and very often students will be asked to engage in specific contexts in order to read those cultures and discern how to minister within them. Sometimes *missiology*, the study of Christian mission, will be included within this discipline and will look at the questions raised by inculturation, enculturation, the nature of evangelism, witness and the practicalities of sharing the faith. Those who must preach may well study that art within the sub-discipline of *homiletics*, while others may make a *comparative study of religions* in which many faiths will be compared and contrasted.

In this brief survey I have limited my description to the more conventional sub-disciplines of theology, and I am not intending to describe the more radical or contextual strands of the subject which are now emerging as substantial contributions to theology. These new strands, such as the black, feminist and liberation theologies, are mentioned more specifically in the body of this book and, I believe, have begun radically to alter how we are to understand the role and nature of the other sub-disciplines here described.

Selected bibliography and contact addresses

ADULT EDUCATION AND GROUP WORK

Peter Ball, *Adult Believing* (Mowbray, 1988).

Anton Baumohl, *Grow Your Own Leaders* (Scripture Union, 1987).

Neville Black and Jim Hart, *Learning Without Books* (EUTP, PO Box 83, Liverpool L69 8AN).

David Boud, Rosemary Keogh and David Walker (eds), *Reflection: Turning Experience into Learning* (Kogan Page, 1985).

Tom Douglas, *Basic Groupwork* (Tavistock, 1978).

Paulo Freire, *Pedagogy of the Oppressed* (Penguin, 1972).

Laurie Green, *Power to the Powerless* (Marshall Pickering, 1987). Now available from Poplar Rectory, London E14 0EY.

John Hull, *What Prevents Christian Adults from Learning?* (SCM, 1985).

Michael Kindred, *Once Upon a Group* (M. Kindred, 20 Dover Street, Southwell, Notts NG25 0EZ, 1987).

A. Patrick Purnell SJ (ed.), *To be a People of Hope* (Collins, 1987).

John Staley, *People in Development* (Search Press, 1982).

Norman Todd with Michael Allen, Laurie Green and Donald Tytler, *A Thing Called Aston: An Experiment in Reflective Learning* (CHP, 1987).

Brian Wren, *Education for Justice* (SCM, 1977).

GROUP RESOURCES

General

Donna Brandes and H. Philips, *Gamester's Handbooks I and II* (Hutchinson, 1978, 1982).

Jean Grigor, *Grow to Love* (St Andrew Press, 1980).

Eugene Raudsepp, *Creative Growth Games* (Putnam Perigee Books, 1977).

William C. Schutz, *Joy: Expanding Human Awareness* (Grove, 1967).

Worship and meditation ideas

Anthony de Mello, *The Song of the Bird* (Image, 1984).

Charles Elliott, *Praying the Kingdom: Towards a Political Spirituality* (Darton, Longman and Todd, 1985).

Janet Morley and Hannah Ward (eds), *Celebrating Women* (WIT & MOW, 1986).

John Vincent (ed.), *Community Worship* (ACT, 239 Abbeyfield Rd, Sheffield S4 7AW, 1987).

World Council of Churches, *Ecumenical Decade, 1988–1998, Prayers, Poems, Songs and Stories* (WCC, 1988).

BIBLE STUDY METHODS AND SUGGESTIONS

John D. Davies and John J. Vincent, *Mark at Work* (Bible Reading Fellowship, 1986).

Christine Dodd, *Making Scripture Work* (Geoffrey Chapman, 1989).

Walter J. Hollenweger, *Conflict in Corinth* (German original 1978; Paulist Press, 1982).

The Taletellers, *Let there Be . . . And there Was, Expelled from Eden, Us and Them*, and other titles to be published (SPCK, 1988).

Hans-Ruedi Weber, *Experiments with Bible Study* (WCC, 1981).

Walter Wink, *Transforming Bible Study* (SCM, 1981; new edn, Mowbray, 1990).

ADDRESSES

The following produce useful Bible study materials:

Bible Society, Stonehill Green, Westlea, Swindon SN5 7DG.

Board of Education, Adult Network, Church House, Dean's Yard, Westminster, London SW1P 3NZ.

British Council of Churches, Inter-Church House, 34–41 Lower Marsh, London SE1 7RL.

CAFOD, Resources, 2 Romero Close, Stockwell Road, London SW9 9TY.

Catholic Truth Society, 38–40 Eccleston Square, London SW1V 1PD.

Christian Aid, Films and Publications, PO Box 100, London SE1 7RT.

Churches Training Groups, c/o Board of Education, Church House, Dean's Yard, London SW1P 3NZ.

Laos Publications, Lay Training Dept, 48 Union Street, London SE1 1TD.

Scripture Union, 130 City Road, London EC1V 2NJ.

USPG, Partnership House, 157 Waterloo Road, London SE1 8XA.

SOCIAL ISSUE MATERIALS AND CONTACTS

Contacts at local diocesan level or through central church agencies can be augmented by contacting some of the following organisations.

Board of Social Responsibility, Church House, Dean's Yard, London SW1P 3NZ.

Christian Action, St Peter's House, 308 Kennington Lane, London SE11 5HY.

Christian Aid, CAFOD, USPG, etc., addresses as above.

Christian Rural Centre, Dovedale House, Ilam, Ashbourne, Derbyshire DE6 2AZ.

Church Action on Poverty, 27 Blackfriars Road, Salford, Greater Manchester M3 7AQ.

Evangelical Coalition for Urban Mission, SU House, 130 City Road, London EC1V 2NJ.

Evangelical Urban Training Project, PO Box 83, Liverpool L69 8AN.

Institute for Social Research and Education, 20 The Glebe, Cumnor, Oxford OX2 9QA.

Quaker Home Service, Woodbrooke College, 1046 Bristol Road, Birmingham B29 6LJ.

Saltley Trust, Grays Court, 3 Nursery Road, Birmingham B15 3JX.

Urban Mission Training Association, Laurie Green, Poplar Rectory, Newby Place, London E14 0EY.

Urban Theology Unit, 210 Abbeyfield Road, Sheffield S4 7AZ.

William Temple Foundation, Manchester Business School, Manchester M15 6PB.

THEOLOGY

G. Ahern and G. Davie, *Inner City God* (Hodder & Stoughton, 1987).

S. Amirtham and J. Pobee (eds), *Theology by the People: Reflections on Doing Theology in Community* (WCC, 1986).

Tissa Balasuriya, *The Eucharist and Human Liberation* (SCM, 1979).

Clodovis Boff, *Theology and Praxis: Epistemological Foundations* (Orbis, 1987).

Leonardo Boff, *Ecclesiogenesis* (Collins/Orbis, 1986).

Leonardo and Clodovis Boff, *Introducing Liberation Theology* (Burns & Oates, 1987).

José M. Bonino, *Doing Theology in a Revolutionary Situation* (Fortress, 1975).

James H. Cone, *God of the Oppressed* (Seabury, 1975).

Vincent J. Donovan, *Christianity Rediscovered: An Epistle from the Masai* (SCM, 1978; rev. edn 1982).

Ian M. Fraser, *Reinventing Theology as the People's Work* (USPG, n.d.).

Ian M. Fraser and Joseph E. O'Brien (eds), *A Theology for Britain in the 80's* (ATFB80, 232 Burley Road, Leeds 4, 1982).

Timothy Gorringe, *Redeeming Time: Atonement Through Education* (Darton, Longman and Todd, 1986).

Laurie Green, *Power to the Powerless: Theology Brought to Life* (Marshall Pickering, 1987). Now available from Poplar Rectory, London E14 0EY.

Gustavo Gutiérrez, *A Theology of Liberation* (SCM/Orbis, 1974).

Gustavo Gutiérrez, *We Drink From Our Own Wells: The Spiritual Journey of a People* (SCM, 1984).

Robert Schreiter, *Constructing Local Theologies* (SCM, 1985).

Juan Luis Segundo, *The Liberation of Theology* (Gill & Macmillan, 1977).

David Sheppard, *Bias to the Poor* (Hodder & Stoughton, 1983).

Aylward Shorter, *Toward a Theology of Inculturation* (Geoffrey Chapman, 1988).

Derek Winter, *Putting Theology to Work* (CFWM, BCC, 1980).

MISCELLANEOUS

John Atherton, *Faith in the Nation* (SPCK, 1988).

Edward Bailey (ed.), *A Workbook in Popular Religion* (Partners Publications, 1986).

Joe Holland and Peter Henriot SJ, *Social Analysis: Linking Faith and Justice* (Orbis/The Center of Concern, 1983).